All Consumers Are Not Created Equal

All Consumers Are Not Created Equal

The DIFFERENTIAL MARKETING STRATEGY for BRAND LOYALTY and PROFITS

Garth Hallberg

JOHN WILEY & SONS, INC.

New York • Chichester • Brisbane • Toronto • Singapore

Copyright © 1995 by Garth Hallberg.
Published by John Wiley & Sons, Inc.

Library of Congress Cataloging-in-Publication Data:

Hallberg, Garth.
    All consumers are not created equal : the differential marketing
  strategy for brand loyalty and profits / Garth Hallberg.
      p. cm.
  Includes index.
  ISBN 0-471-12004-9 (alk. paper)
    1. Database marketing. 2. Direct marketing—Data processing.
 I. Title.
HF5415.126.H35   1995
658.8′4—dc20   95-11214

For Nancy

FOREWORD

If you are a marketer of consumer brands, particularly a CEO, you had better read this book. It will open your eyes to a new marketing concept that may well turn out to be of major importance to you.

It is called Differential Marketing. It means building the loyalty and profits of your most valuable customers by communicating with them more directly. The key to it is the database—a computerized list of names and addresses and important marketing information about your most valuable customers.

Garth Hallberg, who is Worldwide Director of Differential Marketing at Ogilvy & Mather, wrote this book. But before doing so, he set up a task force that spent *four years* picking the brains of people who know all there is to know on the subject. They came up with some remarkable information:

- Most of the profits of many brands—even big brands—derive from less than 10 percent of all households.
- The most valuable consumers rarely have a dominant brand—as few as 20 percent of them buy the same brand more than half the time.
- As much as 80 percent of brand volume is bought by consumers who don't count or don't care.

- Communicating directly with your best customers can increase their purchases as much as 40 percent.
- Procter & Gamble and Kraft Foods have already built databases of more than 40 million households. And there are other marketers close behind them.
- Consumers who are on the database do not resent the mailings they receive. On the contrary, they *like* them.

Garth's book is laced with information of this kind, but its most valuable information has to do with the *economics* of Differential Marketing. He reveals almost all he knows with prodigal generosity—even if he holds back a few discoveries that he insists on confining to his colleagues at Ogilvy & Mather.

What he tells you about the economics of Differential Marketing strikes me as conclusive.

Direct response has always been my first love and secret weapon. For many years I have wondered when ways will be found to use it for building brands. Now, at last, the great day has come.

DAVID OGILVY

PREFACE

This is a book written by a marketing practitioner for other marketing practitioners. And their bosses. In other words, for any manager interested in the future of brands and brand loyalty, and concerned about remaining competitive in a rapidly evolving, brand-hostile marketing environment.

It is based on real life and rock-hard reasoning. The experiences belong to the author, his colleagues at Ogilvy & Mather and elsewhere, and his clients. When confidentiality is a problem, the specifics are disguised but the learning is shared. When numbers need to be used, they are used unabashedly. When important detail threatens to slow down the argument, it is broken out separately in Closeups at the ends of the chapters.

Those of us who practice marketing for a living are struggling through a time of immense uncertainty and change. The consumer has changed, the retailer has changed, the media have changed. We have changed.

About the only thing that has remained constant is the pressure to perform. The need to deliver volume and profit every quarter has forced us to make some painful adjustments in how we bring to market those maddening yet wonderful creations—half ours, half the consumer's—that are called brands.

This is not a book for anyone looking for all the answers, for instant pain relief. All the answers are not yet in. And those that are in are not complete. But there is a wealth of knowledge and experience to be shared that pretty clearly indicate where the answers are pointing.

The key issue, framed by the concerns of two eminent marketers, is the productivity of the marketing communications budget—today and tomorrow. John Wanamaker, the famous nineteenth-century merchant who invented the department store, knew and reluctantly accepted that half his advertising was wasted. Edwin Artzt, CEO of Procter & Gamble, knows and does not accept that the half that is not wasted is endangered by yet more change.

The solution for both of them can be found in this book. It is a new conceptual approach to marketing thinking that:

- Recognizes that all consumers are not created equal, that a relatively small group controls the overwhelming majority of volume and profit in the category, providing a differentially greater profit opportunity for the brand.
- Recognizes, as well, that all purchases are not equal, that brand loyalty affects profitability by influencing not only how much consumers buy but how much they're willing to pay.
- Seeks to increase brand sales and profits by building the loyalty of those consumers who offer the greatest profit opportunity by communicating with them more directly.
- Employs a consumer database and other data-based techniques to direct more loyalty-building communications against high-profit consumers, both through specially crafted brand-loyalty programs and improved targeting of conventional advertising and promotion vehicles.
- Serves one overriding purpose—to build the new kind of brand loyalty that leads to old-fashioned brand growth and increased profits, without incremental marketing investment . . . and that, in the process, creates a sustainable competitive advantage for the marketer.

This is the essence of the concept called Differential Marketing.

GARTH HALLBERG

Waccabuc, New York
August 1995

ACKNOWLEDGMENTS

As David Ogilvy wrote in his foreword, this book is the outgrowth of an Ogilvy & Mather Direct task force that was established in 1992. The purpose was to collect and systematize the knowledge and learning of the entire Ogilvy network about new tools and concepts that could help our clients build stronger, more profitable brands in a rapidly changing, and increasingly brand-hostile, marketing environment. So any thanks must begin with all the Ogilvy & Mather professionals around the world, too numerous to list, who gave of their time and their thinking to help us accomplish our mission.

A special hats-off is due the members of the task force: Brian Fetherstonhaugh in Toronto, Frits Hirschstein in Amsterdam, Nina Mynk in London, and Oscar Prats in Madrid.

And a sincere and hearty thank-you goes to our management godfather, Reimer Thedens, who conceived the idea of the task force, found the financial support, freed up our time, recognized the merit of the findings, and above all, who has been unflagging in his zeal for spreading the gospel of Differential Marketing throughout our company.

The book could not have been written without extensive help and input from friends and colleagues outside of Ogilvy & Mather as well. Dr. David Learner, Ken Murphy, and Mike Carini of MRCA provided me with an invaluable treasure trove of information and experience. Their "Retention Marketing" philosophy is very much in line with Differential Marketing thinking.

Lynn Wunderman, of Marketing Information Technologies, provided a graduate education in the arcane mysteries of database and data-based technology. My apologies to her, as well, for never quite understanding when it was appropriate to use "geodemographic" rather than "geographic and demographic."

John Cummings, founder of *DBM/scan*, served as my eyes and ears, and occasionally as my copy editor. Mike Naples and Roslyn Arnstein opened wide the gates of the Advertising Research Foundation library. Mel Stevens was a font of information from IRI.

Three clients who taught me more than I care to admit are John Kuendig of Kraft Foods, Ric Shaw of the House of Seagram, and Rich Weber of DowBrands. Extra credit goes to Rich, from whose lips I first heard uttered the fateful words, "Differential Marketing."

My agent, Nancy Stauffer, gave me on-the-job training and 60-second psychoanalysis, both of which I learned are critical in getting through the process of writing and publishing. My editor, Janet Coleman, knew when to hold 'em and knew when to fold 'em and, mercifully, found me a perfect title.

The only thing more difficult than writing a book seems to be getting someone to read it, at least in manuscript form. So special thanks are due to Bill Carmody, Mitch Collins, Lissa Couch Seeberger, Peter Flatow, Philip Greenfield, Howard Lelchuk, John Maher, Michael Mesic, Bill Morrissey, David Ogilvy, Jerry Pickholz, Ray Simko, and Jon Swallen. And to Julianne Ramaker for helping the examples come to life in pictures.

Thanks, too, to my office family of Chuck Guariglia and Karen Rodriguez, both of whom kept advising me to keep it short and punchy, one because he's a headline kind of guy, the other because it was her responsibility to turn a diskette into a readable and organized manuscript.

And the biggest thanks of all, of course, to my real family, especially to my wife Nancy, who not only read the manuscript but who nursed me through the comments of all my other readers. And how can I not thank my nine-year-old daughter Charlotte, who inspired me on more occasions than necessary by standing next to the word processor with awe in her eyes and asking, "Daddy, are you still writing that *same* book?"

G.H.

CONTENTS

1 A Call to Change 1

2 The Making of a Brand-Hostile World 13

3 Why All Consumers Are Not Created Equal 27

4 The Changing Nature of Brand Loyalty 49

5 A New Strategy for Brand Growth 71

6 The Promotion Paradox 93

7 The Right Place with the Right Message 119

8 Involving the Consumer with the Brand 139

9 The Measured Impact of Brand-Loyalty Programs 165

10 Enabling Differential Marketing Through Technology 179

11 Advertising in the Differential Marketing Plan 195

12 Sales Promotion and Trade Relations in the Differential Marketing Plan 219

13   PUTTING DIFFERENTIAL MARKETING TO WORK   **241**

14   MAKING DIFFERENTIAL MARKETING PAY   **259**

15   DIFFERENTIAL MARKETING: THE CONCEPTUAL ON-RAMP
         TO THE INFORMATION SUPERHIGHWAY   **275**

EPILOGUE: THE CHALLENGE TO CHANGE   **297**

ENDNOTES   **301**

INDEX   **309**

All Consumers Are Not Created Equal

1

A CALL TO CHANGE

"Is brand loyalty dead?"

That was how a senior marketing executive of a Fortune 500 packaged goods company calmly opened the 1994 planning meeting for one of his brands.

Glancing at the startled faces around the conference table, he continued, "What I mean is, does it really pay to continue to try to build this brand? Do consumers care about brands anymore? All they seem to want is the lowest price. Give them a dollar off and make their day."

Could this experienced marketer be serious? Was he really contemplating turning a crown jewel into a commodity? Did he truly believe his company should radically reshape its core strategy and attempt to compete in the future not as a maker of value-added brands but as a low-cost provider? Judging by the silence that had suddenly descended on the conference room, his audience didn't seem convinced he was kidding. Worse than silence actually. Averted eyes. Frozen smiles. A quick nosedive into the coffee cup or nervous fingers flipping distractedly through a presentation deck.

The marketer shrugged. "We've tried a new advertising campaign ... from our new agency," he added pointedly. "Management's asking for another million in profit contribution. The trade ... the trade?" He rolled his eyes. "Who knows how many million more *they're* looking for?"

From the pessimistic tone, an outsider might have assumed the brand under discussion was a niche product or a marginal line extension, or maybe a tired old name nearing the end of the product life cycle. Not even close to the truth. In fact, it happened to be one of the best-known and largest and most profitable brands in the company's portfolio, even though its volume had been under severe pressure for more than a year.

Why didn't one of the other marketing professionals who were gathered around the conference table—from brand management, sales promotion, media, market research, and the agency—immediately speak up and politely restate the eternal verities of their trade? Weren't brands and the loyalty of consumers to those brands the very cornerstones of marketing? Weren't future profits dependent on the willingness of consumers to continue to pay a premium price for the inherent value, perceived as well as real, of a strong brand?

Why was the only response, when it finally came, a flippant one? "Let's hope brand loyalty isn't dead," someone wise-cracked in a half-hearted attempt to thaw the air, which by that point was indistinguishable from the atmosphere of Jupiter. "At least not within *our* career horizons."

Hyperbole aside, the marketing executive had voiced a fear that had been nagging everyone in the room since the wake-up call of what had come to be called "Marlboro Friday." On April 2, 1993, the financial markets, in their own inimitable fashion, had posed exactly the same question about brand loyalty, gutting the value of Philip Morris, one of Wall Street's darlings, by more than $13 billion, almost 25 percent of its market capitalization, in a single day. The giant tobacco and food conglomerate had just announced an aggressive price cut for Marlboro, arguably the most esteemed and valuable brand name in the entire world, in an effort to defend its market share from further erosion by lower cost cigarettes.

If it could happen to Marlboro, it could happen to any brand. The bear was loose. In the weeks that followed, the rampaging animal devoured a healthy chunk of the share price of many of the other glamour stocks in the consumer goods sector, like Pepsico and Gillette.

Predictably, the news media were quick to jump on the bandwagon, proclaiming the nineties a "value decade." The number of reports that consumers now always shopped for the lowest price and bought only on sale swiftly eclipsed sightings of Elvis.

Certainly no one in that planning meeting was likely to panic prematurely. Thoughtful professionals all, none of them believed branding and brand loyalty were truly dead. On the other hand, it wasn't necessary to sacrifice a sheep and read its entrails to comprehend that their once brand-friendly world was being overrun by brand-hostile market forces. Marlboro Friday was only the most recent and the most dramatic of a growing list of warning signals.

The predatory demands of the trade. The relentless incursions of private label. A promotional habit that couldn't be kicked and that consequently was becoming more addictive year by year. Consumers as well-trained as Pavlov's dogs, reaching for their wallets only when the sale bell was rung. Even venerable Procter & Gamble, the inventor of brand management, systematically pruning and grafting its stable of brands and adopting an "Every Day Low Price" policy. And to top it all off, alarming reports that a media world already turned upside down was in danger of being atomized.

Although they may have been reluctant to admit it, it had to be clear to everyone in the room that the old solutions weren't working. Or at least that they weren't working nearly as well as they once had. And that they would work even less well in the future.

And if for some strange reason it wasn't clear to them, it certainly was crystal clear to the CEO of the company, who had prodded his marketing director to think the unthinkable. CEOs had to make tough decisions about resource allocation every day. What was so sacred about the marketing budget? In this new environment, this post-mass-market world, what kind of return was marketing actually delivering to the company? Was there a better way to spend that money?

It was a different time and a different business climate when that otherwise savvy merchant, John Wanamaker, could cavalierly admit that he knew half his advertising budget was wasted. The CEO damn well wanted to know which half.

"Change is not made without inconvenience, even from worse to better" wrote Samuel Johnson in the preface to his *Dictionary of the English Language*, published in 1755. He was quoting a nugget of wisdom from Richard Hooker, an English theologian, which was already almost two centuries old at the time. And which was written large on the freeze-framed faces in that conference room more than two centuries later.

Numerous ideas being floated around the industry hold out the promise of constructive change. Each has its advocates, its success stories. Could relationship marketing be the magic elixir to revive brand loyalty? Or database marketing? Integrated marketing? Micromarketing? Infomercials? Electronic couponing? Interactive TV? The Internet? The information superhighway?

What do these ideas add up to, other than a boon to those companies who put together marketing conferences and seminars? Is one of them right and the others wrong? Are they the pieces of a jigsaw puzzle? Or are they fragments of a larger picture, more tantalizing than illuminating, the central meaning still obscure?

The thesis of this book is that, in all probability, none of them are wrong, and some of them are likely to be very right indeed, as a means to an end. But before specific solutions can be evaluated, the true dimensions of the problem must be understood. And a controlling strategy must be in place to deal with it—a strategy that reflects the realities and the limitations of the post-mass-market world.

The current state of brands and brand loyalty is in many cases very different, and even less pleasant, than marketers imagine. The future prospects of most brands, even big brands, rest in the hands of a surprisingly small number of consumers.

All consumers are not created equal.

Often, less than 10 or 15 percent of households—the "high-profit buyers" in the category—produce the overwhelming majority of current or potential brand volume and profits. As many as 85 or 90 percent of consumers are either immune to the blandishments of the marketer, or, if they do succumb, do not buy enough to make a significant impact on the bottom line.

Effectively finding and influencing those category high-profit buyers with the mass marketing tools developed for a different kind of world is increasingly problematic. "Loyalty parity" is on the rise.

A marketer's best customers are also the competitor's best customers.

The threat to packaged goods brands is particularly acute. More and more, the most valuable consumers have no dominant brand. "Loyal" high-profit buyers, those who give at least half their purchases to a single brand, are rapidly becoming nonfactors in the brand franchise.

The risk to the brand is compounded by the unintentional side effects of current marketing practices on these most valuable consumers, sensitizing them to price and shortchanging them on loyalty-building advertising.

*** *** ***

The price of excessive sales promotion is the loyalty of high-profit buyers.

A brand that spends twice as much in sales promotion as in advertising is actually spending anywhere from *five to ten times* as much in promotion against the small group of category high-profit consumers. And spending as much as *twenty times* more in sales promotion than in advertising against the high-profit consumers who currently buy the brand.

This disturbing pattern, together with the profusion of other brand-hostile forces, has produced a situation that should elevate sleeplessness to an art form for anyone who practices marketing for a living.

*** *** ***

The fate of most brands is in the hands of consumers who don't count or who don't care.

As much as 80 percent of brand volume is generated by consumers who are essentially disloyal to the brand, or who don't make enough purchases to make any real difference to brand profitability. Given this perilous state of affairs, it may seem that we as marketers have but two choices, neither of them good: a hopeless fight or an unseemly flight. That is, either a rear-guard action against brand-hostile forces with outdated or unproven weapons, or a wholesale abandonment of branding for an alternative marketing paradigm that provides an acceptable return on investment. The former seems a sure-fire ticket to early retirement. As for the latter, a realistic alternative has yet to be discovered.

Over the years, the business of building brands has served both marketers and consumers very well. Moreover, it is a business that may sometimes seem to be on life-support but that still has a vital pulse. The most successful private label is nothing more than the retailer's own brand. And the evidence is clear that the biggest and strongest brands in every category have the greatest return on investment (ROI). Conversely, commodity manufacturers have verifiably low margins.

Besides, branding is too ingrained in human nature to be so casually cast aside. Not just in "shopaholic" America, but in China, and Russia, and every developing country around the world. And not just in the "age of consumption," but across the centuries, from medieval guilds back to ancient Mesopotamia and Egypt, where "distinct grades of branded bricks paved the paths to the pharaohs' tombs."[1]

The purpose of this book is to give marketers a third choice other than fight or flight: change.

We can—and we must—change the way we do business without changing our mission.

First, the book will help marketers understand the severity of the problem by providing new and startling facts and insights about brand loyalty, brand profitability, and consumer buying behavior. Second, it will place the solutions being explored by the industry in a larger context, so that marketers can decide intelligently what makes the most sense for their particular brands. That larger context is a new conceptual framework for marketing decision making called Differential Marketing, or DFM.

Differential Marketing is an overarching vision that embraces the best marketing practices of the past but deals effectively with the circumscribed realities of the present, all the while looking forward to a digitalized and individualized future. It puts to rest John Wanamaker's old marketing math, once and for all. The new math of DFM identifies *which half* of the marketing budget is wasted: the half, or more, that is directed against low-profit or no-profit households.

The way consumers truly differ is in the inherent profit opportunity they present to the marketer—their profit differential.

The profitability of individual consumers varies by the amount of purchases made, as well as by whether those purchases are motivated by loyalty or a promotional incentive. For the vast majority of products and services, *profit differential* is a far greater discriminator between consumers than demography, geography, lifestyle, psychographics, or desired benefits. Recognizing the leverage of this profit differential leads to a very simple formula for success, what might be called the Differential Marketing equation for brand growth and profits.

The brand with the most high-profit buyers—and the most loyal—always wins.

It is a proven fact that in category after category, the largest brand is the one that has made the greatest inroads with the small group of highly profitable consumers. Invariably, the brand leader has attracted the largest number of category high-profit buyers. And those high-profit buyers give the brand leader a greater share of their business than the share that high-profit buyers of competitive brands give those brands.

Winning over and building the loyalty of these high-profit consumers is the most productive path for profitable growth for most brands. For that reason, the *core strategy* of DFM is to direct more loyalty-building activity and resources against this high-profit segment—more than they would normally receive if only conventional marketing practices were employed.

All consumers should not be treated equally.

Marketers cannot afford to be democratic. They must invest their efforts and their budgets where they will produce the most return. The most valuable customers deserve special treatment to build and retain their loyalty. The risk of not giving it to them is great. If a marketer treats high-profit consumers like everyone else, they will treat the marketer's brand like any other.

The overriding need to attract and build the brand loyalty of high-profit buyers manifests itself in all aspects of the Differential Marketing communications plan: targeting, objectives, strategies, allocation between disciplines, media choice, even creative approach. New data-driven techniques and technologies are brought to bear on traditional media and sales promotion to improve their ability to target and win over high-profit buyers. In addition, direct marketing and direct marketing thinking are integrated with the other disciplines to communicate more directly and more relevantly with these key consumers.

The direct marketing "brand-loyalty programs" that are at the heart of most Differential Marketing plans are a powerful new tool for giving a brand's most valuable consumers the special treatment they have earned. Through special privileges and benefits, special channels of communication, and special information-intensive messages, they *involve* the consumer with the brand.

Consumer involvement is the key to greater loyalty.

The involvement generated by adding brand loyalty programs to the communications mix produces measurably higher levels of brand equity and profitable volume for the brand. And as part of a total DFM plan, it does so without incremental marketing investment.

The marketer who wondered out loud if brand loyalty was dead was determined to improve the performance of his business. The issues he raised, and the response or lack thereof, were his spring-board for leading his colleagues into a discussion of Differential Marketing and the test already underway of a brand-loyalty program directed at the small group of high-profit consumers who controlled the majority of sales and profit in the category. The program was the first deliverable of a small, visionary task force from both his company and Ogilvy & Mather—a task force whose mission was nothing less than to stand traditional thinking right on its head in a search for better answers.

Nine months after the planning meeting, the brand team reassembled to hear the results of that initial test. Changes in the brand purchase habits of this key group of high-profit buyers who received the DFM loyalty program had been measured by panel data, the most rigorous methodology available for determining actual consumer sales. Their purchases were compared with those of a control cell of similar buyers who only received the brand's traditional marketing activities.

Brand sales volume in the test cell was almost *30 percent higher* than control cell volume during the twelve-month test period. Consumers in the test cell used the brand at a greater rate, used more of the brand at the expense of the competition, and were far less likely to discontinue usage.

Moreover, when adjusted for constant budget levels and the true incidence of those high-profit buyers in the general population, the combination of traditional and new forms of marketing activity in the test cell significantly outperformed the traditional mix by itself. In other words, as the DFM plan was implemented, it was projected to deliver substantially more profitable volume with *no increase* in the marketing budget.

Not bad for a brand that had been struggling to maintain its position in the market. Brand loyalty, stimulated in an unconventional fashion, was very much alive and well indeed.

Ogilvy & Mather offices around the world have worked with many forward-looking marketers like the one just described—marketers who are both willing to ask the tough questions and seek new solutions to ensure that loyalty for their brands will remain the key driver of brand profits, now and in the future. These early adopters of DFM—several dozen brands across a half-dozen countries—have helped to shape and hone the brand-loyalty programs that are the

foundation of most DFM plans. Extending the learning into traditional advertising and sales promotion is nothing more than marketing horse sense—taking tried-and-true approaches and vehicles
and adapting them to new ends.

The principles and practices of Differential Marketing have been
proven to work—always consistently, often spectacularly. They
have demonstrated their worth over a wide range of categories, from
high-priced considered purchases like automobiles to frequently
purchased, low-priced products like packaged goods. And with every passing day, they will become more effective.

Differential Marketing is neither revolution nor
evolution. It is simply a return to our marketing roots,
newly enabled by information and technology.

Marketing may be the last branch of the business world to benefit
from the transforming power of information technology, but that
transformation, which is already well under way, will be among the
most profound. Consumer marketing and its handmaidens, advertising and sales promotion, are practiced today in pretty much the
same manner they were practiced ten or fifteen years ago. Ten or
fifteen years hence, our current practices will belong in a museum.

The first harbinger of the transforming power of information technology is the consumer database. The breathtaking free fall in the
cost of data processing and storage has made giant databases of
households and their purchasing habits not only possible but affordable. And not just for companies like R. J. Reynolds, with its
high margins, or American Airlines, with its ability to capture the
details of every transaction, but for every marketer who needs to
find a better way to build brand loyalty and profitability. Even for
the broad run of frequently purchased but relatively low-priced
packaged goods, the kinds of brands that are still a major, if no
longer dominant, player in the media and who compete in the most
brand-hostile of marketing environments.

In fact, for most brands, the question may very well soon be not
whether they can afford to reorient their marketing program around

a consumer database and other related information technology, but whether they can afford not to.

Differential Marketing will be, by necessity if not by choice, the predominant driver of marketing activities on the information superhighway.

The "grave new world" that Edwin Artzt, chairman and CEO of Procter & Gamble, warned about at the 1994 annual conference of the American Association of Advertising Agencies need not be grave at all, despite the fact, as Artzt correctly noted, that advertisers "will have a hard time achieving the reach and frequency we need to support our brands."[2] What advertisers *will* have is a wealth of new avenues for targeting their most valuable consumers, and a wealth of new ways of treating them as special customers and involving them with their brand. Those of us who lay down our buggy whips and begin thinking about "who" and "how impactfully" rather than "how many" and "how frequently" will discover opportunities undreamed of during our days of sitting behind a horse.

And so, on that whimsical but dead serious note, ends this brief introduction to Differential Marketing. The chapters that follow expand and elucidate these ideas and this vision to provide a deeper understanding and appreciation of the DFM concept as well as practical advice on how to implement it on behalf of a brand. *Your* brand.

2

THE MAKING OF
A BRAND-HOSTILE
WORLD

Executive Preview

Some of the brand-hostile forces at work are beyond marketers' control. They include on-going changes in demography, consumer behavior and attitudes, media, and the retailing environment. But others are actually precipitated or aggravated by marketers' own actions. Brand proliferation. Loss of brand distinctiveness. The shrinkage of the "quality gap." Price inflation. And most critically, the excessive reliance on promotion, both consumer and trade, at the expense of loyalty-building advertising, driven by the need to make short-term sales and profit goals.

Marketers are driven to overreliance on promotion because we are disadvantaged in our pursuit of profit. One of our major assets never appears on the balance sheet: the brand names under which we bring our products and services to market. As a result, any funds used to create that asset must be expensed when they are paid, not amortized over the life of the asset. This condition helps create a mind-set where brand-building is viewed as a cost rather than an investment, and where, seemingly, the wisest spending is that which produces the most immediate results.

The same mind-set leads us into the habit of thinking about profits like accountants: revenues minus expenses. We feel if enough volume can be generated, we can always cut spending to make the profit number. Spending which more often than not was earmarked for building loyalty to the brand.

13

Marketers are finally realizing that the short-term pursuit of profit and the long-term building and maintaining of a healthy brand cannot be mutually exclusive objectives. Not if we are to survive, much less prosper. Thus, reconciling these two goals is the first challenge of Differential Marketing.

Marlboro Friday was a single event, but the threat to brand loyalty and the old ways of doing business is an ongoing process. Fundamental changes in demography, consumer behavior and attitudes, the media, and the retailing environment have created a very different world from the one that existed when the techniques of television-age mass marketing were being developed and refined. The impact of these changes affect brands of every persuasion, big or small, old or new, goods or services, durable or fast-moving.

Before plunging into an examination of the havoc these changes have wrought, and how Differential Marketing helps address them, a quick review of the trends and market forces that are at work is in order. A fuller understanding of the problem will help inform the solution, especially because our own actions are too often major contributors to the very problem we are attempting to solve.

SAY GOOD-BYE TO A BRAND-FRIENDLY WORLD

At the top of the list of forces over which marketers have little or no control are the demographic trends that are having such a significant impact on traditional marketing targets. Population growth is near zero, depriving us of a steady source of new consumers. Worse news, the first wave of baby boomers are on the brink of fifty, portending smaller households and lower consumption rates of many goods and services. And historically, older consumers have been more set in their ways, lengthening the odds against new product introductions.

Growth may have slowed to a crawl but diversity has blossomed.

By the year 2000, people of African, Hispanic, and Asian descent will account for a third of all consumers. By 2010 they are projected to outnumber all other ethnic groups combined in California and Texas.[1] Household composition is changing as well. As late as 1970, 40 percent of households fit the "traditional" model of husband, wife, and at least one school-age child. Today, that category describes only 25 percent of households, and that figure is still declining.[2]

Consumers themselves are also doing their part to undermine a "one-size-fits-all" approach. The pressure to conform has been replaced by rampant individualism and a desire to be different and stand out. Advertising media have responded by going "special interest." More than fifty networks fill the cable channels. Four hundred magazines have circulations greater than one hundred thousand.

Growing diversity is reflected as well in the way people *use* the media, especially television. What once was the absorbing center-piece of family life—Mom, Dad, Junior, Sis, and Rover transfixed in front of the tube in the living room—is now intensely personal and frenzied. Almost 70 percent of households have at least two televisions. A third have three or more.[3] Ninety percent have remote controls, which are used to "zap" and "surf" and otherwise subvert the advertiser's reason for underwriting their entertainment.

In this kind of chaotic viewing environment, just finding the right consumers can be a problem, much less engaging their attention. That second task has been made especially daunting by the economics of television, which have shrunk the standard commercial length from sixty seconds to thirty or fifteen and crammed fifty commercials into the typical prime time hour.

And even when the advertising does break through the clutter, it's no longer axiomatic that consumers will *respond* to it. Consumers are more cynical and less trusting of authority figures in general, and they make no exception for advertisers. Moreover, people have learned a lot about the tricks of the marketer's trade from the 700 or so product messages they're exposed to over the course of an average day.[4] And, tellingly, brand decisions for many products, particularly packaged goods, don't weigh so heavily on the 80 percent of "women 18–49" in the labor force who no longer have to find their self-esteem in housekeeping rather than in a career.

Brand decisions are also affected by the growth in dual-income families which has made time the ultimate constraint. The traditional Saturday grocery shopping trip has been increasingly supplanted by a series of guerillalike raids by various family members at various times of the night and day on various outlets—supermarket, drugstore, club store, mass merchandiser, health store, convenience store, even gas station. These alternate channels limit the distribution of many brands, upsetting brand buying patterns. And the widespread availability of many kinds of grocery products further marginalizes the brand decision by making them seem even more commoditylike.

New channels are the least of the marketer's troubles from the distribution chain.

Retailers are helping to make a brand-hostile world more hostile.

Thanks to the laser scanner at the cash register, retailers have better and more timely information about product movement than marketers can ever hope to have. And thanks to the tireless efforts of marketers to introduce more brands and line extensions to grow revenue and profit, retailers, as well as consumers, have more choices than they could ever hope to want. This deadly combination has given the retailer the upper hand in buying negotiations, encouraging them to demand a bigger and bigger slice of the marketing pie, as well as giving birth to the infamous slotting and stocking allowances that require marketers to first pay chains to carry their brands and later pay chains not to delist them, literally to not throw them out of the store.

Retailers have also taken advantage of marketers' troubles to open a second front—the new wave of private label products. Not just low-cost, low-quality knock-offs but *lower*-cost, high-quality retailer's-own brands. Aggressive grocery retailers, such as Loblaws out of Canada, are now franchising their successful private label products to rival chains in markets where they themselves have no presence. In the drugstore channel, retailers stock their generic equivalents next to the brand names with a shelf-talker that reads "Compare and Save."

To add insult to injury, even when they are not so blatantly competitive, the operating and merchandising strategies of retailers in certain channels can tend to devalue brands. This tendency is especially true in the packaged goods world. The row upon row of narrow aisles that dominate the central part of many conventional supermarkets, resembling the bars of a cell, has been aptly nicknamed "the prison." The home of most packaged goods brands is often poorly lit and displayed, haphazardly organized (from the consumer's point of view), and an obstacle course created by stacks of unopened cartons and illegally parked carts. It suffers greatly in comparison with the wide open spaces around the perimeter where the "fun" shopping takes place and the retailer's real profits are made—at the well-lit, temptingly displayed, and largely nonbranded bakery, deli, butcher, produce department, and florist.

THE LONG-TERM CONSEQUENCES OF SHORT-TERM SOLUTIONS

In the face of these trends, marketers have understandably been forced to adopt new game plans to keep sales and profits growing. Unfortunately, many of the actions that work well initially only add to the problem.

When baby boomers were growing up they could spot the difference between a Buick and Oldsmobile a block away. Today, thanks to manufacturing efficiencies, they need a checklist. And "margin improvement programs" are too often euphemisms for product debasement, taking quality out of the brand in return for short-term savings. At the same time, technology has made acceptable quality in many categories cheaper to achieve. As a result, the size of the "quality gap" between leading brands and their imitators has shrunken considerably.

Rather than "better," marketers have focused their energies on "more." Packaged-goods marketers have flooded the market with new products and line extensions. Between 1983 and 1993, the number of items available in the average grocery chain store nearly doubled, from about 11,000 to over 20,000.[5] But because the opportunities for real product breakthroughs are always few and far between, these new introductions have tended to be only marginally different than existing products. Predictably, when the real differences between brands are minimal, the distinctiveness of any single brand is blurred.

In an effort to recapture that distinctiveness, many marketers have sought to differentiate their brands by their emotional appeal rather than by a tangible benefit. While emotion has always been an important component of branding, emotion in the absence of a point of difference that can be articulated and firmly seated in the memory is arguably a recipe for consumer confusion.

But perhaps the most pernicious short-term solution is the simplest strategy: raising prices faster than the rate of inflation. This approach has been especially evident in the packaged goods world, where 8–10 percent price increases were the norm throughout the 1980s. *Forbes* magazine reported the case of an 18-ounce box of Quaker Oats that retailed for $.73 in 1980 and for $1.73 in 1991. During this stretch the wholesale price of oats *declined* by a third.[6]

One of the reasons that excessive price increases are so harmful is that they strike at the heart of the unwritten contract between the consumer and the brand. Ultimately, the value of a brand is measured by how much more the consumer is willing to pay for it over and above the price of a similar, unbranded product. When the price differential becomes unacceptable, consumers stop buying. And stop believing that the brand is truly that much better. This is precisely what happened to Marlboro.

But there is another reason that bloated prices are so insidious. The cure, in the form of temporary price reductions, is often no less debilitating than the disease.

---

*Excessive sales promotion is sensitizing consumers
to price and desensitizing them to quality.*

From 1980 to 1993, the total number of coupons distributed more than tripled, from about 100 billion to more than 300 billion, the equivalent of more than 3,000 coupons per year for every household in the United States. During the same period, promotion's share of the typical packaged-goods marketing budget, consumer and trade combined, increased from about half the budget to 75 percent. And it increased at the expense, naturally, of equity- and loyalty-building advertising, which appears to be bottoming out at about 25 percent of brand spending.[7]

What has this glut of promotion achieved? Marketers acknowledge that much of the trade support never gets passed on to the consumer. As for consumer promotion, the number of coupons *redeemed* has grown only by about a third since 1981, and is showing signs of having peaked at about 7 billion redemptions per year. Two major coupon processors reported *declines* in coupon redemption in 1994, with free-standing-insert redemption at 2.0 percent or less.[8] In other words, promotional activity seems to have reached the saturation point. Any additional increases are likely to be largely wasteful.

But wasteful or not, the sheer quantity of promotional activity has certainly taken a toll on attitudes, signalling that brand names are customarily overpriced and heightening consumers' sensitivity to what they're willing to pay. Consumers don't make the distinction that marketers do between "advertising" and "sales promotion." It's all the same to them. So it's not uncommon for marketers to discover, to their horror, that according to their advertising tracking studies, the "Sunday coupons" that tumble out by the bushel from the weekend newspaper are the principal source of their brands' ad awareness.

To compound the problem, marketers are increasingly using what's left of their brand advertising to single-mindedly focus on price. Price promotion clearly has an important role in the marketing mix, but when it hogs the stage, one of two things happens. Either consumers take marketers literally and only buy on sale, like the unfortunate rebate situation in the automotive market a few years back, or they don't buy at all, because what they hear is "cheap steak" rather than "steak cheap."

The compulsion to promote pours gasoline on the retailer fire as well. Does any marketer doubt that retailers have been emboldened in their demands by our unwillingness or inability to draw a line on promotional spending, even if in sand? And that one of the reasons that "category killers"—huge stores with rock-bottom prices—are the dominant force in so many retailing categories is that we have become overly dependent on pushing product through the system, rather than having it pulled through by consumers? Addicted to the tremendous volumes that these stores can generate, marketers, like all addicts, are forced to pay a higher and higher price, in the form of shrinking margins.

"The time has come to sound an alarm, to warn manufacturers what is going to happen to their brands if they spend so much on deals that there is no money left for advertising to build their brand."

So declared David Ogilvy in a speech in 1955. Similar pronouncements by other advertising agency luminaries through the years have been generally received like the revelations of Cassandra, the Trojan prophetess who was fated never to be believed. Whose bottom line was it, anyway, that they were worried about? The agency's or the marketer's?

Some forty years later it became necessary for ten trade groups, including the 4 A's (the American Association of Advertising Agencies) and the ANA (the Association of National Advertisers), to "bring together advertisers, agencies, and the media in an attempt to stem the tide of brand erosion caused by flawed marketing practices."[9] And so was born The Coalition for Brand Equity, the ultimate self-help group for the marketing and advertising industry.

The first deliverable of the Coalition was a booklet in defense of branding entitled *The Trustmarketer's Road to Enduring Profitable Growth*, researched and written by Larry Light, a widely respected industry thinker and the chairman of the Coalition. Released in January, 1994, the booklet sold out 8,000 copies in the first thirty days, mostly on the basis of word-of-mouth.

The material in the booklet was previewed by Light in the closing speech of the ANA convention the previous November and was greeted by thunderous applause. The need to reevaluate current marketing practices and reinvigorate branding was something very much on the mind of the ANA audience, at last. In fact, of nine speakers on the program, seven addressed themselves to this topic. Said Richard Garvey, vice president of marketing of Lego Systems, Inc., and the 1993–1994 chairman of the association, "We're living in the era of the battered brand."[10]

DR. JEKYLL VERSUS MR. HYDE

How did it get to this point? Why have otherwise intelligent and sane business people made a difficult environment nearly impossible by persisting in such self-destructive behavior? The answer is not hard to fathom. Marlboro Friday demonstrated the priorities of a brand-hostile, post-mass-market world.

Marketing decision making is ruled by the tyranny of corporate profits, particularly short-term profits.

Platitudes aside, the mission of any multi-billion-dollar, publicly held consumer marketing-driven company is no different from that of an oil exploration business or an aerospace firm: to increase shareholder value. And that value is constantly being poked, prodded, palpated, and otherwise appraised by a legion of analysts, money managers, and assorted Wall Street pundits, who as a group are about as charitable and forgiving as the previsitation Ebenezer Scrooge.

Little wonder, then, that the quarterly earnings statement long ago ceased to be merely a bland beige report card. It comes in pink or green, leading management either to "other opportunities" or stock-option heaven. And not surprising that this bottom-line fixation extends right down to the bottom rung, where the lowliest assistant brand manager quickly learns the mantra for success: "make the number."

Certainly there can be no dispute that this hard-nosed crusade for ever increasing corporate profitability has been of great benefit in increasing the efficiency and productivity and return-on-investment of American industry in general. It allowed scores of companies to remain competitive in the pressure-cooker of a global economy, as well as helping millions of investors realize substantial gains in their invested capital.

But this "survival of the fittest" mentality has severely handicapped a major sector of the corporate gene pool: consumer marketing companies.

Marketers are disadvantaged in their pursuit of profit.

There is a fundamental difference between an enterprise that sells household cleaners or cosmetics or carbonated soft drinks or fast food or financial products or long-distance telephone services and one that designs space shuttles or drills for oil. One of the greatest assets of consumer marketers cannot be touched, measured, counted, surveyed, or even all that easily valued. Often, well over half of a marketer's assets never appear on the balance sheet: the *brand names* under which we bring our products and services to market.

The asset of the brand is not treated as an asset—financially.

Every year *Financial World* magazine takes a stab at emulating accounting practices in England, where brands can and do appear on the balance sheet, by valuing some of the world's most well-known brand names as corporate assets. The basis of the valuation is the estimated difference in current and future earnings of the brand versus a similar, but generic, version of the same product.

Leading *Financial World*'s list in 1992 was the eponymous Marlboro, which was calculated to be worth $51.6 billion to Philip Morris (PM). In 1993, post-Marlboro Friday, the brand value had dropped by more than a third to "only" $33.0 billion. That left Marlboro

$3 billion behind the new, most valuable brand, Coca-Cola. Jell-O desserts, another brand in PM's stable, was more modestly appraised at $1.5 billion.[11]

In Philip Morris's 1993 annual report, which carried the theme of "The World's Best Brands," total tangible assets—cash and receivables and the machinery, plants, inventory, trucks, real estate, and other holdings necessary to make and distribute Marlboro and Jell-O and almost a hundred other well-known brand names—were stated as only $25.8 billion, $7.2 billion *less* than the estimated value of Marlboro alone.

The accountants' concession to the asset value of brands was listed under "goodwill" and did add $19.7 billion. This figure was largely the price paid for the acquisitions of Kraft and General Foods, less accumulated amortization. Financial and real estate investments contributed another $5.7 billion to the balance sheet. It wouldn't take too many more brands like Jell-O combined with the $33 billion value of Marlboro to surpass Philip Morris's total reported assets of $51.2 billion. A rebound by Marlboro to its 1992 valuation levels would accomplish that feat by itself.

Startling anomalies like these are not the only by-product of this critical accounting difference. There are some very practical financial implications, on the P&L as well as the balance sheet, which directly impact marketers' spending decisions and the investment community's reaction to those decisions. Unlike the case with other assets, money spent to build the brand cannot be amortized over the life of the investment but must be expensed in the same quarter it is paid out. The result is predictable:

Brand-building is viewed as a cost rather than an investment.

The on-going need to meet short-term volume and profit projections creates a marketing mind-set where advertising is considered as just another expense, and where the wisest spending is seemingly that which produces the most immediate results.

Adding the accounting disadvantage to all of our other problems, is it any wonder that expediency has a way of edging out the long-term view? Marketers may not want to weaken the branding paradigm further, but we're all susceptible to the path of least resistance. Building consumer loyalty may safeguard the brand, but making short-term volume and profit goals safeguards the bonus, or even the job.

And with population growth barely discernible, line extensions and new products a glut on the market, no rising tide of inflation to lift all boats, and margin improvement programs having already wrung out any excess costs from manufacturing, there aren't a lot of places to look when the time for delivering the numbers comes rolling around every three months. The surest way to make those short-term goals still seems to be converting the advertising budget into profit or "renting volume" with more promotion.

In fact, it often seems as if marketers have developed a Jekyll-and-Hyde-type personality. Our better instincts are overwhelmed by a compulsion to think about brand profits like accountants—as *total revenue minus total expenses*. While that definition of profits is certainly accurate, it too easily leads us astray from our traditional and rightful focus: the consumer and the brand.

When marketers think like accountants, our first priority is revenue—which equals sales volume.

Brand managers today typically function as *volume* managers, not as business managers. They are judged by revenue, not by the bottom line, and certainly not by the long-term strength of the brand. It is often not until reaching the VP-marketing level that profitability—*division* profit contribution rather than *brand* profit contribution—becomes a critical evaluation of how well a marketer is doing his or her job. As for contribution to brand equity, that high-minded, Dr. Jekyll-like quality is not an item that customarily appears on the performance appraisal.

When marketers think like accountants, we make "trade push" a priority over "consumer pull."

The volume that counts is measured by factory sales, not by Nielsen or IRI (Information Resources, Inc.). The customer is the retailer, not the consumer. And naturally the customer gets the lion's share of the marketing budget, in the form of ever escalating trade promotion.

Unfortunately, growth of volume is no guarantee of growth in profits, especially when that volume growth is achieved through a massive infusion of promotional spending. Thus, Mr. Hyde's job is to be a demon for cost-control.

When marketers think like accountants, we generate profits by cutting spending.

Budget cuts become the universal answer to short-term profit goals. And those cuts usually fall where they will have the least short-term effect: on the funds intended to build consumer loyalty to the brand.

In fairness, there are many reasons why sales volume is extremely important to the health of a brand. Strong volume ensures the attention and affection of the trade, contributes mightily to manufacturing efficiencies and economies of scale, and helps perpetuate the brand by keeping it in front of and in frequent use by a great number of consumers. Also in fairness, there are even more good reasons why marketers must act like prudent businessmen, and deliver the profits that we have promised to management and stockholders. But we cannot allow any of these reasons to obscure the effect of our actions on the ultimate source of our livelihood.

Marketers need to think like marketers—sooner rather than later.

We need to consider the impact of our spending decisions on the consumer, and how the consumer feels about the brand. In dealing like accountants with the big numbers that appear on the brand's operating statement, it's easy to lose sight of the small numbers that go into those big numbers, the numbers that are crucial for real profitability—the profits derived from *individual* consumers who buy the brand. Decisions about the big numbers have an immediate and very apparent impact on the P&L. But they also have an impact on the small numbers, which may not be so immediate and is not at all likely to be apparent, unless we take the time and effort to look for it; an impact frequently contrary to what we might expect. And an impact that, if given proper consideration, might cause us to modify some of our decisions about the big numbers, or even change them completely.

These then are the challenges that Differential Marketing seeks to meet. To refocus marketers on the real source of profitability of our brands: *the individual consumers* who buy the brand. To prove that those profits can be increased over the long haul, while still making the quarterly numbers. And to demonstrate how long-term brand building activities truly do generate meaningful profit—*individual consumer profits*, which will aggregate to brand profits, and ultimately to division and corporate profits that will please accountants and marketers alike.

Let Mr. Hyde R.I.P.

3

WHY ALL CONSUMERS ARE NOT CREATED EQUAL

Executive Preview

Individual consumers represent the true source of profits for any brand.

Consumers who do buy the brand are a source of positive profit-flow. Consumers who don't buy the brand often contribute negative profit-flow, because of marketing expenses wasted by producing no return in sales. Brand profitability is the aggregate of the profitability of all consumers, whether they buy or whether they don't. Surprisingly, some consumers can generate a loss even if they do buy the brand, because marketing expense exceeds profit margin.

Implicit in this analysis is the fundamental truth that, from the standpoint of profitability, all consumers are not created equal. The so-called Pareto Principle has entered the marketing lexicon as the "20/80 rule," that is, 20 percent of the customers account for 80 percent of the sales.

Differential Marketing capitalizes on this skew by means of "profit segmentation"—dividing all consumers into groups based on the profit opportunity they provide the marketer. For frequently purchased categories, profitability correlates with buying rate. For other categories, such as durables, with the proximity in time to the purchase occasion.

New data shows that for most categories, one-third of the buyers account for at least two-thirds of the volume. This "high-profit seg-

27

ment" generally delivers six to ten times as much profit as the low-profit segment.

Moreover, they are critical not only because of their profit contribution but also because of their relatively small number.

The profits of most "mass market" brands clearly, then, do not come from the mass market. The small segment of profit-producing consumers must have a high priority in the marketing plan.

A t its simplest, the core idea of Differential Marketing (DFM) is to make profitability the driver of all marketing strategy, *individual consumer* profitability.

At first blush, this might not appear to be a very revolutionary concept. Certainly not one that necessarily would lead to the radical rethinking of the marketing plan. Where else would profits come from, if not from the consumers who buy the marketer's goods or service? Yet in practice, the care and feeding of this singular source of profitability is too often neglected.

Contrary to the implication of remarks frequently overheard in annual planning meetings, or at crunch time at the end of the quarter, profits do not mysteriously materialize out of sales volume or market share or budget reductions. No more than they are delivered by storks.

There is only one source of profits: the individual consumers or households who buy the brand.

Profits come from current consumers. The profit is the price consumers pay, less the retailer's margin, less the cost of raw materials, manufacturing, sales and distribution, less marketing expense.

Profits from current customers are offset by losses from consumers who do not buy the brand.

There is always more *positive profit-flow* than actual *profit*. Consumers who do *not* buy the brand produce losses that drain money from the positive profit-flow. These losses are generated by marketing expenses that produce no return in sales because they are directed at nonbuyers. In fact, positive profit flow from some customers can also be offset by losses from other customers who, nonetheless, *do* buy the brand. These losses are incurred because the marketing expense to generate the sale exceeds the available margin.

Total brand profitability is the sum of the individual returns of all buyers and nonbuyers combined.

The total profits for the brand are calculated by adding up the profit or loss of *all* consumers, irrespective of whether they buy the brand. Overhead and general and administrative expenses may be deducted at this point, or deferred until brand profit contribution is aggregated at the division or corporate level. That decision is safe to leave to the accountants.

This is an unreconstructed marketer's way of thinking about profits. Like everything else that we do, it places consumers at the center of the marketing universe. Product features and package design and advertising platforms revolve around them. Why not the profitability of the brand?

Perhaps the most startling notion inherent in this definition is that many consumers actually produce losses for the marketer, even if some of them do buy the brand, because marketing expenditures exceed margin. This observation suggests it is equally important not to overinvest on low-profit consumers as it is to invest those funds wisely against the high-profit segment. John Wanamaker would undoubtedly applaud.

Another inference, which shouldn't be as startling as some marketers find it, is that some consumers are far more profitable than others. Some consumers do indeed provide differentially higher levels of profit, some differentially less, and consequently do deserve higher or lower levels of marketing support. These differences logically lead to a new way of thinking about—and segmenting—consumers: on the basis of the *profit differential* they present to the marketer.

THE CONCEPT OF PROFIT SEGMENTATION

It was the Italian economist and sociologist, Vilfredo Pareto, who, in a work published in 1896, *Cours d'Economie Politique*, first observed the general phenomenon of the few controlling the majority of influence. Critics attacked Pareto's assertion that the distribution of income and wealth in a society was not random but followed this consistent pattern throughout history. Had he only been content to focus on product consumption, there could have been no debate.

In any event, the so-called Pareto Principle has entered the marketing lexicon as the 20/80 rule. Conventional marketing wisdom holds that, on average, about 20 percent of the users of a brand or a category account for about 80 percent of the volume and, other factors being constant, about 80 percent of the profits.

While some marketers might quibble about the degree of the skew, few would deem it insignificant. Nonetheless, it has been largely ignored in practical marketing applications. Historically, there seemed to be no cost-effective way of identifying the 20 percent of heavy users, much less communicating with them. More important, there was no compelling reason to single them out, considering the high degree of efficiency achievable through the mass media that permitted the marketer to ignore the inevitable waste.

Times have changed, though, in more ways than one, as demonstrated in the preceding chapter. But one of the few things that has remained constant is Pareto's basic principle, which has become one of the key building blocks of DFM.

Differential Marketing systematizes the fundamental truth that all consumers are not created equal through the concept of *profit segmentation*.

Differential Marketing segments consumers on the basis of the amount of profit they are capable of delivering to the marketer.

Instead of dividing consumers on the basis of demographics or lifestyles or attitudes, DFM divides consumers into groups of *varying profit opportunity.* All consumers in each profit segment have generally similar levels of profit potential for the marketer and different levels from consumers in the other profit segments.

A key word is "potential." Consumers are not segmented on the basis of their *current* profitability, but rather on the level of profit they will generate if the marketer's efforts to win them over are successful.

Similarly, profit opportunity is measured by gross profit, *before* marketing expense. Net profit is not used to determine profit segmentation because according to the marketer's definition of profitability, marketing expenses are a charge against positive profit-flow. As such, they are both variable and discretionary. For example, if two consumers make the same amount of purchases, but one is currently less profitable than the other because of a higher level of purchases "on deal," that may be the result of the marketer's current promotional practices rather than some behavior pattern inherent to the consumer. If so, the real profit opportunity of the two consumers is equal.

The most common and most useful profit segmentation for DFM is four groups: high, medium, low, and no profit. Consumers in the high-profit segment represent at least six times the profit opportunity to the average packaged goods brand as low-profit consumers, almost as much for the average consumer service business, and usually all of the profit for the durables marketer.

For most brands, in most circumstances, the profit differential is the greatest discriminator between consumers.

With few exceptions, the skew of potential profit is far more pronounced than skews for seasonality, demography, geography, lifestyle, or desired benefits. Thus, profit opportunity affords marketers the greatest leverage for targeting their marketing activities.

The magnitude and the consistency of this pattern have become increasingly evident since the mid-1980s, especially for packaged goods, because of the extensive use of scanning panels by marketers. Even scanners, however, can sometimes understate the predominance of the heavy-buying households, who make their frequent purchases from a wide variety of outlets. Static diary panels, like that operated by one of the leaders in consumer behavior research, MRCA Information Services, of Stamford, Connecticut, have the advantage of capturing all of the household purchases from all outlets and all shopping trips.

To satisfy the need for highly accurate and objective but non-confidential information to validate and illustrate the principles of DFM, MRCA undertook a series of special analyses of its proprietary data file exclusively for this book. The MRCA sample is statistically balanced to replicate a true cross-section of consumers and, perhaps most critical, stable enough to measure trends over extended periods with relatively small groups of reporting households. As a result, highly reliable comparisons of the consumer buying behavior patterns prevalent today can be made with those of fifteen or more years ago, when scanners were still in their infancy.

One of MRCA's fundamental tasks was to verify the concept of profit segmentation by examining consumer buying habits across a variety of categories and brands where profit opportunity logically correlates with category buying rate.

The one-third/two-thirds rule prevails for category buyers.

Over a wide variety of packaged-goods and soft-goods categories, 33 percent of category buying households account for at least 67 percent of category volume. This means that the top third of category buyers purchase *at least* three times as many boxes of cereal or pairs of blue jeans as the middle third and six times as much as the bottom third. Thus they constitute the high-profit segment. In fact, as the Closeup at the end of the chapter demonstrates, heavy category buyers often make as many as ten times more purchases than the bottom third. And, all other things being equal, they contribute ten times as much profit.

This relationship between sales and buyers is illustrated in Figure 3.1, in the form of a visual mnemonic device called the Profit Matrix

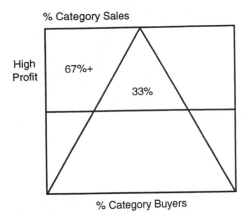

Figure 3.1   The packaged-goods Profit Matrix. (Source: MRCA Information Services.)

that will be used extensively throughout this book. The numbers inside the triangle represent the percentage of buyers or buying households (33%), and the numbers outside represent the percentage of sales (67%). The point is made visually that a relatively small number of buyers, the tip of the triangle, account for a relatively large proportion of sales. In other instances, this mnemonic device is used to demonstrate the nature of different relationships, like that of marketing spending to size of profit segment. But the numbers inside the triangle are, in general, always inversely proportional to the numbers outside.

As categories go, so go brands. MRCA looked at recent data for twenty-seven well-known, established brands in thirteen food, beverage, and personal and household product categories. They are all nationally distributed and advertised, and they range from market leaders to niche players. While no special effort was made to make the sample statistically representative of all packaged-goods brands, there is no reason to believe it is not reasonably representative, given the diversity of the brands selected. The typical packaged-goods Brand Profit Matrix is illustrated in Figure 3.2.

The one-third/two-thirds rule extends to the brand.

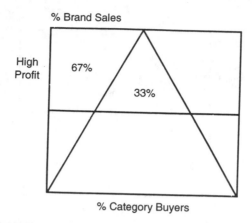

Figure 3.2 Typical packaged-goods Brand Profit Matrix. (Source: MRCA Information Services.)

On average, the top third of category buying households accounted for at least two-thirds of brand volume. For three of the brands, heavy category buyers accounted for more than 80 percent. For two others, they actually accounted for more than 90 percent of brand volume.

As a double check, MRCA examined data for the same brands for a period about fifteen years earlier. On average, the top third of category buying households consumed 68 percent of volume.

MRCA also examined buying behavior for eighteen well-known brands of apparel and footwear. The Profit Matrix for the typical soft-goods brand is illustrated in Figure 3.3. On average, the top third of category buying households accounted for 77 percent of soft-goods brand volume.

This same skew is evident among consumer service businesses. According to data collected by MRI (Mediamark Research, Inc.), which surveys the media and buying habits of 20,000 households each year, the top third of credit card holders accounted for 66 percent of credit card charges. And only 21 percent of movie-goers accounted for 80 percent of the attendance.[1]

The "long-distance wars" between AT&T, MCI, and Sprint revolve around the same phenomenon. The steep calling rate discounts are directed at the top third of personal long-distance callers, who

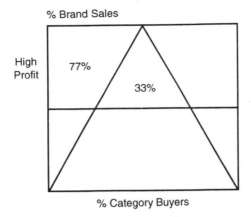

Figure 3.3 Typical soft-goods Brand Profit Matrix. (Source: MRCA Information Services.)

account for 68 percent of long distance billing.[2] The reason MCI's "Friends and Family" program was initially so devastating to AT&T was that it motivated those high-profit callers not only to sign up themselves but also to recruit other high-profit callers to sign up with them. Equally important, the plan was of little interest to the 30 percent of AT&T's customers who make less than $10 a month of long-distance calls,[3] and who in many cases wouldn't provide enough profit to cover the cost of AT&T's—or MCI's—billing system.

The Pareto Principle is also evident in retail businesses. MRI reports the top third of diners at family restaurants account for almost 90 percent of the visits.[4] And a new survey conducted for the Coca-Cola Retailing Research Council discloses that the top third of shoppers account for 80 percent of the grocery spending in any particular supermarket.[5]

The principle even holds true for the *range* of brands marketed by a single company. "It even surprised us when we did a special analysis of our database," observed John Kuendig, vice president of Marketing Development for Kraft Foods, one of the marketers leading the way in implementing the principles of DFM. "The top third of our households account for almost 70 percent of total Kraft volume—that's *all* the brands we sell, from cheese to coffee to Jell-O—and they buy almost ten times as many pounds of Kraft products as the bottom third. Why wouldn't you want to concentrate on them?"

Nor is a pattern this pervasive confined to the U.S. market. Data from marketers and market research organizations throughout Europe, Asia, and Latin America confirm that this kind of skew is a universal fact of consumer buying behavior.

The phenomenon of the few accounting for the most is consistent from category to category, country to country, brand to brand, and year to year.

But what about the sector of consumer durables—products that last for years, like personal computers, television sets, and automobiles? In most instances there is no such thing as a heavy buyer in those categories, at least over the course of the normal budgeting and planning period of twelve months.

For durables, profit segmentation is based on the timing of the purchase.

What makes a durables shopper high-profit is *how soon* they are going to buy rather than *how much*. The closer the consumer is to the purchase occasion, the higher the profit potential for the marketer.

In any given year, only a small percentage of consumers think about buying and an even smaller group actually make a purchase. These consumers are the equivalent of heavy buyers for the durables marketer. The "medium buyers" and "light buyers" are those consumers who will be in the market at some time in the future, typically one year out and two years or more, respectively.

In the luxury car market, for example, only about 25 percent of consumers who will buy or lease a new luxury car in the next four years will make the purchase during the current year. For the automaker intent on making the annual sales and profit plan, these consumers deserve more attention and resources than the 75 percent who will not buy this year. Importantly, this does not mean that the 75 percent are unimportant. They are only less so, and just for now.

For seemingly any category or brand, the pattern of the few delivering the most volume seems unchallengeable. But what about *profit*? Can we truly assume that "all other things are equal," that volume always correlates with profit? Perhaps for durables, where it is an all or nothing proposition. But what about fast moving goods and services? If we accept the marketer's definition of profitability, we *can* make the assumption with confidence.

The high-profit segment is high profit, not just high volume.

In fact, the percentage of total brand profit delivered by high-profit consumers is virtually always *larger* than their percentage of volume. The reasoning is simple, once the mathematics are understood. The no-profit segment is not only no-profit but always-loss, because nonbuyers receive marketing expenditures but produce no return in sales. Thus, the combined profit, the positive profit-flow, derived from the high-, medium-, and low-profit segments always *exceeds* total brand profitability. The loss generated by the no-profit segment offsets this larger number to produce the actual brand profits.

Moreover, the profitability of the low-profit segment often is marginal, because the profit contribution they do make barely offsets the marketing expenses directed at them. As a result, they contribute proportionately less profit than they do volume.

The drag on profitability of the no-profit and low-profit segments ensures that the positive profit-flow produced by the high-profit and medium-profit segments is a greater percentage of total brand profitability than it is of total brand volume. This lost profit can be thought of as the *mass-media tax* imposed on brand profitability by the exclusive use of mass vehicles, like television, traditional print, and free-standing inserts.

---

*Ten to twenty percent of the profits the brand actually
earns typically are paid to the mass-media
tax collector.*

Despite the best efforts of media planners and buyers, this degree
of waste is inevitable against low- or no-potential households. To
review the calculations, see the Closeup at the end of the chapter
detailing why the high-profit segment's share of total profit always
exceeds their share of total volume.

THE SHRINKING HIGH-PROFIT SEGMENT

Based on the evidence, the critical importance of high-profit consumers to brand profitability seems undeniable. But there is also a
second truth revealed by profit segmentation. A differentially high
profit potential is not the only reason that makes high-profit consumers such an opportune target.

Never have so few bought so much.

At first glance, it may seem that the one-third of the buyers who
account for two-thirds or more of the volume may be a large enough
group to justify the inevitable waste in mass media and promotion,
as long as they are reached effectively. But the one-third/two-thirds
rule overstates the true picture of the world in which marketers
must operate, often by a considerable margin.

---

*In terms of total households, the one-third/two-thirds
rule is more like the one-fifth/two-thirds rule.*

The mass audience that is reached by mass media and sales promotion no longer uses many mass products. The market forces driving population diversity, combined with marketers' own actions to satisfy the needs and tastes of every nook and cranny of that diverse population, have virtually eliminated the "average" household. Households differ not only in terms of the brands they use but in the *kinds of products* they buy.

Thus, when *category penetration* is factored in, the size of the high-profit segment is diminished significantly. For those categories still enjoying broad appeal, like breakfast cereal, about twenty-six million households—roughly a quarter—account for two-thirds of the volume. But the MRCA panel demonstrates how quickly that number can shrink—to twenty-one million for coffee, fifteen million for yogurt, and only thirteen million for toilet bowl cleaners—less than 15 percent of all U.S. households. Figure 3.4 shows the 1992 Category Profit Matrix for yogurt, where 16 percent of households account for 83 percent of volume.

The same pattern holds true outside the world of packaged goods. MRI reports that the top third of cardholders who account for two-thirds of credit card volume represent only 15 percent of households. For family restaurants, just over 20 percent of households account for 90 percent of the visits.[6]

As relatively small as those heavy buyer groups are at the cate-

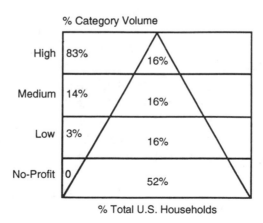

Figure 3.4 Yogurt Category Profit Matrix. (Source: MRCA Information Services 1992 data.)

gory level, they can diminish even further when looked at on a brand basis.

For high-profit brand buyers, the one-third/two-thirds rule is more like the one-tenth/two-thirds rule.

For twelve of the twenty-seven packaged-goods brands analyzed by MRCA, high-profit category buyers who bought the brand numbered less than 10 percent of households. The average was 12 percent; the highest, 27; the lowest, an astonishing 2 percent.

The situation in soft goods is even more pronounced. Heavy category buyers of sixteen of the eighteen apparel and footwear brands totaled less than 5 percent of households. The *average* was below 2 percent. Among the bigger brands, 5 percent of households buy 85 percent of Levi's blue jeans and 3 percent buy 82 percent of L'eggs pantyhose.

Folger's coffee provides a typical packaged-goods example. It is the leading brand in a category bought by well over half of all households, and the brand itself is purchased by 38 percent of all households over the course of a year. Yet, 70 percent of its volume is accounted for by only 15 percent of households.

Or take Diet Coke, a well-known, heavily advertised brand in a carbonated soft-drink category that has an overall penetration level of almost 90 percent. About a quarter of all households buy Diet Coke at least once during the year, and it commands an 8 percent market share, not insignificant in this extremely large but fractionated market. *But*, two-thirds of its volume is accounted for by eleven million heavy category buying households.

And even these figures do not tell the whole story about the stunning concentration of buying power. Many of the heavy category buyers who buy Folger's or Diet Coke do not buy *as much* of it as some more loyal medium category buyers. When current brand buyers, irrespective of profit segment, are divided into three groups, from heaviest to light, the top third can have an extraordinary skew. Figure 3.5 shows the pattern for Diet Coke. The top third of Diet Coke buyers, some seven million households, account for 84 percent of Diet Coke's annual sales.

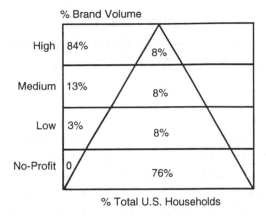

Figure 3.5   Diet Coke Brand Buyer Profit Matrix. (Source: MRCA Information Services.)

For "mass-market" brands like Diet Coke and Folger's, it seems very obvious where profits really come from—and where they don't.

The profits of mass-market brands don't come from the mass market.

It seems equally obvious that the care and feeding of this relatively small group of profit-producing consumers should have a high priority in the marketing plan. This observation is especially true for brands in the kind of market-share dogfight typical of mature markets and brand-hostile marketing conditions. In other words, the prevailing weather pattern. In fact, their loyalty is critical not only to keep them buying, but to keep them buying *profitably*. Just as all consumers are not created equal, neither are all the purchases they make equal. How brand loyalty affects profitability is discussed in depth in Chapter 4.

CLOSEUP

The Packaged-Goods Profit Matrix

MRCA data shows that, on average, the top third of category buyers—the high-profit segment—accounts for at least two-thirds of
category volume. That relationship is illustrated in a Profit Matrix
shown in Figure 3.6. The triangle represents total households. It is
divided into four profit segments—high-, medium-, low-, and no-
profit. The figures inside the triangle represent the percentage of
total households that fall into each of the four profit segments.

Forty-nine percent of households make no purchases in the widget category over the course of the year. They constitute the no-
profit segment. The 51 percent of households that do buy widgets
are divided into three groups of equal size, based on the number
of widgets they buy. The top third of widget-buying households
becomes the high-profit segment; the second third, the medium-
profit; and the bottom third, the low-profit. Each represents 17
percent of total households.

The figures to the left of the triangle are the percentage of total
category volume accounted for by each of the segments. Thus,

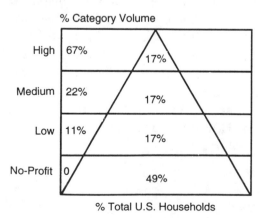

Figure 3.6   Widget Category Profit Matrix.

the heavy-buying high-profit segments account for 67 percent of volume, medium-profit for 22 percent, and low-profit for 11 percent.

As shown in Figure 3.7, a similar kind of Profit Matrix can also be used to demonstrate the relative amount of purchases made by individual households in each segment. The figures to the left of the triangle now represent the total amount of purchases, as expressed in dollars, of all households in the profit segment. The widget category has $1 billion a year in sales. So the high-profit segment, which accounts for 67 percent of category volume, has $670 million in sales.

The numbers inside the triangle now represent the number of households in each segment rather than the percentage. Each of the top three profit segments accounts for 17 percent of households, or 16,150,000 of a total of 95 million households.

To the right of the triangle are the total category expenditures of the average household in each segment. This figure is obtained by dividing the total segment dollar volume by the total number of households in each segment.

To take the high-profit segment as an example, $670 million divided by 16,150,000 households yields an average household expenditure of $41.49. This compares with $13.62 for the medium profit segment, and only $6.81 for the low-profit. Or, to put it another

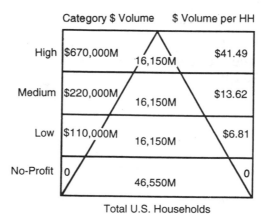

Category $ Volume $ Volume per HH

High	$670,000M	16,150M	$41.49
Medium	$220,000M	16,150M	$13.62
Low	$110,000M	16,150M	$6.81
No-Profit	0	46,550M	0

Total U.S. Households

Figure 3.7 Category Profit Matrix for widgets showing relative amount of purchases made by individual households in each segment.

way, for a category where one-third of the buyers account for two-thirds of the volume, the high-profit buyer buys more than six times as much as the low-profit buyer.

This ratio can increase dramatically if more volume is concentrated in the high-profit segment. Figure 3.8 demonstrates what happens when high-profit households account for 75 percent of category volume, not the least atypical for packaged goods brands. In this case, the number of consumers in each segment remains constant, as does the total category dollar volume. But $750,000 million is accounted for by the high-profit segment, resulting in an average household purchase of $46.44. This is more than *ten times* as much as the $4.33 spent on widgets by the average low-profit household.

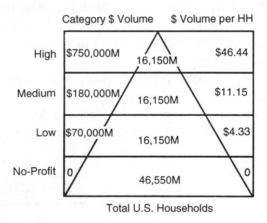

Category $ Volume $ Volume per HH

	Category $ Volume		$ Volume per HH
High	$750,000M	16,150M	$46.44
Medium	$180,000M	16,150M	$11.15
Low	$70,000M	16,150M	$4.33
No-Profit	0	46,550M	0

Total U.S. Households

Figure 3.8 Widget Category Profit Matrix showing high-profit households accounting for 75 percent of category volume.

CLOSEUP

Why the High-Profit Segment's Share of Total Profit Always Exceeds Share of Total Volume

Because brand profitability is the major driver of Differential Marketing, it's important to understand exactly how the various segments can produce profits or losses for the brand. It's also important to know why the share of total brand profit contributed by the high-profit segment is always greater than its share of total brand volume.

As explained in the text, profit from a DFM perspective has only one source: the consumers who buy the brand. Individual consumer and aggregate profit segment profitability can be calculated using the following equation:

$$
\begin{array}{l}
\text{Retail Sales} \\
- \text{ Retailer Margin} \\
\hline
= \text{ Gross Revenue} \\
\\
- \text{ Raw Materials} \\
- \text{ Manufacturing} \\
- \text{ Sales \& Distribution} \\
\hline
= \text{ Gross Profit} \\
\\
- \text{ Marketing Expenses} \\
\hline
= \text{ Net Profit}
\end{array}
$$

The sum of the bottom lines of this equation for each consumer in each profit segment represents total brand profitability.

Most costs are associated with the product per se, either making it or selling it into the distribution system. As such, they are offsets to the revenue produced by the sale of the product. And from a profit segment perspective, they are properly accounted for only in those segments where product purchases are actually made—the high-profit, medium-profit, and low-profit segments.

Marketing expenses are different. They are incurred in the *expectation* of making the sale. And with the inevitable waste in mass media and promotional vehicles, some of those expenses will be incurred by reaching consumers who simply are not in the market for the category, much less the brand—the no-profit segment. Thus, from a profit segment perspective, the no-profit segment, which produces no revenue, does have expenses associated with it. Therefore, the no-profit segment produces a loss to brand profitability.

Figure 3.9 illustrates the Gross Profit Matrix for Widget-X, a typical brand of widgets. The widget category has a household penetration rate of 51 percent, divided equally into high-, medium-, and low-profit segments of 16,150,000 households each. Widget-X's total annual volume is $200 million, 75 percent of which, or $150 million, is accounted for by the high-profit segment. With a gross margin of 50 percent, gross profit totals $100 million, $75 million of which falls into the high-profit segment. The ratio of gross profit to volume is consistent across all profit-earning segments, but marketing expense must be factored in to determine *net* profit, as shown in Figure 3.10.

Widget-X spends $20 million a year in advertising. (Widget-X also spends a considerable sum on sales promotion, but for purposes of simplicity, marketing expenses in this example will be limited to advertising. Excluding sales promotion does not change the conclusions of the analysis.) Widget-X's advertising agency is skillful in

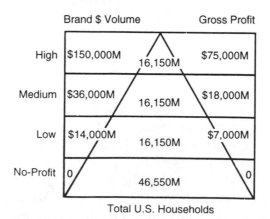

Figure 3.9   Widget-X Gross Profit Matrix.

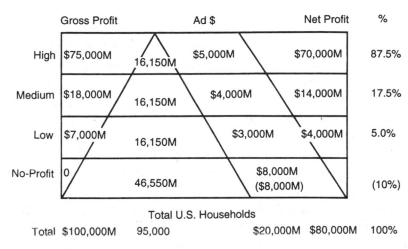

Figure 3.10 Net Profit Matrix for Widget-X brand widgets.

media targeting. Of those impressions that do reach widget buyers, substantially more reach high-profit households, $5 million worth versus $4 million for medium-profit and $3 million for low-profit households. Nonetheless, a large proportion of impressions still falls on the deaf ears of the no-profit segment, 40 percent or $8 million worth to be exact.

Subtracting those advertising expenses from gross profit produces a net profit figure of $80 million. But the actual positive net profit-flow from Widget-X sales totals $88 million. The difference is the loss of the $8 million invested in advertising to consumers who have absolutely no interest in purchasing a widget, at least not this year.

Calculating net profit by segment reveals an interesting and important phenomenon. The $70 million delivered by the high-profit segment represents 88 percent of total net profit, and 80 percent of positive profit-flow, in both instances greater than the 75 percent share of volume. The reason is twofold.

First, the marketing expense directed against the high-profit segment is proportionately lower in relation to the profit produced than that of any other segment. Even with a substantial impression skew, advertising only accounts for $5 million/$75 million or 6.7 percent of the high-profit segment's gross profit. This compares with $3 million/$7 million or 42.9 percent of the low-profit segment's gross profit. Because proportionately more of the low- and medium-profit segments' gross profit is offset by marketing expenditures, the percentage of net profit delivered by the high-profit segment is larger in relation to positive profit-flow—80% ($70,000,000 ÷ $88,000,000) rather than 75%.

Second, the inevitable loss produced by the no-profit segment means that the combined positive profit-flow of all profit-making segments *exceeds* the net profit—in this case by $8,000,000, or 10%. When each segment's positive profit-flow is repercentaged on the smaller base of net profit, all segments show a higher percentage of net profit than they did of positive profit-flow—88% for the high-profit segment, and 17% and 5% for the medium- and low-profit segments respectively. The high-profit segment's increase is dispro-portionately larger than that of other segments—from 80% to 88%—because it accounts for 80% of the positive profit-flow and therefore of 80% of the "overage" (80% of 10% overage = 8% + 80% = 88%).

Sharp-eyed observers will note a critical assumption in the pre-ceding analysis: that gross margin is identical in each profit seg-ment. That is not necessarily the case if the type or form of product that high-profit buyers customarily buy is markedly different for those purchased by medium- and low-profit buyers. One notable example would be categories where heavy buyers buy significantly more "bulk sizes," which customarily have a lower mark-up. In that case, percent of profit may be somewhat lower than percent of volume, although the share of total profits will still be considerably higher than that of the other segments. If not, then the wrong stan-dards have been used to classify "high-profit" buyers.

Interestingly, that circumstance does not typically come into play for packaged goods brands. MRCA data shows that although heavy buyers of packaged goods buy somewhat more product on each pur-chase occasion than medium and light buyers, their higher volume is due primarily to buying considerably more frequently than other buy-ers, not to buying "in bulk." Another exception is when heavy-buyers actually pay *more* for the same product, as often happens in the travel industry. Frequent fliers tend to fly on shorter notice than leisure travelers, so they are unable to take advantage of the steep discount structure offered to consumers who plan ahead. As a result, the mar-gins of heavy airline ticket purchasers are higher, and their profit skew is even more pronounced than that of their volume.

4

THE CHANGING NATURE OF BRAND LOYALTY

Executive Preview

The number of high-profit consumers a brand attracts is clearly critical to growth and profits. But so is the loyalty of those high-profit buyers.

Marketers are often afflicted by "loyalty blindness." They believe that a consumer either "belongs" to them, or to a competitor, or is a confirmed price-switcher. This is too simplistic a model to produce the most effective strategies for brand growth. Packaged goods is a good indicator of how brand loyalty in the post-mass-market world is relative rather than absolute. Consumers distribute their purchases over a group of brands they find acceptable. "Share of customer" for each brand serves as the best measurement of relative brand loyalty.

High-profit buyers buy the largest number of brands, almost six per category on average, and have the lowest average share of customer. Moreover, an analysis of new data conclusively demonstrates that the loyalty of high-profit buyers has declined markedly since the late 1970s. In fact, the very nature of brand loyalty seems to be changing.

Less and less do high-profit buyers have a dominant brand to which they give 50 percent or more of their purchases. More and more, they distribute their buying across the brands in their repertoire. Loyalty parity is on the rise.

As a result, as much as 80 percent of a brand's sales are made

49

to consumers who are essentially disloyal to the brand, or who do not make enough category purchases to truly make a difference to brand profitability.

As startling—and as ominous—as this situation is, if the root causes are correctable it opens up a potentially lucrative source of additional sales and profits: more business from current high-profit buyers.

Because of their greater number of purchases, the high-profit segment will always present the greatest profit opportunity. But the actual *amount* of profit they deliver to the marketer will depend on the loyalty of individual consumers within the segment.

Loyalty affects brand profitability in two ways. The degree of loyalty has a strong influence on the share of total category purchases consumers give to any particular brand. It also has a significant effect on the price the marketer can charge for the brand.

The more loyal the consumers, the more they will pay.

MRCA data shows that loyal high-profit packaged-goods buyers actually pay, on average, 7–10 percent more for a brand than non-loyal buyers. That's the price differential they accept in order to buy their brand of choice rather than the brand on sale.

The less loyal the consumers, the more marketers must deal.

Conversely, when loyalty is low and marketers resort to price promotion to drive volume up, they drive profitability down. Just because it's so self-evident doesn't mean it's not worth repeating: A purchase made "on deal" will always deliver less profit to the marketer than a purchase made at full price. The cost of the incentive has to come from somewhere. That "somewhere" is the profit margin. In fact, it's not uncommon for the cost of the incentive to exceed the available margin, and actually produce a loss.

Even if the transaction is "profitable," the promotion may still cost the marketer profits. The *incremental* effect on sales and profits must be considered. If many or most of the purchases would have been made anyway, even in the absence of the promotional incentive, the marketer ends up losing money. Studies of packaged-goods brand purchase data from IRI (Information Resources, Inc.) have reported that 84 percent of trade promotions have a negative impact on the brand's bottom line.[1] Similarly, news stories quoting IRI executives have also reported that 89 percent of consumer promotion is unprofitable.[2]

The more marketers must deal, the less they make.

What's true for a single promotion is also true for a general overreliance on promotion. A study of the PIMS (Profit Impact of Market Strategies) database, maintained by The Strategic Planning Institute (SPI), revealed the correlation between a high level of sales promotion in the marketing mix and lower profits. Focusing on packaged-goods businesses, the study's authors, Robert D. Buzzell, Professor of Marketing at the Harvard Business School, and Bradley T. Gale, SPI's Managing Director, concluded that "those businesses that allocate most of their marketing budgets to promotion *tend* to have lower profit margins and rates of return on investment." Businesses that on average spent 77 percent of their marketing funds in promotion achieved an average return on investment of 18.1 percent. Those who averaged only 44 percent in promotional spending had an ROI of 27.3 percent. While those who placed only 34 percent of their funds in sales promotion, versus 66 percent in advertising, had the highest ROI of all—30.5 percent.[3]

The link between brand loyalty and profitability has been so firmly established that it hardly needs to be belabored. In *The Fourth Wave*, the second booklet published by the Coalition for Brand Equity, coauthors Larry Light and Richard Morgan cite no less than fifteen different marketing experts who have found a clear correlation between the two.[4]

Nowhere is brand loyalty more critical to profitability than in the dog-eat-dog world of packaged-goods marketing, where mature markets and mature brands are the norm and the battleground is share of market. And nowhere does the prevailing view about loyalty so often seem so muddled.

It's instructive to study packaged-goods brands in detail because they serve as the "white mice" of marketing. They have enough genetic similarities with most brands to use them to predict what might happen in other sectors. And it is easier to understand exactly what *is* happening because of the extensive amount of information available and their frequent sales turnover, which makes patterns and trends easier to spot.

When packaged-goods marketers are not bemoaning the death of loyalty, they are prone to a highly simplified view of their markets, to wit, that buyers of the category are divided into three camps, "mine," "theirs," and "nobody's." They either buy the marketer's brand or the competitor's or they are faithless price-buyers. Keeping things simple is always to be admired. But oversimplification can be counterproductive.

Most consumers are "ours."

Consumers spread their purchases across many brands, making a binary, on/off model of brand loyalty simply too blunt an instrument to allow marketers to determine where the greatest profit opportunity lies for their brands.

LOYALTY BLINDNESS

"I still don't get it." That was the first response from a young packaged-goods brand manager upon being presented the results of the Differential Marketing (DFM) test described in the first chapter. "Why would I want to waste more resources on my current buyers?

I'm married to them already. What I want to do is go after the other guy's users. Or maybe even pull new consumers into the category."

Rather than debate the issue in front of the brand manager's boss, the presenter nodded at the chart on the screen, showing a 30 percent increase in volume from those very same consumers to whom the brand manager believed he was "married."

"I don't care what it says," the brand manager continued heatedly. "I'm not sure I buy your data about low loyalty. Every presentation I've ever seen around here shows that we've got one of the highest loyalty rates in the category."

"What about the loyalty of *heavy* category buyers?" the presenter asked.

"What about it? If anything, heavy buyers are going to be more loyal, right? They're the most involved, so they find the brand they like and stick with it. Unless they're a price-buyer, in which case they either buy what's on sale or go for the store brand."

The symptoms exhibited by the brand manager were not the least bit extreme or unusual. The underlying condition might be characterized as "loyalty blindness." It afflicts a large portion of the marketing world, and it is brought on by equal measures of wishful thinking and flawed research techniques. Ignored is the basic DFM proposition that all consumers are not created equal. And relied upon are consumers' impressionistic descriptions of what they *think* they buy, rather than what they actually purchase.

When actual buyer behavior is examined *on a profit segment basis* by means of *panel* data, a very different picture emerges. The incidence and importance of true "price-switchers" is often exaggerated. Some buyers in all segments do buy exclusively or nearly always on deal. The level varies category to category, but generally MCRA data shows that the group is dominated by the low-profit segment.

"Price buyers" tend to be light buyers.

Unlike heavy buyers who need and therefore buy the product frequently, lighter buyers have the luxury of shopping around or waiting for the next coupon. In the yogurt category for example, high-profit price buyers, those heavy buyers that make 70 percent or more of their purchases on deal, account for only 13 percent of heavy-buyer volume. Only 5 percent of heavy buyers make *all* their purchases on deal in comparison with 23 percent of light buyers.

"Loyal buyers" tend to be light buyers.

Similarly, most solo brand buyers and other "loyalists" are found in the low-profit segment. They have little opportunity to switch brands because they make relatively few purchases. In *extreme* cases, light buyers have no occasion to be disloyal.

In the air freshener category for example, MRCA data reveals that more than 60 percent of the light buyers make only one category purchase per year. In other words, by definition they are 100 percent loyal. When these kinds of low-profit buyers are lumped in with all buyers, they distort the true picture by significantly inflating the average.

By comparison, the high-profit segment is indiscriminate in its affection. Heavy category buyers of the leading air freshener give it only 29 percent of their business, on average. And they purchase 3.6 different brands over the course of a year.

Loyalty is relative, not absolute.

The concept of *share of requirements*, like the 20/80 rule, is too often a victim of collective amnesia. Marketers know that consumers tend to spread their purchases around a group of brands they find acceptable—the *considered set* or the *brand repertoire*. We know, too, that any single purchase decision is dependent on a variety of factors, including brand availability and promotional incentives as well as the consumer's degree of conviction about the distinctiveness of the brand.

But loyalty blindness has lulled us into a false sense of security and caused us to overlook the dramatic consequences of that behavior pattern among the heaviest, and most profitable, buyers. And we persist in that mind-set until we see data like that about air fresheners, which is not the least uncommon. Only then can we accept the facts about what truly constitutes brand-loyalty in a post-mass-market world.

SHARE OF CUSTOMER

The academic-sounding term "share of requirements" somehow fails to do justice to a very important and practical marketing concept. It might better be called what it actually is: the *share of customer* that the brand commands of the total purchases of the household or consumer.

Share of customer is the brand's market share of the individual.

Share of customer—or SOC—is measured by dividing the total brand purchases of an individual by their total category purchases. The period measured is commonly a year so that multiple purchase cycles are included. And because of the way the data is collected, from consumer panels, SOC is most often expressed on a household basis. If a household bought twelve packages of air freshener during the course of twelve months, and four of them were Glade, Glade's SOC in that household would be 33 percent.

Share of customer is not a perfect measure of brand loyalty, but it is a practical one. Conceivably, a household might be more or less loyal to a brand than the SOC would indicate. For example, if a brand were frequently out of stock, another brand might be bought in its place, even though the first brand was strongly preferred. But any minor flaws are outweighed by the ease of measurement and the simplicity of calculation. Thus, share of customer has become the most common yardstick for evaluating brand loyalty of packaged goods.

In fact, the utility of the concept of SOC extends far beyond these kinds of products. Of the eighteen apparel and footwear brands that MRCA examined, category heavy buyers gave them an average of 38 percent of their purchases. Similarly, according to Mediamark Research, Inc. (MRI), heavy fast-food eaters distribute their patronage over an average of 2.9 different chains, and heavy credit card users carry 6.2 cards.[5] In all of these cases, and in many similar ones, share of customer is a simple and convenient method for gauging brand loyalty.

When the marketing situation warrants, the concept can even be extended across categories. Gatorade, for example, earns virtually a 100 percent share of customer in the "sports drink" category, which it invented and continues to dominate. But a more useful way of thinking about Gatorade brand loyalty might be to measure its share of customer across all "thirst quenchers," including carbonated soft drinks, iced tea, and lemonade. These other kinds of products may be, in fact, the true competitive set.

The core principle of share of customer—that consumers have a repertoire of brands they consider acceptable and from which they choose among on any given purchase occasion—can even be useful in thinking about infrequently purchased categories like automobiles, appliances, and other durable goods. Rarely do consumers shop only one brand when they are making a considered purchase. Sears recognized the necessity of offering shoppers national brand names in addition to its own Kenmore line and now carries GE, Whirlpool, and other major appliance brands in its "Sears Brand Central" departments. And auto dealerships, which were once a captive distribution network, more often than not offer a choice of makes under the same roof.

The consumers in the market for this kind of purchase—the high-profit segment—are multiple-brand "considerers" rather than multiple-brand buyers. So for durables, loyalty can logically be measured by "share of mind" or "share of consideration," and not just by straight repurchase rate.

Share of customer is a fundamental analytical tool of DFM. Not only does it demonstrate that loyalty is relative and measure the degree, it also illuminates a startling challenge facing many brands in the current marketing environment, especially packaged-goods brands. By most common definitions of "loyalty," very few high-profit consumers in the brand franchise are loyal to that brand.

A brand's best customers buy more from the competition than they do from the brand.

Of the packaged-goods brands that MRCA studied, the average share of customer of category heavy buyers who bought those brands was *less than* 20 percent. In other words, heavy category buyers who did buy the brand, bought it on average less than one in every five times they made a purchase in the category. They bought one of the brand's *competitors* four out of five times. The highest share of customer for any single brand was 48 percent, for Butterball turkeys. The lowest was 5 percent for a brand in the highly fractionalized cheese category.

Nor is this low loyalty rate a mirage created by statistics, a large loyal core group "averaged down" by an even larger number of heavy buyers buying the brand only one time. If a reasonable definition of "brand loyal" is a share of customer of 50 percent or more, very few high-profit consumers in the brand franchise qualify. Only 11 percent of the high-profit buyers who bought these brands bought them at least 50 percent of the time or more when they made a purchase in the category.

Of the brands analyzed, Folger's coffee had one of the highest loyalty rates. As reported in Chapter 3, heavy coffee buyers who buy Folger's represent almost 15 percent of the total population, or roughly fifteen million households. Yet only about four million of them buy Folger's rather than a competitive brand at least half the time. And this is an outstanding ratio in comparison with many brands.

If this is a marriage, it is certainly of the most permissive kind. The Closeup at the end of the chapter, while not as titillating as the average supermarket tabloid, provides more eye-opening facts about the state of marital bliss in the packaged-goods marketing world.

The corollary to this picture of the brand franchise as a broad group of consumers who "sample" the brand from time to time, is that the relatively few high-profit buyers who *are* loyal to the brand must be very valuable indeed. And they are. When it comes to profitability, a brand's true "core franchise"—the heavy category buyers who give more than half their purchases to the brand—are the crown jewels. The four million heavy buying households that give Folger's at least 50 percent of their business account for nearly half of the brand's annual volume. To put that four million in perspective, there are roughly ninety-five million households in the entire country, and about thirty-six million who buy Folger's at least once over the course of the year.

The implication of this stunning concentration of buying power is profound.

The brand's core franchise of loyal, high-profit buyers must be protected at all costs.

Without a core group of loyal, heavy buyers, there conceivably might be no brand. Unfortunately, judging from trends in consumer buying behavior through the 1980s and early 1990s, brands in general have but a tenuous hold on their core groups. Based on MRCA data, Folger's provides a shining success story relative to the plight of many brands.

TOWARD LOYALTY PARITY

Most marketers have a vague sense that "brand loyalty is declining." Yet how much loyalty has actually declined or what that decline means for the formulation of marketing strategies is poorly understood. The publicly available data is at best sketchy, and at times even contradictory. For every "Chicken Little" there is a "Pollyanna" to defuse the warnings.

Once again, the packaged-goods "white mice" may provide the clue. Conclusive new panel data from MRCA shows that declines in brand loyalty are both pervasive and substantial. There are wide variations from brand to brand and category to category, but the overall direction is clear: downward. And the degree is often unnerving.

MRCA conducted a special analysis of loyalty trends for twenty-six of the twenty-seven selected major brands, generally covering the period from 1977 to 1992. One brand, Pampers disposable diapers, was eliminated from the analysis because its extreme decline in loyalty reflected a significant increase in competitive activity which was not representative of most other categories. At both the beginning and end of the period the U.S. economy was halfway through a recovery from a recession, minimizing any economic bias.

The reporting dates vary slightly for a few brands because of data availability, but in all cases they provide a long-term perspective on changes in loyalty over a critical fifteen or so years, when the market forces and marketing actions discussed in Chapter 2 were intensifying, particularly the explosion of sales promotion budgets. Importantly, the relative stability of the panel and the consistent methodology allows a valid comparison of loyalty measures, dating back to a time when household scanning data was not widely available.

The analysis also reveals why there is so much confusion about the extent of brand loyalty declines, and even some question about whether they have truly occurred.

Declines in brand loyalty are most pronounced in the critical high-profit segment.

Whatever the measure of loyalty, declines among heavy category buyers have outpaced those of the other profit segments. Less severe declines among medium and light buyers, who represent two-thirds of all buyers, have served to mask the true extent of the problem.

Moreover, it is not just that loyalty measures have declined, but the very *nature* of brand loyalty seems to be changing among category heavy buyers. Specifically, the tendency of these high-profit buyers to have one "dominant" or "favorite" brand and several alternatives seems to be giving way to a repertoire without any clear-cut favorites.

The concept of a "dominant brand" is losing meaning.

One of the simplest ways of judging loyalty is to determine the number of brands in the category that a consumer bought over the course of a year. For a fast-moving packaged-goods brand, this should be an adequate measurement of the size of the considered set. Over the fifteen year period, the number of brands bought in each category by medium and light category buyers increased on average from 3.7 to 3.9. But the number bought by heavy category buyers rose from 5.3 to 5.7.

By itself, these increases may appear more reassuring than troubling, considering that over the course of the reporting period the number of products sold in the average supermarket more than doubled. But the absolute number of brands purchased in each category—almost six for the heavy buyer—begins to give pause, even though some of the categories, like salty snacks, are inherently so broad that multiple brand purchase is to be expected.

Share of customer declined in a similar fashion. Average share of customer of medium and light buyers for the average brand fell from 27 percent to 23 percent. Eight brands increased SOC, eighteen brands declined. But share of customer of *heavy* category buyers for the average brand *fell* from 23 percent to 18 percent. Heavy category buyers of ten brands increased their SOC, sixteen declined.

While this data is unsettling, many brands actually increased their share of customer. Overall declines in the range of 20 percent seem reasonable and consistent with the increases in the number of brands purchased. Based on these measures alone, it could be argued that the Pollyannas have a point. It is only when the *nature* of multiple brand buying is examined that the true declines in loyalty become evident. What seems to be happening is that the gap between the "favorite brand" and other brands in the consumer's repertoire is *narrowing*.

Loyalty parity is on the rise.

The crown jewels of the franchise, the high-profit brand-loyal consumers who give, or once gave, more than 50 percent of their category purchases to the brand, seem especially prone to "loyalty parity." As demonstrated in Figure 4.1, the percentage of brand-loyal, high-profit buyers in the franchise have declined on average by more than a third, from 17 percent to 11 percent of category heavy buyers buying the brand.

And even this average was cushioned by the nine brands that marginally increased or managed to maintain their loyal heavy buyer penetration. For the remaining seventeen brands, the average percentage of loyal high-profit buyers declined by roughly half.

This means that almost 90 percent of the high-profit buyers of a brand give it less than half their business. And because the brands studied were chosen more or less randomly, it also means that

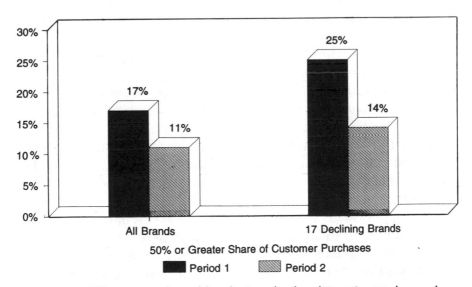

Figure 4.1 Fifteen-year brand loyalty trends showing category heavy buyers of twenty-six brands. (Source: MRCA.)

almost 90 percent of the high-profit buyers in the category don't give *any* brand more than half their business.

Whatever brand-hostile forces are at work, they are harder at work in the high-profit segment.

The decline in brand-loyal buyers was almost an exclusive phenomenon of the high-profit segment. While high-profit, brand-loyal buyers in the average franchise were decreasing by more than a third, brand-loyal buyers in the medium- and low-profit segments fell by just 10 percent, from 30 percent to 27 percent of all buyers. Granted, because of their greater number of purchases, there was more opportunity for a decline in the high-profit segment. A difference of this magnitude, however, suggests that *something else* was happening as well, that whatever was driving the declines had an unequal effect on the different profit segments. (This phenomenon is examined more closely in Chapter 6.)

Nor can the precipitous drop in heavy buyer loyalty be blamed on the inclusion of brands in categories where variety is not necessarily a vice, like breakfast cereal. When the brands in those categories are excluded, the situation hardly improves. Among brands in "non-variety-seeking" categories, brand-loyal, high-profit consumers in the franchise have also declined by more than a third, from 32 percent to 20 percent of category heavy buyers buying the brand. And only two of the thirteen brands managed to increase their proportion of 50-percent loyal heavy buyers.

As might be expected, many of the largest declines in loyalty occurred in brands who going-in had the highest loyalty rates. They had the most to lose. Windex, for example, had an extremely high percentage of 50-percent loyal category heavy buyers in the first reporting period: 59 percent according to MRCA data. By 1992, that figure had fallen to 33 percent, twenty-six percentage points.

The smallest declines, and the majority of the gains, occurred for brands that from the start had relatively low levels of loyal heavy category buyers, 10 percent or less. And most of them were in variety-seeking categories. The level for Pringle's potato chips, for example, dropped from 4 percent to less than 1 percent, and the level for Oreo cookies increased from 3 percent to 4 percent. But even though as a group there was less of an absolute drop in loyalty, *relatively* these smaller brands behaved much the same.

The coup de grace for any determined wearers of rose-colored glasses is delivered by a look at the "extremely loyal" heavy buyers, those who gave 80 percent or more of their purchases to a single brand. Extremely loyal heavy category buyers have virtually disappeared from the average brand franchise, falling from 10 percent to 5 percent of category heavy buyers of the brand. The decline is similar when brands in variety-seeking categories are excluded. The remaining brands drop from 18 percent to 9 percent.

Few high-profit buyers can now be considered brand loyal by any definition.

The practical impact of such a low level of loyal buyers is that their contribution to brand volume is modest. Only 20 percent of the average brand's volume is accounted for by loyal heavy category buyers, and only 10 percent by extremely loyal heavy buyers. Eliminating brands in variety-seeking categories, where high loyalty rates would not be expected to be the norm, improves the picture only slightly. For the remaining brands, only a bit more than *one-third of brand volume* is contributed by those heavy-category buyers who are at least 50 percent loyal.

The corollary to these findings is *not* better than the proverbial sharp stick in the eye.

The majority of brand sales and profits come from consumers who are essentially disloyal to the brand . . . or who don't buy enough to make a difference.

About two-thirds of a representative brand's volume is accounted for by buyers who choose the brand less than half the time they make a category purchase. Or who do not buy enough of the product category to substantially add or detract from brand volume and profitability. Figure 4.2 illustrates the contribution of marginal consumers and brand *disloyalty* in a representative packaged-goods brand franchise.

There is some tantalizing evidence from the automotive industry that what is true for the "white mice" is also becoming true for the more general population. The phenomenon of the decline of a dominant brand, or at least a brand that dominates consideration, is not restricted to packaged goods. In a recent J.D. Power & Associates survey, the top five makes whose owners describe themselves as "loyal to the brand" are Toyota, Acura, Honda, Cadillac, and Lincoln, in that order. For these customers, these brands might be described as the equivalent of the "dominant brand" in packaged goods.[6]

But how "dominant" that brand *is* varies widely. Cadillac and Lincoln are the two makes with the highest repurchase rate, about twenty to twenty-five percentage points higher than the category. And they are also the two makes with the highest percentage of owners who say they will definitely repurchase. Surprisingly, the other three makes are generally average or below average on these repurchase measures.[7] When it comes time to buy, the younger owners of Hondas, Acuras, and Toyotas who claim to be more loyal

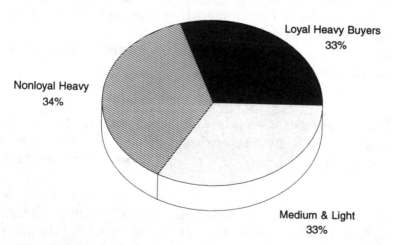

Figure 4.2 Source of representative brand volume by profit segment and 50-percent-plus loyalty. (Source: MRCA.)

than Cadillac and Lincoln owners seem to want to shop around more, and do. For them, their current car is simply not as dominant in their mind, despite their self-described high rates of loyalty.

The evolving behavior pattern of loyalty parity is absolutely critical to an understanding of what constitutes brand loyalty in a post-mass-market world.

The high-profit consumer is not the marrying kind.

It is far different to have one brand to which one is primarily faithful, despite a few flings on the side, versus no faithfulness at all. Marketers may aspire to marriage, even if the consumer is already married to another. But marriage is not in the cards for marketers if the only thing their true love is committed to is playing the field.

Moreover, this clear-eyed look at what brand loyalty is, and what it is not, has significant implications for the development of marketing strategies to increase brand profitability. Surely for those brands like Folger's or Cadillac who still have a group of core buyers that contribute an extraordinary percentage of volume and profit, hanging on to them must be made a top priority, even as new buyers are brought into the franchise. And for brands for whom that core franchise is rapidly disappearing, stemming the desertion rate is an obvious necessity.

But aside from defensive measures, the relative lack of loyalty among a large proportion of high-profit consumers in the brand franchise reveals an exciting new opportunity.

Current high-profit buyers may be the best source of future profit growth.

If the root causes of loyalty parity are correctable, or if they can at least be positively influenced, the greatest source of incremental profits for the brand may be those consumers who are already contributing the bulk of the brand's profits.

The reasoning is straightforward. Much of the hard work is done. The brand is already part of the considered set, even though there is certainly room to grow loyalty. There are not many current high-profit buyers, so the marketer should be able to target them with a special effort without severely crimping the rest of the marketing budget. What's more, incremental profit can be earned by relatively modest changes in share of customer. It's not necessary to displace a dominant brand in the consumer's repertoire, or even to become the dominant brand. For example, going from a 20 percent to a 30 percent share of customer increases the profitability of the household by 50 percent.

Why this often overlooked opportunity—getting more profits from current high-profit consumers—is a key strategy for growth in a Differential Marketing plan is explained in more detail in Chapter 5.

CLOSEUP

Brand Loyalty for Packaged Goods

One of the most difficult habits for marketers to break is thinking of consumers as being in one of three opposing camps: "mine," "theirs," and "nobody's." Even when the concept of share of customer is well accepted and understood, there is a natural tendency to assume that within the repertoire one brand is dominant, with the others bought from time to time, for a change of pace, perhaps, or because of a special price incentive. And also to assume that if the marketer's brand is dominant, he or she "owns" that consumer.

Nothing could be further from the truth in the packaged-goods sector. Those consumers who have a dominant brand, one to which they give 50 percent or more of their purchases over the course of a year, are relatively few and far between. And they are concentrated in the medium- and low-profit segments, where so-called dominance is often achieved by virtue of making so few purchases over the course of the year that buying the brand once or twice makes it appear dominant. Dominance among those consumers who buy two-thirds or more of all category purchases—the high-profit segment—is the exception rather than the rule, as MRCA data amply demonstrates.

The brands included in the MRCA sample described in the text can be broadly divided into two groups:

1. Brands in categories where variety for variety's sake is of little or no benefit, such as air fresheners.
2. Brands in categories where variety is arguably a natural benefit, such as cheese or breakfast cereal, thus lowering expectations about how high a share of customer can be reasonably achieved.

The two groups are reported separately to eliminate any suspicion that the choice of brands in the sample introduces a bias to the findings. The numbers in each column of Table 4.1 represent the percentage of brand buyers in the respective profit segments for whom the brand is "dominant," that is, who buy it at least 50 percent of all purchase occasions over the course of the year. For example, 44 percent of medium- and low-profit consumers who bought any of the brands in nonvariety categories, bought those brands at least 50 percent of the time.

Even among those brands in categories where variety for variety's sake should not be an influence, only 20 percent of all high-profit brand buyers buy it as their "dominant" brand. Not shown in the table is the range among the nonvariety brands, which was from 41 percent to 2 percent.

The numbers in each column of Table 4.2 represent the percent of brand buyers in the respective profit segments who are virtually "sole buyers," that is, who bought it on at least 80 percent of all category purchase occasions over the course of the year. For example, 30 percent of medium- and low-profit consumers who bought any of the brands in nonvariety categories, bought those brands at least 80 percent of the time.

As for finding many of those rare sole buyers in the high-profit segment, "Fergeddaboutit," as they say in Brooklyn. Less than 10 percent of high-profit buyers give 80 percent of their purchases to a dominant brand, even in the nonvariety categories. Not shown on the chart is the range, which was from 24 percent to 1 percent.

TABLE 4.1   PERCENTAGES OF 50-PERCENT LOYAL BUYERS

Average Brand	All	High-Profit	Medium/Low Profit
Nonvariety	36%	20%	44%
Variety	8	2	11
Average	22%	11%	27%

TABLE 4.2   PERCENTAGES OF 80-PERCENT LOYAL BUYERS

Average Brand	All	High-Profit	Medium/Low Profit
Nonvariety	23%	9%	30%
Variety	3	1	4
Average	13%	5%	17%

Hard data like this should cause marketers to rethink their notions of what constitutes brand loyalty, not to mention to wonder whatever happened to their "marriage," a subject more fully elaborated upon in Chapter 6.

5

A NEW STRATEGY FOR BRAND GROWTH

Executive Preview

The key to increasing profit is changing consumer behavior—either by attracting new consumers into the franchise, or stimulating more buying from current consumers, or retaining consumers who would otherwise leave the franchise. But which approach should take priority?

Most marketers have an ingrained instinct to focus their efforts on seeking out new buyers. But in a paradox of the post-mass-market world, attracting new buyers is rarely the problem for most brands. As much as 50 percent of a typical packaged-goods brand's buyers are likely to be "new" each year.

But the typical brand doesn't grow by 40 or 50 percent for several reasons. Many of the new buyers are low-profit buyers, who can contribute little to brand sales. Most brands suffer from an equally large outflow of buyers. And changes in the buying rate of current buyers, especially current high-profit buyers, can have a significant impact on brand sales.

Two tools have been developed to help marketers assess which change in consumer behavior is likely to produce the most growth for the brand: the Profit Cycle and the Profit Opportunity Matrix. The Profit Cycle is the consumer life cycle from the marketer's point of view. It segments consumers by buying stage, from the time they enter the brand franchise until the time they leave it. The Profit Opportunity Matrix shows the relative contribution to volume change of each profit segment and phase of the Profit Cycle.

For many brands, these two tools reveal a fundamental truth. The

71

most likely path to growth is not accelerating an already healthy flow of new buyers. Rather, it is retaining high-profit buyers in the franchise, and continuing to grow their loyalty and profitability.

J ust as marketers need to refocus on the true source of brand profits, we need to rethink our strategies for increasing that profit. If profits come from the individual consumers who buy the brand, the key to greater profits is, logically, to change individual consumer buying behavior, either by attracting new consumers into the franchise or stimulating more buying from current consumers or retaining consumers who otherwise might cease to buy. Or, most likely, some combination of all of the above.

But which, if any, should the marketer make the top priority? And how, and at what cost, can the marketer influence that change in behavior? These questions are central to the Differential Marketing (DFM) business proposition.

Simply establishing a priority for a specific change in consumer behavior can be a departure from traditional planning practices. Very often, we don our accountant's hats, and couch our strategies for growth in "big number" terms, like "maintaining share of voice" or "dominating the promotional period" to produce more "tonnage." When we do consider the dynamics of consumer buying behavior, the priority is highly predictable.

Finding new buyers is too often not just an objective but an obsession.

"Bring me more customers," is the customary, almost knee-jerk, command to the advertising and promotion troops. Either win over competitive buyers by convincing them that our brand is better, or cheaper, or attract nonbuyers of the category by demonstrating that they can't live without it. And stay within the budget, please.

Or, if the marketer has happened to absorb the lessons of the previous chapters: Bring me new *high-profit* buyers whose share of customer is currently zero.

This instinct to reach out for new buyers is certainly explainable. Intuitively, the growth of the brand franchise seems linked with the growth of the customer base. Who of us has ever seen a market research study or sales report that didn't confirm that the biggest brand was the one bought by the most consumers? And collectively, there is a long memory of the heyday of mass-marketing in the 1950s and 1960s when the population was growing at more than 2 percent a year, and a brand that didn't get its share of new buyers was on the road to oblivion. But that does not necessarily mean that an all-out effort to acquire new customers is the shortest path to victory in the current environment.

It is one of the paradoxes of consumer buying behavior in this post-mass-market world that attracting new customers is rarely the problem marketers envision it to be.

When loyalty is weak, wanderlust is strong.

Conventional advertising and promotion, coupled with consumers' wayward affection, do an excellent job of producing a steady stream of new recruits. If they didn't, automakers would soon be out of business with an average repurchase rate of only about 35 percent.[1] And the households in MRCA's sample, who spread their buying over as many as six brands in each category, don't necessarily buy the same six brands each year. As a result, as much as 50 percent of a typical packaged-goods brand's buyers over a twelve-month period are likely to be "new."

But the typical packaged-goods brand certainly doesn't *grow* fifty percent a year. Why it doesn't, and what marketers in every sector can do to better take advantage of their success in attracting new buyers, can be best understood by examining the purchase dynamics of consumers as they move through the brand franchise. The *Profit Cycle* and the *Profit Opportunity Matrix* are key tools for helping marketers plot their strategies for the future growth of their brand.

THE PROFIT CYCLE

The concept of the Profit Cycle gives marketers a simple and useful framework for understanding how buyers in different stages of development deliver profit to the brand.

The Profit Cycle is the consumer life cycle from the marketer's point of view.

It is a vertical segmentation of the brand's consumer franchise that follows the brand buying patterns of consumers over time, from first purchase to last.

When consumers make their initial purchase and enter the franchise they are *new buyers*. If they continue to buy they become *retained buyers*. When they stop buying they are *lapsed buyers*.

For fast-moving categories, like packaged goods, retained buyers can be further divided on the basis of the trend in their buying rate. They are either *growing* or *declining* because of changes in usage or share of customer. In theory they can also be "stable," but this group is normally so small that for all practical purposes they can be lumped with either growing or declining retained buyers.

This new DFM tool is really an update of the time-honored metaphor for the dynamics of consumer buying behavior.

The Profit Cycle is a data-driven version of the "leaky bucket."

The bucket represents retained buyers, the leaks the lapsed buyers, and the faucet refilling it the new buyers.

The profit contributed by new buyers and retained buyers is the total brand profitability in any given reporting period. The profit that would have been earned from lapsed buyers, had they bought at the same rate they did the previous year, may be thought of as *opportunity profit*, as in lost opportunity. Figure 5.1 provides a schematic illustration of the process.

Thinking about brand profitability in terms of the Profit Cycle illuminates the importance of new buyers in relation to retained or lapsed buyers. Kellogg's Corn Flakes, illustrated in Figure 5.2, is a good example of a mature brand in a mature category. What makes it especially noteworthy is that it is a brand that has been around for as long as anybody can remember. Yet MRCA reports that of total households buying the cereal in 1990, fully 42 percent were *new* buyers. But, and there are several buts, the number of buyers who lapsed in 1990 was the equivalent of 40 percent of total buyers. And all the new buyers put together only accounted for 20 percent of total brand volume.

For a brand that is as familiar to most consumers as Kellogg's Corn Flakes, finding ways to improve on an already healthy flow of new buyers would seem to be a formidable challenge, and not necessarily the strategy of choice for further growth if other possibilities exist. One possibility is to stem the losses from lapsed buyers.

The volume and profit from a buyer who does not lapse is every bit the equivalent of that from a buyer gained.

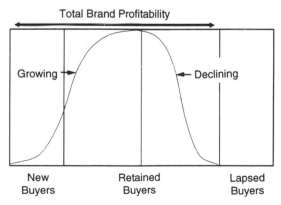

Figure 5.1 The Profit Cycle.

Figure 5.2 Profit Cycle for Kellogg's Corn Flakes. (Source: MRCA Information Services, 1989–1990.)

Another strategy would be to drive more business from retained buyers. Corn Flakes' share of customer of the brand's retained buyers is low, as would be expected in a variety-oriented category like breakfast cereals.

Modest increases in retained high-profit buyer share of customer can produce as much volume and profit as all new buyers combined.

Less than a four percentage point increase in the share of customer of retained heavy buyers—from an average of 10 percent to 14 percent—would be as important to the brand in terms of volume and profitability as all the new consumers that it gained. For a more detailed look at the mathematics, see the Closeup at the end of the chapter.

Turning to the other end of the spectrum, the Profit Cycle for Yoplait yogurt, illustrated in Figure 5.3, is more typical of brands in dynamic categories. During this two year period, yogurt eating habits continued to evolve and several new products were introduced. The velocity of consumers through the franchise reflects that unsettled market situation.

Figure 5.3 Profit Cycle for Yoplait yogurt. (Source: MRCA Information Services, 1991–1992.)

In 1992, 51 percent of Yoplait buyers were new buyers, while only 49 percent were retained buyers, split relatively evenly between growing and declining. But the equivalent of 45 percent of 1992 buyers were lapsed buyers; that is, they bought the brand in 1991 but not in 1992.

Just as important was the amount of volume rushing through the franchise. New 1992 buyers contributed 44 percent of total 1992 Yoplait volume, while growing retained buyers contributed 34 percent, and declining retained buyers produced only 22 percent of total volume. The volume of Yoplait bought in 1991 by buyers who lapsed in 1992 was the equivalent of 28 percent of 1992 volume.

At first glance, the Yoplait Profit Cycle may seem to prove that marketers' instincts are correct. New buyers were certainly critical for Yoplait volume and profits in 1992. But the question for DFM is not if new buyers are important or unimportant.

The key question for Differential Marketing is:
Which phase of the Profit Cycle offers the greatest
incremental profit opportunity?

Just looking at the Profit Cycle won't answer that question, but it certainly will demonstrate that there is more than one hypothesis. The immense influx of new buyers and volume for Yoplait was achieved with traditional marketing efforts. Those same traditional marketing efforts, however, failed to prevent both a substantial outflow and the obvious loss of brand volume from declining retained buyers, who are poised to become 1993 lapsed buyers.

Where would the greatest improvement have been likely to come from in 1992 if a DFM plan had been implemented? By increasing an already sizable group of new buyers? Or by slowing down the defection of existing buyers, almost half of whom deserted the franchise in 1992,[2] and of those who stayed, almost half of whom significantly decreased their purchases? And which strategy would lay the strongest foundation for the brand in 1993?

These may be premature questions, in that the evidence for the ability of DFM loyalty programs to build business from current customers has not yet been presented. But the Yoplait Profit Cycle figures should at least throw the door open wide to the possibility that more growth was obtainable by slowing the losses from both declining retained buyers and lapsed buyers. At the very least they should send a cautionary signal that current buyers are not to be taken for granted, that far from "mine" or "theirs," they belong to anybody and everybody.

The Profit Cycle should also alert marketers to the fact that there is rarely a one-to-one correlation between additional buyers and additional volume. For both Kellogg's Corn Flakes and Yoplait, it wasn't just the number of consumers who were leaving, entering, and staying put that determined the impact on the brand. It was also their *degree* of profitability.

Low-profit buyers usually dominate both ends of the profit cycle of mature brands.

Superimposing horizontal profit segments over the vertical profit cycle provides a more precise analysis of the impact of buyer flow on brand volume and profits. For mature packaged-goods brands in mature markets, like Kellogg's Corn Flakes, this analysis usually

reveals that lighter buyers enter and leave the franchise disproportionately more than heavy buyers. The low-profit segment will commonly account for almost 60 percent of lapsed buyers during a
twelve month period. But only about 20 percent of those consumers
who cease buying will typically be from the heavy category buying,
high-profit segment. As a result, the volume loss from lapsed buyers
is often far less than their number would suggest.

Similarly, the preponderance of new brand buyers will also be
light category buyers, in roughly the same proportion as those that
left the franchise. And they will naturally be light brand buyers as
well, at least initially. Thus their contribution to volume is relatively
small.

On reflection, the reasons for this pattern are easy to explain.
Heavy category buyers already have an average of five or so
brands in their repertoire. They are *running out* of brands to add.
Moreover, because of their high frequency of purchase, dropping
a brand completely is not something that is likely to happen regularly. High-profit buyers of air freshener, for example, make over
eight category purchases a year. That gives them more than ample
opportunity to buy each of the 3.6 brands in their considered set
at least once.

On the other hand, light category buyers with low purchase frequency have little margin for demonstrating that a particular brand
is still in their considered set. Sixty-two percent of light buyers of
air freshener make only one purchase per year. So a light buyer
"dropping out" of a franchise may be nothing more than a consumer
who succumbed this year to a competitive promotion, but who very
likely may return to the franchise next year for their one annual
purchase. In that case, they would become a "new" light buyer.

The other reason for the dominance of low-profit buyers at both
ends of the profit cycle for brands like Kellogg's Corn Flakes is that
in many cases lapsed and new buyers are not "lapsed" or "new" at
all. They are simply extremely light buyers whose interval between
purchases is greater than the reporting period. Extremely light buyers of air fresheners make do with one purchase every two years.

This relatively benign impact of buyer flow on brand volume is
the rule for mature brands in mature categories, but the exception
can be costly for the brand in question, as the following example
demonstrates.

	New	Retained	Lapsed	Total
High	+11%	-5%	-18%	-12%
Medium	+ 8%	0%	-12%	- 4%
Low	+ 3%	0%	- 5%	- 2%
Total	+22%	-5%	-35%	-18%
% 1991 Buyers	34%	50%	50%	

Figure 5.4 Taster's Choice Profit Opportunity Matrix showing contribution to volume change, 1991–1992. (Source: MRCA.)

THE PROFIT OPPORTUNITY MATRIX

According to MRCA data, Taster's Choice coffee suffered an 18 percent volume decline between 1991 and 1992. The causes of this precipitous drop in sales is best understood by use of another tool of DFM called the Profit Opportunity Matrix.

The Profit Opportunity Matrix pinpoints problems and opportunities in the Profit Cycle.

Rather than show the absolute amount of buyers and volume contributed by each buying group, the Profit Opportunity Matrix shows their *relative* contribution to volume change, year to year. By using this matrix, marketers can determine at a glance how their current marketing efforts are faring with each profit segment and phase of the profit cycle. When the Profit Opportunity Matrix is applied to Taster's Choice, as shown in Figure 5.4, the effect of lapsed buyers, particularly lapsed high-profit buyers, is immediately apparent.

The percentages in each box represent the percent of total volume gain or loss accounted for by each group, using 1991 as the base year. Thus, the volume lost to 1991 buyers who lapsed in 1992 would have produced a 35 percent volume loss for the brand if no new buyers had entered the franchise and retained buyers had kept their purchases constant. Eighteen percentage points of the 35 percent were directly attributable to lapsed high-profit buyers.

New buyers entering the franchise in 1992 offset this loss to a degree, adding the equivalent of 22 percent of 1991 volume. The difference between that number and the 35 percent of volume that was lost accounted for a net decrease of 13 percent of sales. The remaining 5 percent of the decline was due to retained buyers buying less.

The figures speak again. As usual, conventional media and promotion did an excellent job for a brand in attracting new buyers. For Taster's Choice, new buyers in 1992 accounted for the equivalent of 34 percent of 1991 buyers. But it would have taken far more new buyers than that, particularly high-profit buyers, to make up for the 50 percent of 1991 buyers who lapsed from the franchise, a massive defection that occurred despite that same advertising and promotion.

And this is not the whole story. As will be seen shortly, a DFM plan aimed at keeping consumers in the franchise might have had an even broader impact because of similar trends that were at work inside the bucket of retained buyers.

THE TRUTH ABOUT THE LEAKY BUCKET

The image of the "leaky bucket," which marketers have been operating with for years, is so descriptive and memorable that it tends to get in the way of clear thinking. Most of us can't see the bucket for the leaks, which are the salient feature. Hence, the ever-present anxiety about winning over new customers. How else can the bucket be kept full?

The answer lies in looking at the bigger picture, first, by understanding the nature of lapsed buyer leaks, and, second, by analyzing what's happening inside the retained buyer bucket. Very often, the same brand-hostile forces are at work in both Profit Cycle phases, producing the same kind of drain on brand sales and profitability. When this is the case, the potential impact of DFM on these buyers is magnified considerably.

All leaks are not created equal.

True *leaks* are those that occur when a consumer leaves both the brand and the category as a result of a fundamental change in needs. For example, a child who is potty-trained no longer requires diapers. High profit or low, there is very little a marketer can do about them.

Churn, on the other hand, looks like a leak and has the same impact as a leak, but is far more controllable. Churn occurs when a consumer leaves the brand for some reason *other* than a fundamental change in underlying needs. When a mother stops buying Pampers, for example, and buys only Huggies and Luvs. Churn can be precipitated by a variety of factors: a bad experience with the brand, a reappraisal of the brand's benefits in relation to competition, or simply the perceived need to "try something new." Or perhaps there is no apparent reason.

Churn happens.

A consumer who churns out of the brand may or may not churn out of the category as well.

Churn is more likely to occur in categories where there is a great degree of substitutability. The more the competitors, the more opportunity for the consumer to drift away from the brand. This is not only true within categories but *across* categories. For example, a consumer might "discover" a thirst-quenching powdered soft drink like Crystal Light, drink it religiously for a summer, then change over to iced tea the following year. Or a confirmed zippered food-storage bag user might go wild at a Tupperware party.

Although it is not always possible to distinguish between true leaks and churn, for some brands and categories the incidence of churn can be surprisingly high, even among heavy-buying, high-profit households. For example, an MRCA analysis of the toilet bowl cleaner category shows a 35 percent loss of buyers year to year, and a 29 percent loss of high-profit buyers. On a brand basis, those figures are much larger, 60 percent and 49 percent respectively for Vanish, for example. Assuming that most of these consumers continued to have toilet bowls and continued to clean them, then the culprit must be churn. A high degree of churn can be expected in this category, where more economical general purpose cleaners might serve nearly as well as a specialty product.

From the marketer's point of view, churn has one very intriguing and leverageable characteristic. Churn is not necessarily directly linked to *dissatisfaction* with the product itself. The consumers who abandoned Crystal Light or Vanish may very well have continued to *like* the brands. But for whatever reason, they no longer *bought* them.

Probably the best documented example of high degrees of product satisfaction and high degrees of churn coexisting peacefully, and frustratingly, comes from the automobile category. J.D. Power & Associates periodically reports the bad news: satisfaction is high, repurchase is low. In a survey released in March, 1994, 90 percent of owners claimed to be satisfied with their current car. Yet only 36 percent of them had repurchased the same make, and a mere 27 percent were confident that they would definitely buy the same make again.[3] But the bad news can be good news as well.

Churn is the kind of leak that can be slowed or even plugged.

Much churn would seem to be driven by a *lack* of positive reinforcement rather than by a negative judgment about the product. It is as though in this brand-hostile environment, consumers have a limited ability to sustain their interest in the distinctiveness of any particular brand, or sometimes even in the benefits of a particular category. In that sense, churn may be a corollary to the trend away from a dominant brand in the considered set.

Churn can be slowed by a DFM plan that places more resources against *current* buyers. It's no coincidence that brand loyalty programs are multiplying in the automobile category, where churn is a major factor. Cadillac benefits from a churn rate that is much smaller than the category average, 38 percent versus 64 percent according to J.D. Power data.[4] If Cadillac buyers churned at the category rate, sales would be reduced significantly, perhaps as much as a third, depending on the number of new buyers. Conversely, if Toyota had Cadillac's churn rate, instead of a rate that was only average for the category, its franchise would be likely to increase by a similar amount.

What's more, the same DFM approach that helps to plug leaks at the source will also help control the *evaporation* of profits from retained buyers.

Evaporation is a slow leak.

Evaporation is the *gradual* loss of share of customer to competitive brands, or of brand usage to other alternatives. For a brand hemorrhaging volume, evaporation can be as destructive in its impact as churn. But evaporation, like churn, can be controlled. For a relatively healthy brand, preventing or reducing evaporation represents a key opportunity for additional growth.

Taster's Choice once again provides a cautionary example. According to MRCA data, Taster's Choice lapsed-buyer problem in 1992 was aggravated by a high rate of evaporation among retained high-profit buyers. In the version of the Profit Opportunity Matrix illustrated in Figure 5.5, the retained buyer group is separated into its two components, growing and declining retained buyers. The percentages in the matrix represent the absolute change in volume year to year for the consumers in that group, expressed as a percent of total Year I sales. Thus, new high-profit buyers contributed the equivalent of 11 percent of total 1991 volume in 1992. Growing retained high-profit buyers increased their volume by the equivalent of 15 percent of *total* 1991 sales. All lapsed buyers in 1992 accounted for 35 percent of 1991 sales.

Two observations are immediately apparent. Almost all of the changes inside the bucket are the result of changes in the high-

	New	Growing	Declining	Lapsed	Total
High	+11%	+15%	−20%	−18%	−12%
Medium	+ 8%	+ 2%	− 2%	−12%	− 4%
Low	+ 3%	+ 0%	− 0%	− 5%	− 2%
Total	+22%	+17%	−22%	−35%	−18%
% 1991 Buyers	34%	25%	25%	50%	

Figure 5.5 Taster's Choice Profit Opportunity Matrix as in Figure 5.4, but showing here the retained buyer group separated into its two components: growing and declining retained buyers. (Source: MRCA.)

profit segment. And the combined impact of evaporation and churn on high-profit buyers borders on the catastrophic.

When a brand is in trouble, cherchez la high-profit franchise.

In 1992, growing retained buyers *increased* their purchases by an amount equal to 17 percent of 1991 volume. The high-profit segment was responsible for the overwhelming majority of that increase, 15 percent. But declining retained buyers *reduced* their purchases of Taster's Choice by the equivalent of 22 percent of 1991 volume, and almost all of that evaporation, 20 percent, was attributable to the high-profit segment. Since both groups of retained buyers were roughly equal in size, the net effect of the activity within the bucket was the relatively modest decline of 5 percent (22% minus 17%) shown in Figure 5.4.

But the net effect is as misleading as the fact that the average person in the world has one testicle. The 20 percent evaporation of volume from declining high-profit buyers is even *greater* than the 18 percent loss contributed by lapsed high-profit buyers. Together, the loss of volume from high-profit buyers, churn and evaporation combined, is the equivalent of an astonishing 38 percent of the brand's 1991 volume.

It is not within the province of this book to comment on the cause of this decline, other than to identify its source. But the characteristically large inflow of new buyers suggests that it was not the result of some marketing catastrophe. The brand retained its attractiveness for many consumers.

This kind of situation aptly illustrates the futility of chasing new buyers while ignoring current customers.

For every customer lost, another customer has to be found.

Short of divine intervention, a DFM program targeted against high-profit buyers would have been the best hope of softening the blow to the brand's volume. If that loss could have been cut in half, instead of a precipitous decline in sales of 18 percent the brand would have had a modest growth rate of 1 percent.[5]

Case closed. Nothing could be further from the truth than the classic picture of the bucket as a passive receptacle for in-flow and out-flow of consumers. Beneath the apparently placid surface, currents ebb and flow and, occasionally, as with the case of Taster's Choice, even surge, sometimes putting a substantial portion of volume and profit at genuine risk—or presenting an often overlooked growth opportunity.

TOWARD A NEW STRATEGY FOR GROWTH

The obvious leverage in the retained customer base should not obscure the real need of every brand to have an ongoing supply of new buyers. For new brands, new buyers are by definition a priority. For mature brands, all leaks are not preventable. Churn can only be reduced, not eliminated. So too evaporation.

New buyers are also an absolute prerequisite for brand longevity. For mature brands under brand-hostile conditions, brand penetration has a distinct tendency to drift south. Over a fifteen year period, nineteen of the twenty-six brands that MRCA analyzed suffered declines in household penetration. The average decline was almost 30 percent. During the same period, the absolute number of households increased by roughly 15 percent, which meant that for these nineteen brands the absolute number of buying households *actually decreased* by 20 percent.

Nonetheless, marketers often get into trouble by thinking that they can't do enough to refill the bucket. The Profit Cycle suggests this is not the case.

Conventional advertising and promotion do an excellent job in attracting new buyers.

Between 40 and 50 + percent of the buyers of Corn Flakes, Yoplait, and Taster's Choice were new buyers. Realistically, how many more new buyers could their brand managers expect to attract?

There is simply no good marketing reason to make the pursuit of new buyers the *only* priority, even for brands with strong growth aspirations. The dynamic state of the bucket underscores the fallacy of dismissing marketing to the current customer base as "defensive," as it often is by those of us who suffer from employment-related elevated levels of testosterone.

Marketing to current high-profit customers is a classic growth strategy.

Growth is a by-product of all phases of the Profit Cycle, not just sales produced by new buyers. In terms of "making the number," the cases or pounds or dollars or units that are *not lost* count just as much as any that are hard won. Moreover, a modest increase in usage or share of customer of heavy retained buyers has the potential to offset most of the volume lost from lapsed buyers, and make the new buyers flowing into the franchise truly "plus" business.

These conclusions are as true of durables as they are of frequently purchased goods and services. What's declining, or accelerating, in the durables marketer's bucket is "share of consideration" rather than share of customer, consideration that only makes its presence or absence felt at the time of the next buying occasion.

The critical importance of a balance between seeking new buyers and cementing the loyalty of current customers is reflected in a finding that could be described as the mantra of DFM, the new equation for brand growth and profits.

The brand with the most high-profit buyers—and the most loyal—always wins.

Actually, that's not just the bottom line of DFM. It's the bottom line of marketing, period.

The leading brand in every category is the brand with the largest number of high-profit buyers in its franchise, and also the most *loyal* high-profit buyers. For categories where purchase is infrequent, like consumer durables, the leading brand is, by definition, the brand with the most buyers. For frequently purchased categories, like packaged goods, the proof is in panel data. Numerous examples reveal that in category after category, the brand with the largest market share has both a higher penetration of category heavy buyers and a share of customer from those category heavy buyers that is greater than that earned by other brands from *their* category heavy buyers.

But even though the correlation of share of customer with market share is generally acknowledged, it has been largely ignored when developing marketing strategies. The prevailing thinking, among those who have thought about it, seems to be that penetration and loyalty move pretty much in lockstep as a brand grows bigger. So, blasting the marketplace with advertising and sales promotion will make the brand more popular, and that popularity will manifest itself in two ways: more buyers, and more loyal buyers.

Andrew Ehrenberg of the South Bank Business School in London characterizes this thinking as the Law of Double Jeopardy,[6] in that less popular brands are small for two reasons. Because they are not as well-liked as larger brands, fewer people buy them. And those buyers they do attract buy them less often. Conversely, more popular brands are bigger for just the opposite two reasons.

This may be a practical perspective for a mass-marketing world, where the only communications tools are blunt instruments. Available tools to *only* increase penetration, or *only* increase loyalty, are relatively few and far between, especially on the advertising side of the ledger. But that situation is rapidly changing, as is demonstrated fully in subsequent chapters. And, even in a mass communication environment, many leading brands have, wittingly or not, developed loyalty levels that ensure that they will remain leaders. Because the *loyalty* of their high-profit buyers is considerably more important than their *number* in explaining the difference in volume between those leading brands and the competition.

High-profit share of customer is often more important than high-profit penetration in determining the size of the brand.

Folger's, for example, led the coffee category with a 25 percent share in the 1992 MRCA panel. Traditional Maxwell House, the "blue can," lagged behind at 15 percent. Yet Folger's penetration of heavy category buyers was only six points higher than Maxwell House, 58 percent versus 52 percent. The major part of the difference in market share between these two brands was attributable to the loyalty of their heavy buyers.

Folger's share of customer of heavy category buyers that bought the brand was 38 percent. Maxwell House's SOC from its category heavy buyers was only 24 percent. If Maxwell House heavy-buyers had been as loyal as Folger's, Maxwell House's market share would have been 22 percent instead of 15 percent. Conversely, if Folger's heavy buyers' SOC fell to the Maxwell House level, Folger's market share would have been only 18 percent versus Maxwell House's 15 percent.

Why this situation exists is a matter of speculation. But that similar situations abound is clearly evident in the MRCA data, confirmed by numerous proprietary consumer panels. Many leading brands have managed to establish differentially high levels of loyalty, despite the paucity of targetable communications tools previously available. But as the number of tools expands, so does the opportunity to make the loyalty of the high-profit segment, particularly current high-profit buyers, a priority of the marketing plan.

A Differential Marketing plan geared to building the loyalty of high-profit buyers is the strategy of choice for brands that aspire to category leadership—or, for that matter, for brands with growth aspirations of any kind.

Unfortunately, the need for that loyalty stands in stark contrast to actual trends in consumer buying behavior, detailed in Chapter 4. Even worse, unless changed, marketers' own actions will continue to tug those levels downward. Inadvertently but unquestionably, traditional marketing practices exert the greatest drag on both the loyalty and the profitability of those consumers who are most prized: the high-profit segment. Exactly how that happens is the subject of Chapter 6.

CLOSEUP

Leveraging Retained Buyers

The volume and profit potential inherent in modest improvements of share of customer or usage rate of current buyers is often obscured by the bloodlust for "new buyers." But it shouldn't be.

As shown in Figure 5.6, MRCA data reports that in 1990, 20 percent of Kellogg's Corn Flakes volume was attributable to new buyers. And 18 percent of volume was lost as current buyers churned out of the brand franchise. The Kellogg's Corn Flakes Profit Cycle illustrates the relative contribution to volume of each group.

Fifty-eight percent of 1991 volume was derived from retained high-profit buyers. Breakfast cereal is a category where variety is the norm, so the share of customer that those high-profit buyers gave to Corn Flakes that year was relatively low—only 10 percent. That means that every point of SOC for these buyers represented 5.8 percent of total volume:

$$58\% \div 10 = 5.8\%$$

	New	Retained	Total	Lapsed
High	10%	58%	68%	10%
Medium	7%	14%	21%	6%
Low	3%	8%	11%	2%
Total	20%	80%	100%	18%
% 1990 Buyers	42%	58%	100%	40%

Figure 5.6 The Kellogg's Corn Flakes Profit Cycle showing total 1990 volume. (Source: MRCA.)

If SOC could be increased from 10 percent to 13.5 percent, then these same retained heavy buyers would contribute an additional amount of volume equivalent to all the volume gained from new users or lost to lapsed users:

$$5.8\% \times 3.5 = 20.3\%$$

Whether or not such an increase is achievable in the variety-seeking breakfast cereal category would have to be determined through testing. Kellogg's may have concluded it is not, considering the 1994 advertising theme, "Try it again for the first time." Clearly, the brand is trying to attract old/new buyers.

But in any case, this example aptly illustrates how small changes in share of purchases of current high-profit customers have the potential for producing significant swings in volume and profit.

6

THE PROMOTION PARADOX

Executive Preview

The dramatic decline in packaged-goods heavy buyer loyalty is most likely the inadvertent outgrowth of current promotional practices and marketing spending patterns.

A brand spending twice as much of its budget in sales promotion as in advertising is actually spending ten to twenty times as much in promotion against its own category heavy buyers. This extreme imbalance is caused by the different ways the two disciplines distribute their impact across profit segments.

Demographic targeting notwithstanding, advertising reaches all profit segments roughly in proportion to the size of the segment. But the bulk of sales promotion spending only impacts consumers who actually purchase, and therefore is proportional to the volume of the segment. Since the high-profit segment is no larger than other segments, but makes the vast majority of purchases, the disparity between sales promotion and advertising spending is magnified.

The ratio of the investment in loyalty-building advertising versus the cost of price-sensitizing sales promotion against an individual household can be thought of as the Brand Loyalty Equation—a fundamental analytical tool of Differential Marketing. This equation illustrates why the loyalty problem in the high-profit segment has become so severe and underscores the need not only to aggravate the problem no further but also to begin to correct it. New data confirms that when promotion declines, loyalty increases.

The argument for Differential Marketing (DFM) has, thus far, centered on the *opportunity* for brand growth and improved brand profitability through increased brand loyalty, particularly the loyalty of current high-profit buyers. There is also an argument that springs from *necessity*, at least to the extent that the packaged-goods experience continues to reflect broader trends.

The declines in brand loyalty measurements noted in Chapter 4 can be attributed to the many brand-hostile forces at work in the marketplace. But one noteworthy fact remains unexplained: declines in heavy-buyer loyalty were far more precipitous than those in the other profit segments. This condition could simply be a manifestation of the old maxim of the boxing ring, "The bigger they are, the harder they fall." Or it could be that one or more of those brand-hostile factors exercised a disproportionate effect on the high-profit segment. There is a substantial body of evidence that suggests the latter is indeed the case.

From a marketing perspective, the most salient change during the period from the late seventies to the early nineties, when the declines in brand loyalty were monitored, was the explosive growth in sales promotion, both consumer and trade. That change did not affect all profit segments equally. The way consumers take advantage of sales promotion produces a distribution of expenditures that is precisely the opposite of what marketers would seek to create in a DFM plan. Left uncorrected, the situation has the potential to further weaken the loyalty of the high-profit segment.

THE IMPACT OF SALES PROMOTION

The massive drain of resources from loyalty-building advertising to price-sensitizing sales promotion since the mid-1970s is well known, but its full impact is not well understood.

Sales promotion has replaced advertising as the primary means of motivating consumers to buy brands.

A generally accepted estimate is that the percentage of the packaged goods marketing budget allocated to both consumer and trade promotion has grown from less than 50 percent in the mid-1970s to about 70–75 percent today. And perceptive observers know that the percentage decline in advertising *spending* understates the real problem in terms of advertising *delivery*. Marketing budgets have not kept pace with the rate of inflation. Media costs have exceeded it.

The predictable result is that consumers are making a great many more of their brand choices with the help of a promotional incentive. MRCA monitored the increase for the twenty-six packaged goods brands over the same fifteen+ year period (1977–1992) as the loyalty measures. Among all buyers, the average percentage of purchases made with any kind of promotional incentive, including trade promotion, increased significantly, from 34 percent of volume to 48 percent.

The trend was distressingly consistent across all profit segments, with heavy buyers affected the most. Their percent on deal averaged about five percentage points higher than that of the other segments. The level for the brand with the lowest percent sold on deal across all segments was 22 percent. The highest was 67 percent. What's not to understand?

Only this: For the average packaged-goods brand, the ratio of promotion to advertising spending across all consumers may be, conservatively, only about 2:1. But it is strikingly higher among the heavy category buyers who buy the brand—the crown jewels who control the bulk of current brand volume and profit and who represent a major source for additional growth.

The overwhelming majority of a brand's promotional spending is spent against its own high-profit buyers.

A brand spending twice as much of its budget in promotion as in advertising is actually spending at least ten times as much in promotion against its most valuable customers. A brand with low category penetration or a higher than average concentration of heavy-buyer volume can spend as much as *twenty times* more in promotion against them. In other words, for every dollar in loyalty-building advertising, current high-profit customers receive anywhere from ten to twenty dollars in price-sensitizing sales promotion.

Compare this with the ratio of spending that was common in the heyday of mass marketing about twenty-five years ago. At that time there was almost twice as much money in the budget for advertising as there was for promotion, and the ratio of promotion to advertising spending against the high-profit segment rarely exceeded 3:1. That is, a doubling of the percentage of promotion spending has tripled or quadrupled the promotional impact against the brand's best customers over the last several decades. The Closeup on the mathematics of disloyalty at the end of the chapter provides a guided tour through the calculations.

How can this be? The fundamental reason is that advertising and sales promotion distribute their impact very differently across the profit segments. Advertising spending correlates with *segment size.*

Traditional media reach all profit segments roughly in proportion to the percentage of consumers in the segment.

If the high-profit segment consists of 20 percent of households, it is likely to receive about 20 percent of advertising impressions, demographic targeting notwithstanding. But sales promotion spending correlates with *segment volume.*

Sales promotion impact is focused on those consumers who actually purchase, and is roughly in proportion to the percentage of sales made to the segment.

If high-profit brand buyers account for about 70 percent of brand volume, they will be the beneficiary of about 70 percent of sales promotion expenditures.

Because high-profit consumers buy more, they take advantage of more sales promotion offers. But they do not receive disproportionately more advertising impressions, only the slight skews that are a by-product of media targeted to broad demographic targets. Therefore, sales promotion spending against the brand's high-profit buyers is a much larger proportion of the spending they receive than it is for the other profit segments.

The balance between advertising and sales promotion spending—the Brand Loyalty Equation—is totally out of balance in the high-profit segment.

The more the balance of the Brand Loyalty Equation is tilted in favor of promotional spending, the more loyalty can be expected to suffer. Which apparently is exactly what has happened for the high-profit segment in general.

A skeptic might ask if spending against the high-profit segment is so disproportionately out of balance, why is the percent of volume bought on deal by the high-profit segment only modestly higher than that of other segments? The answer very likely lies in the different shopping patterns of the various segments. The percent on deal volume of heavy buyers is *deflated* by the way they buy, while that of the medium- and low-profit segments is *inflated*.

Heavy buyers are heavy not just because they buy *more* on each purchase occasion, but because they buy far more *often*. This heavy frequency of buying has been corroborated by MRCA over a wide variety of categories. And it means that many times when heavy buyers are in the market, there is likely to be no promotional incentive available for the brands in their considered set.

Medium and light buyers, on the other hand, have a lower purchase frequency. Whether or not they buy a particular product on a particular shopping trip is more often *discretionary* than it is for heavy buyers. Thus, they can frequently postpone a purchase until an offer becomes available, or conversely, the presence of an offer can stimulate a purchase of a product that is not immediately required. The combination of these factors explains why "price buyers"—buyers who buy all or almost all their purchases on deal—are more often found in the lower profit segments, as noted in

Chapter 4. In effect, the impact of sales promotion spending against these segments is not constrained by buying behavior, and thus it has a disproportionately larger influence on them than it does on heavy buyers.

The Brand Loyalty Equation is a key analytical tool for DFM. It illuminates the counterproductive spending patterns across segments and the disparity between loyalty-building and price-sensitizing efforts. And it demonstrates the necessity for many brands of implementing a fundamental DFM resource allocation strategy: more funding of loyalty building efforts against the high-profit segment. In order to fully understand this important concept, it's helpful to put aside generalizations and look at how it applies to a single brand.

THE YOPLEX BRAND LOYALTY EQUATION

YopleX is not a brand that will be familiar to readers. Nonetheless, it can ably serve as a representative example of how conventional advertising and promotion practices unduly penalize the marketer's ability to build brand loyalty in the high-profit segment.

YopleX is a hypothetical brand of yogurt that generally resembles Yoplait, the number two brand in the category. Understandably, Yoplait's actual advertising and promotional spending is not publicly available. Nor, for that matter, are Yoplait's actual sales figures or those of the yogurt category, only MRCA's reported figures. So the analysis must rely on the best available nonconfidential sources, together with some reasonable estimates.

YopleX was created in order not to confuse illustration with reality, yet to make the illustration as real as possible. Even if all the estimates and reported figures and assumptions for YopleX are not 100 percent accurate, which they're obviously not, the analysis should give the reader a general sense of a typical Brand Loyalty Equation. The results are certainly representative of numerous cases where actual data has been used.

Yogurt is typical of many products in a post-mass-market world. This $800 million category (1992 factory sales) has substantial but by no means universal appeal. According to MRCA data, the household penetration of yogurt buyers is just a shade under 50 percent. The average retail selling price per unit is about $1.00, roughly in the lower-middle range of packaged-goods' pricing. Category percent on deal is 37 percent, lower than the average for MRCA's cross section of brands, but still substantial. The top third of buyers account for 83 percent of category volume, more than in most categories but still within the normative range. Figure 6.1 illustrates the yogurt Category Profit Matrix.

YopleX, the second leading brand behind Dannon with sales of about $150 million, seems to have its sights set on category leadership. It has been a leader in introducing new line extensions and it has promoted heavily to pump up volume. Over 50 percent of YopleX sales are made on deal. But it has also advertised heavily, with a $12 million media budget. Its advertising to promotion spending ratio is close to the average ratio reported in Donnelley Marketing's survey of promotional practices, 25 percent versus 75 percent.

The first step in creating the Brand Loyalty Equation is to determine how much advertising was directed at each profit segment. Approximately 70 percent of YopleX's $12 million advertising budget is placed in television and 30 percent in print. This split reflects the brand's need to target upscale women aged 25–54, a primary

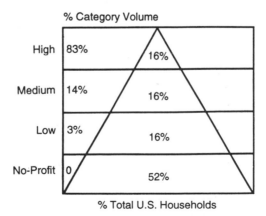

Figure 6.1 Category Profit Segment Matrix for yogurt. (Source: MRCA Information Services.)

group of consumers of yogurt. The relatively heavy use of print, which is more targetable than television, to reach this group will also provide a heavier than normal skew of impressions against the high-profit segment. Even so, for the plan as a whole, an incidence of impressions about 15 percent above average against the high-profit segment would be an outstanding performance. Assuming this most favorable case, if the high-profit yogurt segment represents 16 percent of the population, they receive at best about 18 percent of YopleX's advertising delivery. Conversely, as John Wanamaker would have predicted, nonbuyers receive about 50 percent, less than their percentage of households but still a sizable amount. The relationship is illustrated in Figure 6.2.

Many experienced advertisers are surprised that the skew to the high-profit segment is generally so moderate. After all, media targeting is highly sophisticated and accurate. Target audience delivery indices are commonly 120 or higher, even with an all-television plan. This seeming discrepancy highlights an inescapable fact: Broad demographic target audience definitions are crude tools for identifying high-profit consumers.

All "Women 25–54" are not created equal.

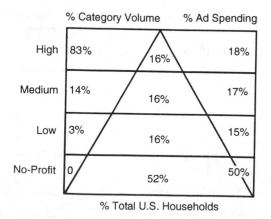

Figure 6.2 The Profit/Advertising Matrix for YopleX. (Source: MRCA, author's estimate.)

There are far more women 25–54 who don't buy YopleX than who do. And only a little more than half the women 25–54 buy yogurt of any kind.

Figure 6.3 illustrates the limitations faced by demographic targeting in trying to reach high-profit consumers. NPD/Nielsen studied five categories, including yogurt, where women 25–54 are an important target audience for media planning. The analysis determined the percent of buyers who were actually in that demographic group and the percent of category volume that they purchased. In all five categories, women 25–54 only constituted a little more than 50 percent of all buyers. And as a group, they only showed a moderate skew to heavy buying, with an average index of percent volume to percent buyers of 111.[1]

Demography is no longer destiny.

In a highly fragmented and individualized world, traditional media planning labors under a severe handicap. Category and brand

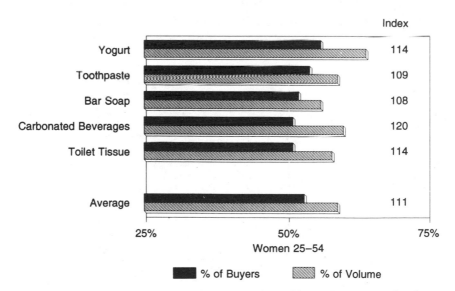

Figure 6.3   Effectiveness of demographic targeting on buyers and volume. (Source: NPD/Nielsen, Inc., Advertising Research Foundation Workshop, November, 1991)

choice is shaped more by personal taste, beliefs, and values, and less by factors such as age and income. Despite the best efforts of advertisers and their agencies, the demographic basis of media planning and buying inhibits them from achieving anything more than a modestly higher level of impressions against the most valuable consumers. But not so for promotion.

As surprised as experienced marketers often are by the moderate skew of advertising, they are usually even more surprised that the promotion skew to the high-profit segment is so *immoderate*. About 70 percent of YopleX's $33 million promotion budget is likely to end up in the pockets of current high-profit consumers, as illustrated in Figure 6.4. Who else is making all those on-deal purchases if not the heavy buyers? MRCA data proves that to be the case.

Observant readers will note that the 70 percent figure, although extremely high, is still less than the 83 percent of the volume that the high-profit segment controls. That's largely because 8 percent of YopleX's total consumer promotional spending is wasted on the no-profit segment, delivering coupons and other offers via FSIs and the like to consumers who do not buy any yogurt.

In fact, the large number of consumers who don't buy a particular category, or who only buy infrequently, distorts the true picture about coupon redemption rates. And that number offers further

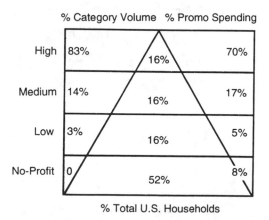

Figure 6.4 The Profit/Promotion Matrix for YopleX. (Source: MRCA, author's estimates.)

reason to worry about the insidious effect of promotion on the high-profit segment's loyalty.

Heavy-buyer coupon redemption rates are three to five times the average redemption rate.

If we assume that YopleX's average coupon redemption rate is 2.5 percent then the heavy buyer redemption rate must be about 11 percent. This much larger figure can be derived mathematically simply by knowing the size of the profit segments, the percent volume they account for, and the overall redemption rate (see the Closeup on the true redemption rate of heavy buyers at the end of the chapter). And, although it isn't necessarily comforting, the higher redemption rate does makes sense, given the relatively small number of heavy buyers and the relatively large amount of promotional spending thrown their way. In fact, all other things being equal, if yogurt penetration were 30 percent rather than close to 50 percent, YopleX's heavy-buyer coupon redemption rate would have to be 17 percent.

As worrisome as the spending patterns and the redemption figures may be, the full impact of the Brand Loyalty Equation does not hit home until advertising and sales promotion spending are compared by segment on a *household* basis. If a brand's profits are derived from the individual households who buy the brand, then the spending against those individual households is critical in terms of understanding what motivates that buying and the trends that are likely to ensue.

YopleX spends an estimated $.16 per household in advertising against category heavy buyers, irrespective of whether or not they buy the brand. This figure is determined by multiplying total spending by 18 percent, the percent of impressions that this segment receives, and dividing by the number of households in the segment. But as illustrated in Figure 6.5, YopleX's total promotion dollars per household against heavy category buyers who buy the brand, is $3.40, or more than twenty times as much as is spent for advertising. (The percent of *brand* volume accounted for by each profit segment is slightly different than the percent of category volume.)

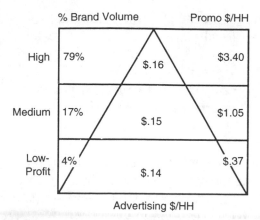

Figure 6.5   The Brand Loyalty Equation for YopleX current buyers. (Source: MRCA, author's estimates.)

This ratio is on the high side of the normative range, but not truly out of the ordinary. Considering the critical importance of these buyers to the health of the franchise, a Brand Loyalty Equation like this one surely sends a loud and clear warning signal to the brand.

IN SEARCH OF SILVER LININGS

Mathematics aside, is the type of analysis underlying the Brand Loyalty Equation an apples-to-apples comparison? Does the ratio of spending of the two different disciplines against the same household really reflect their relative effect on that household's purchasing behavior? And does it equate with the impact on their loyalty to the brand?

Not necessarily. But that doesn't mean mathematics overstates the case, or that it matters. For it's the overriding pattern that counts, and the fact that it has worsened over time.

Clearly, the law of diminishing returns certainly must come into play at some point. A 10:1 ratio of promotion to advertising spending against the high-profit segment is highly unlikely to have twice the behavioral impact of a 5:1 ratio. For proof, look no farther than the overall pattern of coupon usage over the past few years, where coupons in distribution have continued to increase dramatically while redemptions have not.

There's also a valid question about whether the consumer truly sees the impact of all the promotion money marketers spend, particularly trade promotion. If they don't, the equation would be somewhat brighter, although by no means sunny. Making the assumption that only half of YopleX's estimated trade promotion dollars get passed through to the consumer, then YopleX's brand loyalty equation changes from a 20:1 ratio against current heavy buyers to 14:1, an improvement but hardly salvation.

Some marketers would undoubtedly contend that the money spent on certain kinds of promotional vehicles is not purely promotional. "Theme promotions," such as the Pillsbury Bake-Off Contest, are clearly designed to build brand image rather than to move short-term volume. But similar examples are few and far between. The relevant question is how much brand building impact is produced by those vehicles that are most used by marketers—free-standing inserts and trade allowances and other forms of trade promotion?

Few marketers would disagree that trade promotion contributes little to overall brand equity. But the case for FSIs is less clear-cut. Customarily, much of the space on an FSI is devoted to a "beauty shot" of the product and a headline that reinforces the brand's benefits. This certainly gives the piece some of the look of a print ad. But placed in a bank of money-saving offers, to which consumers turn to clip coupons rather than to learn more about products, is it reasonable to expect that an FSI has anything close to the same communications effect as an ad?

Communications effect is, in fact, the heart of the matter for the Brand Loyalty Equation. Does a dollar in promotional spending have the same communications effect as a dollar in advertising?

For advertising, the communications effect is intentional. For sales promotion, the portion that finances the offer is not. But sales promotion always has a much simpler and more easily grasped message: "Buy now and save." And equal or not, there can be no question that sales promotion spending does have a significant impact on how the consumer views the brand.

To deny this fact is to affirm that consumers make the same

distinction that marketers do between advertising and promotion, "above the line" and "below the line" spending. Hardly.

For consumers, an ad is an ad, even if it's a coupon.

It doesn't matter to consumers whether it's one of a sheaf of coupons in the Sunday newspaper or a slick, four-color presentation in a classy magazine, or a thirty second commercial during *Roseanne*. More than one advertiser has noted with chagrin that their advertising tracking studies report that the primary source of awareness of the brand's advertising is "Sunday coupons."

Moreover, the communications effect of all that promotional spending does not come just from what the marketer thinks of as "communication": printed or filmed advertising or incentives for the brand. Just as "body language" is an important factor in communications between two people, "marketing body language," as expressed in the overall selling environment, in-store as well as in the newspaper ad or circular, is likely to be a key contributor to the consumer's changing perceptions of brands. The surfeit of promotion, both in general and for the marketer's brand, sends a clear message.

"Marketing body language" signals that getting a better price is more important than getting a better product.

Consumers are likely to infer that brand choice is not as critical to satisfaction, that it's all right to shop around, perhaps even when a promotional incentive is not available.

The fact that advertising and promotion do interrelate was conclusively proven in the landmark "How Advertising Works" study, based on BehaviorScan data from Information Resources Inc. (IRI). IRI found that "higher levels of trade dealing appear to inhibit the ability of TV advertising to positively affect sales. Specifically, the higher the level of display for an established brand, the less likely that the brand would be able to increase sales given increased advertising weight. Similarly, higher levels of display and store feature inhibit the likelihood of a successful established brand copy test."[2]

It's very important to note that this conclusion is not based on the impact of a competitor's trade promotion on a brand's spending or copy test. It's based on the impact of the brand's own promotion. In other words, the more the brand promotes itself on the shelf, the less chance that the advertising it runs will have a positive impact.

In fairness, it must be noted that IRI came to the opposite conclusion in regard to consumer promotion for established brands, but only in regard to copy tests. "The probability of an established brand copy test being successful increases with higher levels of brand volume sold on vendor coupon."[3] It is likely that the consumer promotion in conjunction with a new selling message did encourage higher levels of trial. But that is a valid tactical use of promotion that in no way changes the overall conclusions about the long-term effect, or about the strategic imperative, for the brand not to employ the tactic on a continuous basis.

In the end, even if the Brand Loyalty Equation is an apples-to-grapes comparison, and arguably sour ones at that, it's still low-hanging fruit and ripe for the plucking by consumers. And the fact that it is being plucked is inescapable, behaviorally, from the MRCA data and attitudinally from the Roper Organization, which periodically polls consumers about which of a dozen factors are most important in their decision to buy a particular brand. In 1993, "a reasonable price" was cited by 64 percent of consumers versus 47 percent for "the manufacturer's reputation for quality." This seventeen percentage-point gap was an all-time high since the measurements began in the mid-1970s.[4]

Even outside the packaged-goods world this price-conscious attitude is taking hold. "Willingness to pay a premium for specific services, from airlines to pay cable, also has eroded markedly in the past few years." So Roper reported in 1993 in *Public Pulse*, a monthly report on consumer attitudes.[5] And it's doubtful that there would be much of an argument from automakers, who have seen the power, and the pitfalls, of rebates—or retailers, who have begun holding Christmas sales prior to Thanksgiving.

And while excessive promotion is not the only brand-hostile force operative in the marketplace, nor the only one contributing to the erosion of brand loyalty, it seems to be the determining one, at least for the high-profit segment. The final bit of proof comes from an examination of loyalty trends in a sector which has not experienced the massive increase in promotional activity seen in packaged goods.

MRCA analyzed eighteen selected brands of footwear and apparel in the same manner as the twenty-six packaged-goods brands to determine changes in loyalty over time. The soft-goods industry is certainly not a model for promotional restraint. In fact, it has an extremely high rate of purchases made "on sale"—52 percent in 1992 according to MRCA data. But it is also an industry that is increasingly more marketing oriented rather than sale driven. The percentage of on-sale merchandise was 57 percent in 1977, five percentage points higher than it was fifteen years later.

Arguably, brand loyalty trends in soft goods over these fifteen years reflect the industry's change in approach. The level of high-profit soft-goods consumers who were brand loyal, that is, who gave the brand more than half their category purchases *increased* from 28 percent to 31 percent. The fact that these levels are considerably higher on an absolute basis than those of packaged goods may be more related to the lower frequency of purchase than to any innately greater loyalty. But the key finding is inescapable.

When promotion declines, loyalty increases.

Loyalty equilibrium, or even modest improvement, was achieved over a period of time when admittedly high levels of promotional activity were stabilized or decreased. The lesson to be learned is clear. Brand loyalty can survive brand-hostile market forces if marketers do not exacerbate them with their own actions. The corollary to that conclusion is best summed up by that shrewd opossum, Pogo, created by Walt Kelly, who more than once uttered the truth to his comic-strip buddies while mired deep in the Okefenokee swamp.

"We have met the enemy and he is us."

So why aren't "we" winning? Because the same excessive promotion that is stealing away our consumers' loyalty is performing a similar function on our hard-earned profits. It's no secret that the margin of pumped-up promoted volume is far lower than that of nonpromoted sales. For YopleX, the difference is an 11 percent net profit margin compared to 40 percent. The difference is even more pronounced in the high-profit segment, 18 percent compared to 53 percent. And those numbers assume all promotion volume is incremental, a fact disputed by common sense, experience, and the analysis of panel data cited in Chapter 4. The final Closeup at the end of the chapter provides more details about why excessive promotion is hazardous to brand profitability.

To a visitor from Mars the entire situation might appear to be an interesting but minor manifestation of a more widespread planetary death wish. For it's not just a brand that's in trouble. Or a category. It's an industry and a paradigm that would appear to be in trouble.

What's wrong with current marketing practices? Do marketers on Earth really need to ask?

Inadvertently, we give our best customers and prospects significantly less than their fair share of media advertising, hampering our ability to build brand equity and loyalty. While at the same time, those best customers and prospects are overwhelmed by a promotional message training them to buy on deal, or, in many categories, heightening their price sensitivity, thus paving the way for private label. And in every category, for every brand, imposing a serious penalty on bottom-line profitability.

As a colleague remarked on being presented with the weight of the evidence, marketers seem to be "looking for love in all the wrong places."

CLOSEUP

The Mathematics of Disloyalty

Packaged-goods marketers are expert in assessing how well their spending delivers against their "target audience," usually a broad demographic subgroup such as "Women 18–49." But historically they have shown very little curiosity about assessing how well it delivers against the one target audience that really counts, the heavy category buying, high-profit segment.

The mathematics favor brand disloyalty because of the very different way advertising and promotion work in the marketplace. Advertising reaches *everybody*, or practically everybody, even if it is skewed to the demographically defined target audience. But except for the distribution cost, the impact of sales promotion is *limited* to those consumers who actually take advantage of the offer. And since heavy buyers have far greater opportunity to take advantage, and do so, the promotional spending against that group is magnified. Moreover, any change in the overall ratio of advertising to promotion (A/P) has an *exponential effect* on the heavy buying, high-profit segment.

Figure 6.6 illustrates what happens when Widget-X shifts the ratio

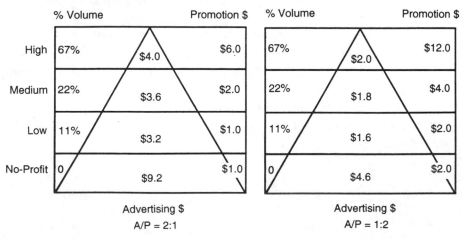

Figure 6.6 Widget-X advertising and promotion spending by segment.

is a constant $30 million. In both cases, the high-profit segment, which represents 17 percent of households, receives 20 percent of the advertising spending, a favorable skew for a brand that employs a typical broad target audience definition. Also in both cases the high-profit segment, which accounts for two-thirds of the category volume, receives two-thirds of the promotional spending that remains after deducting the 10 percent that goes to distributing coupons to noncategory buyers.

When the A/P ratio is 2:1, the high-profit segment receives $4 million in advertising spending and $6 million in promotion, less than twice as much. But when the A/P ratio shifts to 1:2, the high-profit segment only receives $2 million in advertising but a whopping $12 million in promotion, six times as much.

It would seem extremely likely that this kind of shift since the mid-1970s in the spending of most brands has played a large part in the precipitous declines in loyalty observed among heavy buying, high-profit consumers.

CLOSEUP

The True Redemption Rate
of Heavy Buyers

Just as marketers rarely think about the excessive amount of promotion spending that goes against the heavy buying, high-profit segment, they rarely consider what the true coupon redemption rate of heavy buyers must be. And how that high rate might be affecting the loyalty of this critical group.

The more purchases a consumer makes, the more opportunities there are to take advantage of a promotional offer. MRCA panel data reveals a close correlation between the percent of volume and the percent of total deal volume by profit segment. In other words, if the high-profit segment makes 75 percent of the purchases in a category, it accounts for about 75–80 percent of the volume sold on deal, and therefore, it redeems about 75–80% of the coupons.

It stands to reason that if a relatively small group makes a relatively large percentage of the redemptions, the incidence of redemption—the *redemption rate*—should be considerably higher. And it is. Just how much higher can be calculated from the following formula:

$$\text{HB Redemption Rate} = \frac{\text{HB \% Volume} \times \text{Average Redemption Rate}}{\text{HB \% HH} \times \text{HB Targeting Factor}}$$

where the average redemption rate is the overall rate of reported redemptions; HB % volume is the percent of total brand volume accounted for by heavy category buyers; HB % HH is the percentage of total households, not category households, accounted for by heavy category buyers; and the HB targeting factor is the ratio of the percentage of coupons delivered to heavy category buyers versus their percentage in the total population. For example, if, through targeting, heavy buyers received 23 percent of all coupons but represented only 20 percent of total households, then their targeting factor would be 1.15.

In most cases the formula will yield a good approximation of the true heavy-buyer redemption rate. It can be refined by substituting the actual percentage of brand promotional volume accounted for by heavy category buyers for their percentage of total brand volume, which in most cases will be a slightly higher number. If anything, this formula modestly understates the true rate of heavy-buyer redemptions.

The calculation for YopleX is as follows:

$$\text{HB Redemption Rate} = \frac{79\% \times 2.5\%}{16\% \times 1.15} = 10.7\%$$

Thus, the coupon redemption rate of high-profit buyers is four times greater than the average—another by-product of all consumers not being created equal.

CLOSEUP

Why Excessive Promotion Can Be Hazardous to the Profitability of Your Brand

Just as all consumers are not created equal, neither are all consumer purchase occasions. It is self-evident that purchases made with some form of promotional incentive will be less profitable than those made at regular price. Just how much less profitable, however, is not always taken into consideration, or even known, by marketers when allocating their budgets.

YopleX has a 19 percent dollar share of the roughly $800 million yogurt market, or $150 million in annual factory sales. Volume by profit segment is typical of packaged-goods brands. The heavy-buying high-profit segment accounts for almost 80 percent of total brand volume, or $118 million.

To assess total YopleX profitability, some estimate has to be made of the brand's gross margin, that is, the profit remaining after the costs of raw materials, manufacturing, and sales and distribution, but before marketing expenses are deducted. Taking into consideration the incremental cost of maintaining a product in the refrigerated dairy case, the gross margin is estimated at 55 percent. By applying that percentage to volume, gross profit by segment can be easily calculated, as shown in Figure 6.7.

To determine net profit and margin, estimated marketing expenses must be deducted. YopleX spends $13.5 million in advertising, and $33.5 million in sales promotion, including production. The resulting net profit and margin by segment is shown in Figure 6.8.

As expected, YopleX's greatest profitability and highest margin are found in the high-profit segment. The low-profit and no-profit segments produce losses on a total volume basis. The same steps can be followed to assess the difference in profitability between nonpromoted and promoted volume.

MRCA reports that 56 percent of YopleX volume is sold on deal, stimulated by either consumer promotion or trade. This figure is

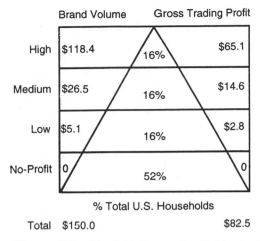

	Brand Volume	Gross Trading Profit
High	$118.4	16%	$65.1
Medium	$26.5	16%	$14.6
Low	$5.1	16%	$2.8
No-Profit	0	52%	0

% Total U.S. Households

| Total | $150.0 | $82.5 |

Figure 6.7 YopleX Gross Profit Matrix (in millions of dollars).

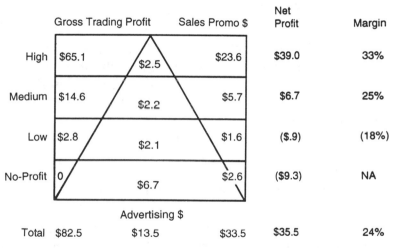

	Gross Trading Profit		Sales Promo $	Net Profit	Margin
High	$65.1	$2.5	$23.6	$39.0	33%
Medium	$14.6	$2.2	$5.7	$6.7	25%
Low	$2.8	$2.1	$1.6	($.9)	(18%)
No-Profit	0	$6.7	$2.6	($9.3)	NA

Advertising $

| Total | $82.5 | $13.5 | $33.5 | $35.5 | 24% |

Figure 6.8 YopleX Net Profit Matrix (in millions of dollars).

considerably higher than the 37 percent on deal reported for the category. The high-profit segment actually has the greatest deal percentage, 57 percent. The medium- and low-profit segments percentages of deal are 55 percent and 47 percent, respectively. By applying these percentages to total sales, volume and gross trading profit can be allocated between promoted and nonpromoted volume, as shown in Figure 6.9.

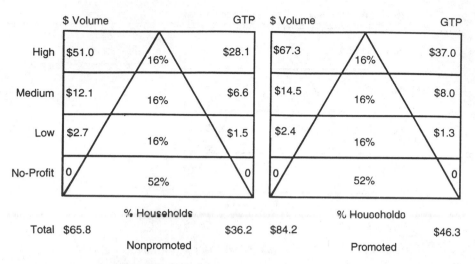

Figure 6.9 YopleX Gross Profit Matrix for promoted versus nonpromoted volume (in millions of dollars).

To calculate net profit, advertising and sales promotion spending must be allocated equitably. A reasonable assumption is that advertising has an influence in all purchase decisions, even those made with a promotional incentive. Therefore advertising spending is allocated to both promoted and nonpromoted volume by segment, in proportion to sales. Those advertising dollars directed at noncategory buyers, the no-profit segment, are charged against nonpromoted volume, under the assumption that the expense is an inevitable by-product of the strategy to drive volume through brand advertising.

Sales promotion expense is allocated totally to promoted volume, which logically is the primary beneficiary of promotional spending. (For those marketers who would argue that sales promotion has a longer-term brand-building impact as well, a reallocation of a modest proportion of the *consumer* sales promotion budget would not materially affect the results of the analysis.) Sales promotion costs to the no-profit segment represent the expense of distributing coupons that are not used. The advertising and sales promotion expense by segment of both promoted and nonpromoted volume is shown in Figure 6.10.

Subtracting these marketing expenses from gross profit reveals some startling findings. As shown in Figure 6.11, nonpromoted vol-

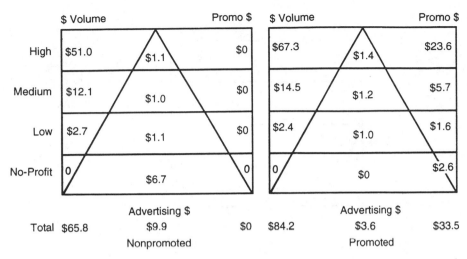

Figure 6.10   YopleX marketing spending for promoted versus nonpromoted volume (in millions of dollars).

ume contributes $26.3 million, or 74 percent of total brand profits. This high level is achieved despite the conservative assumption that nonpromoted volume should absorb all advertising against the no-profit segment. The net margin is a healthy 40 percent. In the high-profit segment it is 53 percent.

The picture for promoted volume is not nearly as rosy. As shown

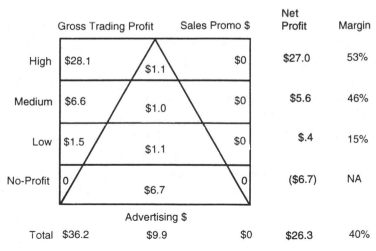

Figure 6.11   YopleX Net Profit Matrix for nonpromoted volume (in millions of dollars).

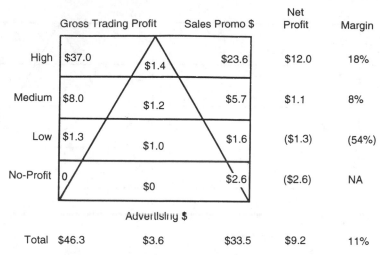

	Gross Trading Profit	Sales Promo $	Net Profit	Margin
High	$37.0	$23.6	$12.0	18%
	$1.4			
Medium	$8.0	$5.7	$1.1	8%
	$1.2			
Low	$1.3	$1.6	($1.3)	(54%)
	$1.0			
No-Profit	0	$2.6	($2.6)	NA
	$0			
	Advertising $			
Total	$46.3	$3.6	$33.5	$9.2	11%

Figure 6.12 YopleX Net Profit Matrix for promoted volume (in millions of dollars).

in Figure 6.12, promoted volume, which represents 56 percent of total volume, contributes only $9.2 million in profit, or 26 percent of total brand profits. But just as important, virtually all that profit from promoted volume is derived from the high-profit segment. Promoted volume in the medium-profit segment is only marginally profitable and actually unprofitable in the low-profit segment.

This pattern of promoted volume profitability is very typical for packaged-goods brands. Promoted volume profitability is essentially restricted to the high-profit segment. All other segments are either marginally profitable or produce a loss.

If sales promotion expenses were decreased, profitability would actually increase in those segments where losses are currently produced. In fact, profitability is likely to increase across all segments if the impact of promotion on incremental volume is taken into consideration. These findings will prove extremely important when developing strategies for revamping sales promotion strategies and reallocating budgets, discussed in Chapters 12 and 14, respectively.

7

THE RIGHT PLACE WITH THE RIGHT MESSAGE

Executive Preview

The goal of Differential Marketing is to communicate more of the right kinds of messages to the "right places"; in other words, more brand loyalty building in the high-profit segment. But demographic targeting of conventional advertising vehicles often falls short in its ability to differentiate high-profit households from all others. To accomplish the goals of Differential Marketing, the targeting of traditional media can be enhanced by utilizing a consumer database and other data-based tools, and the overall impact augmented by delivering a brand-loyalty program via direct mail to individual high-profit households.

Most marketers equate loyalty programs with frequent-flier type programs, which are unaffordable to all but a small group of brands that can afford a lucrative reward structure. But since the mid-1980s, evolutionary offshoots of these programs have been successfully introduced by companies which market everyday, low-priced products, such as Kraft Foods, Kimberly-Clark, and Procter & Gamble.

The incentive in this new kind of "brand-loyalty program" is relevant and useful information, either about the brand or the context in which it is used or both. The first such program nationwide was "The Beginning Years," a series of booklets about child development developed by Ogilvy & Mather Direct for Huggies disposable diapers in the early 1980s. Importantly, each booklet was synchronized with the actual age of the baby in the household.

The success of "The Beginning Years" and many other subsequent brand loyalty programs using information to sell harks back to an earlier tradition that characterized advertising as "the news of the marketplace" and that produced the long-copy ads of David Ogilvy. But creative trends and the desire for greater media efficiency, and thus shorter commercials, have resulted in advertising which generally provides consumers with very little real information. This unmet need sets the stage for the overwhelming acceptance by consumers of these programs and their substantial impact on brand loyalty.

M arketers' misguided search for affection, and its unintended but not insignificant consequences, is precisely what Differential Marketing (DFM) seeks to redress. The first critical step is to help put aside our thoughtless indiscretions and start looking for love in the *right* place. And the "right place" in DFM terms means the *right* kind of message, loyalty-building, directed at the *right* audience, the high-profit segment.

But it should be clear by now that the way to reach the right audience is very different in DFM than it is in conventional media. "Women 18–49" can be satisfactorily delivered by a judicious selection of television programming or magazine titles. But the demographic targeting tools of traditional advertising and promotional vehicles are likely to be far too blunt to effectively reach a marketing target of "the high-profit segment." There are simply too many consumers in every profit segment with the *same* demographic profile. To implement the strategies of DFM, it is often necessary to target and make contact with a far more precisely defined audience.

Differential Marketing targets individual high-profit households.

Targeting individual high-profit households does not mean entirely abandoning conventional communications practices. It does, however, require balancing them with new kinds of programs and activities that, in the aggregate, create a stronger, more productive communications plan, productive from the standpoint of putting greater loyalty-building communications pressure against high-profit consumers.

And it also means exploring new options that enhance the ability of traditional vehicles to help achieve that targeting objective. By use of a *database* and other *data-based* tools, many of the same advertising and promotion vehicles that marketers already use employing demographic targeting can now be targeted to *individual* households. The most notable exception is television, and as is shown in Chapter 11, even in that medium, improvements in the way television is bought and used by marketers can go a long way to improve effective advertising delivery against the high-profit audience. And television is the medium that is likely to become *most targetable* to individual households as the information super-highway is built.

Moreover, the need to target individual high-profit households with more loyalty-building messages makes a powerful communications medium that has historically been underutilized by marketers an attractive new possibility. That medium is direct mail, but of a kind very different from what most marketers think of as direct mail—a brand-building communication rather than merely an offer in an envelope.

In Differential Marketing, direct mail is direct advertising.

And, usually, the direct advertising is of a very specific kind: ongoing brand-loyalty programs designed to build share of customer and buying rate in the high-profit segment.

THE EVOLUTION OF LOYALTY PROGRAMS

Say "loyalty program" and most marketers today will instantly think "frequent flier." A marketing generation ago, they probably would have thought "Green Stamps."

The origin of loyalty programs is the origin of selling.

If the Egyptians branded the bricks for the pyramids, they probably invented consumer loyalty programs as well. The idea of rewarding one's best customers with some kind of special privilege dates back to the first merchant who threw in an extra roll of papyrus to show his appreciation for a scribe's business.

What Sperry & Hutchinson—the originator of S&H Green Stamps—did in the 1950s and American Airlines did in the 1980s was to systematize the loyalty program participation by creating a well-defined, and high-value, reward structure for a huge customer base that operated on the very democratic principle of "the more you buy, the more you get."

Frequent-flier programs brought loyalty programs into the information age.

Arguably, the real breakthrough of American Airlines' "AAdvantage Program" was its ability to piggyback on Sabre, the company's pioneering computerized reservation system, to eliminate a very real drawback of Green Stamps: the need for consumers to go to all the effort to "lick'em and stick'em" in those countless books to keep track of where they stood. Airlines who didn't have American's technology had to scramble to duplicate this benefit when they introduced their own programs.

Aside from helping prevent customers' interest from flagging, the computerization of these programs lead directly to a potentially powerful new communications medium: the mileage statement. Suddenly the airlines, who heretofore were lucky to spell the customer's name right on the ticket, were communicating with their high-profit customers as often as once a month, and giving them something of real value to sustain their involvement with the brand. In no time at all, a glossy newsletter accompanied the statement, providing more information about the program and its rewards, but also alerting customers to news and information about the airline that could be useful for their travel plans.

But the value of that information was overshadowed by the value of the reward structure. Ironically, the success of the "AAdvantage Program," and the numerous imitators it spawned, laid a heavy burden on the development of future loyalty programs. Chief among them was the widespread notion that the programs could not work unless the consumer payoff had substantial monetary value. Programs created by several large hotel chains and rent-a-car companies suffered from lack of interest until they were tied into an airline program as "partners." If free lodging or car rental could not measure up to the lure of a trip to Hawaii, what else could?

The "mileage wars" that broke out as the programs matured also sent a cautionary signal to marketers. It seemed, with some justification, that much of the "loyalty" that these programs were producing was not loyalty at all, but merely repeat purchase.

True loyalty is not for sale to the highest bidder.

Much of the "loyalty" only lasted until a better offer came along. This fact was rediscovered in the 1990s with the "discount wars" between MCI's "Friends & Family" versus AT&T's "True Savings" program. By early 1995, much of the advertising for both programs was focused on disparaging the value of the savings offered by the other.

Despite this shortcoming, there can be no denying the significant impact a "reward" or "volume discount" program can have on a brand's or a company's business, especially for early adopters. "Friends & Family" inflicted significant damage on the AT&T long-distance customer base until "True Savings" was developed to counteract it. MCI's program was especially powerful because the structure had inherently greater appeal to high-volume, high-profit long distance customers. And, it motivated them to *identify* other high-volume, high-profit customers and *recruit* them for MCI.

The aggressive and highly successful introductions of affinity credit cards by both Ford and General Motors are other prime examples. By providing a credit toward the next new car purchase based on the amount of charges on the card, they have created a powerful new weapon to fight their historically disappointing re-purchase rates. And they will retain a head-start advantage even if other automakers attempt to join in.

These variations on the frequent-flier idea, as well as other credit-card based "points" systems, are all lineal descendants of the papy-rus maker by way of S&H Green Stamps and the American Airlines' "AAdvantage Program." They can be a key DFM tool for companies or brands that have high price-points or robust annual volumes, as well as the ability to monitor transactions, either by themselves or through a third party.

"BRAND-LOYALTY" VERSUS "FREQUENT-BUYER" PROGRAMS

The "AAdvantage Program" and its many imitators may have grabbed the headlines, but this concept has since been quietly, and successfully, extended to brands whose fundamental economics make it impossible to reward their best customers with high-value perks like airline tickets, even brands in low-price, seemingly low-interest categories such as packaged goods.

The loyalty programs created by companies such as Kraft Foods, Kimberly-Clark, Unilever, Nestlé, and Procter & Gamble must work within a radically different economic structure. But they still man-age to provide high-profit consumers with rewards that may be less tangible and less valuable in a monetary sense, but that, relatively speaking, are every bit as motivating as a free trip to Hawaii.

In fact, this other kind of loyalty program successfully avoids the major shortcoming of frequent-buyer type programs by creating brand loyalty in the classic sense rather than "transaction loyalty." And, in the process, they show the marketers who can afford true frequent-buyer programs how to better insulate their own partici-pants from the effects of competitive bribery. Such programs are characterized as *brand-loyalty programs* to distinguish them from traditional frequent-buyer programs, which are more focused on creating a repeat purchase pattern than on building the brand. A brand-loyalty program is usually at the core of a brand's DFM plan.

Despite the many differences, brand-loyalty programs were actually born out of an insight from the frequent-flier experience. Free tickets were not the only motivation for businessmen to participate.

Recognition is its own reward.

The special treatment and the "perks" that came with being a frequent flier could often be more important than another airplane trip, even two first-class tickets to a remote and sunny island. These perks included upgrades, special reservations lines, and early boarding, but they also included less tangible benefits, like being greeted by name or "being in the know" through advance information delivered by the program newsletters. Out of these kinds of benefits, the idea of "relationship marketing" began to take hold.

In a leap of faith in 1983, Kimberly-Clark, working with Ogilvy & Mather Direct, began to create the first nontransactional, nonreward-based brand-loyalty program, for Huggies Disposable Diapers. The key element in the program was a series of newsletters called *The Beginning Years* that were sent about once every three months to mothers with diaper-age children (see Figure 7.1). Synchronized with the actual birth date of the recipients' baby, each newsletter educated parents and gave advice about what to expect in the next three months of their own child's development.

The newsletters did include coupons, which was as close as the program came to free trips. But the coupons did not drive the success of the program. Instead, it was the unexpected recognition from the marketer and the information that accompanied it, information that was highly relevant and useful to the target audience.

The ability of "The Beginning Years" to build true loyalty and generate incremental volume was proven in a year-long panel test, and in 1985 the program was rolled out nationally, reaching a large majority of the approximately three million families that annually welcomed the arrival of a new child. Over the next several years, Huggies made steady progress in its market-share battle with

Figure 7.1 A sample of *The Beginning Years*, a series of newsletters from Kimberly-Clark used as a brand-loyalty program for Huggies Disposable Diapers. Reproduced, with permission, from the copyrighted series "The Beginning Years," published and distributed by Kimberly-Clark Corporation, makers of Huggies® Disposable Diapers.

Figure 7.1   Continued

Procter & Gamble's Pampers, finally overtaking it as the leading brand of disposable diapers. The brand-loyalty program was not the only reason for the brand's success, but Procter & Gamble clearly considered it a major contributor. How else to explain why P&G eventually countered with its own on-going information-based brand-loyalty program aimed at new moms?

For all the information-based brand-loyalty programs that have been developed since—and there have been far more of them than frequent-buyer programs—"The Beginning Years" remains a classic. It earns that accolade not only because of its well-documented success in building sales, but also because it was the first of many to demonstrate how the power of a very old and traditional advertising idea can be given new life in the not-so-traditional vehicle of a brand-loyalty program.

Information sells.

"THE NEWS OF THE MARKETPLACE"

Stanley Resor, who presided over the J. Walter Thompson (JWT) advertising agency from 1916 to 1961, and who was instrumental in transforming the company from a collection of regional offices into the world's first advertising giant, had a succinct piece of advice for those who would practice his craft. He characterized advertising as "the news of the marketplace."[1]

Using information to sell is a time-tested advertising technique.

A quick inspection of the ads created by JWT and other agencies in the first half of the century confirms that Resor's dictum was widely put into practice. Magazine and newspaper ads were copy intensive, rich in details about the product and why it was right for the reader. Words dominated the look, and a powerful headline, like John Caples' famous "They Laughed When I Sat Down At the Piano, But When I Started to Play!" for the U.S. School of Music in the 1920s, was everything.

Resor and Caples were bullish on using information to sell because they knew it did exactly that—sell. They knew that in those days before scientific market research was invented because they observed actual sales results, results from advertisements that sold the product directly to consumers, giving them no motivation other than what they read and saw on the page.

The selling power of information was proved by early direct-mail advertising.

When advertising people wax nostalgic about John Caples, they often forget that he was a direct marketing copywriter, and that the ad for the U.S. School of Music was a mail-order ad. The reader could send in the coupon in the lower right-hand corner for a free book, "Music Lessons in Your Own Home," as well as a "Demonstration Lesson" and "particulars of your Special Offer."

Those were the days before the evolutionary lines between advertising and direct marketing, or mail-order as it was commonly called, diverged like the upland gorilla and the chimpanzee. Albert Lasker, who built the most famous and the biggest ad agency of the time, Lord & Thomas, said "I wouldn't attempt to run an agency without a big volume of mail-order business to tell me what to do for my other clients."[2]

What Lasker was referring to was the age-old problem of determining the effectiveness of advertising, and the fact that mail-order was measurable. He believed what was learned from mail-order could then be applied to so-called "general" advertising. After all, the mission of both was the same: to sell. When Lasker hired Claude Hopkins at the turn of the century, a third of Lord & Thomas's business was mail-order advertising.[3] Hopkins, who went on to become one of the most successful and famous copywriters of all time, and the author of a book titled *Scientific Advertising*, absorbed and used mail-order principles throughout his career.

In 1938, the Mather & Crowther advertising agency in London sent the young David Ogilvy to the United States, where he came under the influence of Hopkins and Caples as well as the "hard-sell" school of advertising—notably, Rosser Reeves, who would go on to be the long-time copy-chief at the Ted Bates agency, and the popularizer of the "USP"—the unique selling proposition. On Ogilvy's return, he confronted the agency staff with the lessons he had learned, most of them derived from the experience of mail-order advertisers who measured sales rather than guessed at them.

"Direct response has always been my first love and secret weapon."

So David Ogilvy has stated, on numerous occasions. As the excerpts from his remarks in the Closeup at the end of the chapter show, he adopted the key principles of direct response to develop his signature style of advertising: long, information-filled copy, introduced by a headline that attracted the right prospects with a glance.

A dozen years later, in 1950, the fame of Ogilvy's new agency was assured when he created the classic series of ads featuring the man in the Hathaway shirt. The photograph of the distinguished, mustachioed, middle-aged man with the dashing eye patch is indelibly etched in memory. What is often forgotten is the body copy: fact-filled, detailed, product-focused. Despite the attention-getting photograph that dominated the page, the rest of the ad satisfied Ogilvy's guiding principle of giving readers information, and plenty of it. The first stopped readers in their tracks, the second closed the sale. Read the fine print in Figure 7.2 for all the fascinating details about Sea Island Cotton and its numerous Atlantic crossings.

The use of information to build brands and to sell continued well into the fifties. Photography in ads was by then common, but copywriters continued to hold sway, even for products where a

The Gun is a $2,000 Purdey from England

(The shirt: A Sylex, Sea Island Cotton from Hathaway)

THIS Sea Island cotton is astounding stuff—with fibers *three times longer* than those of ordinary cotton. It is described in the advertisements as "soft as swansdown, lustrous as satin, absorbent as wool, durable as linen." It is grown on St. Vincent, Antigua, St. Kitts, Montserrat, Nevis and Barbados.

Then it travels. Between being plucked in the balmy Caribbean sunshine, and its final apotheosis in a shirt by HATHAWAY of Canada, this nonesuch among cottons has been to England and back.

The Sylex Sea Island yarn is spun with loving care by Thomas Oliver & Sons, then woven on the looms of Ashton Brothers—two of the finest mills in England. Notice the extraordinary sheen. You can almost *feel* its downy softness.

The shirts are superbly tailored, with all the HATHAWAY hallmarks—long tails, single-needle stitching, impeccable collars. Price: $15 in colors and white, at stores that keep up the great tradition.

For the name of the store nearest you, write WELLINGTON-HATHAWAY, Ltd., Prescott, Ontario.

Figure 7.2 One of the Hathaway Shirt ads created by Ogilvy & Mather. Courtesy of C. F. Hathaway, a Division of Warnaco, Inc.

great deal of information wouldn't seem necessary to interest consumers. In a full-page ad for Prom home permanent in a 1951 issue of *Life* magazine, the obligatory picture of the beautiful hair seems almost incidental compared to the explanation of why the product needed no neutralizer and instructions about how to choose the right formula.

In the same issue, fully half of an ad for Clorets gum, not exactly a complicated product, is given over to text. Little, if anything about the gum is overlooked, including a description of the "secret" ingredient, chlorophyll, as well as instructions about when to use the product—after drinking alcohol or eating garlic, and in the morning. If that isn't enough information to tip off the unsuspecting offender, the ad goes into detail about how to conduct a "breath test" to prove Clorets' claims.

Surprisingly perhaps, the emergence of television did not immediately change advertisers' viewpoint that "more was more."

Infomercials have been around as long as commercial television.

In the early years of commercial television, filling the available air-time was sometimes problematic. Advertising to the rescue, with fifteen- and sometime even thirty-*minute* commercials, which were not only broadcast but *scheduled*. The legendary Vita Mix commercial, an early infomercial that alerted the nation about the perils of mashed potatoes to teeth and gums, was broadcast under the guise of a program called "Home Miracles for 1950."

But even as the infant medium matured, advertisers did their best to cram their allotted sixty seconds with information about the product itself, adapting their techniques to the limitations but also the strengths of sight, sound, and motion. The late fifties and the sixties were the heyday of the "mnemonic device," designed to provide a quick, memorable, and unique way of explaining the product's formulation or benefit—such as the clear plastic shield that stopped a baseball just before it struck the announcer, mimicking how Colgate toothpaste's "Gardol" stopped cavities.

And product demonstrations, particularly of the "side-by-side" kind, were ubiquitous. Procter & Gamble was reported to have instructed its advertising managers to attempt to include a side-by-side demonstration in every P & G commercial, and most particularly a demo that a consumer could actually repeat in her own home. Of this was born Rosie's diner and the "quicker-picker-upper" for Bounty paper towels, as well as numberless imitators.

But there was more than one current in the stream. Bill Bernbach, who founded the Doyle Dane Bernbach (DDB) agency in 1952, is widely acknowledged as the father of advertising's "creative revolution."

"Creative" meant "image," not information.

Side by side on the airwaves with Rosie were commercials like the one DDB created for Volkswagen, where, over footage of a seemingly endless funeral procession of expensive limousines, a sonorous voice read the will of the departed, announcing that the driver of the tiny VW bringing up the rear, "who oft times said a 'penny saved is a penny earned,' and also oft times said, 'Gee Uncle Max, it pays to own a Volkswagen'," was to be rewarded for his frugality by being bequeathed his dead uncle's "entire fortune of one-hundred billion dollars."[4]

In the 1970s, Bernbach's tenets of "less is more" and "emotion first" began to be widely accepted in the industry, and copied. Some might even say adulterated, with increasing reliance on flashy cinematography and music, and more recently, a technologically inspired belief in the transforming power of special effects.

Now, some twenty-odd years later, whether the creative revolution has lived up to its promise, or whether there was one revolution or many, let others debate elsewhere. But one observation is certain, irrespective of where we actually are in the revolutionary cycle.

Factual communication about products and services has been sacrificed on the twin altars of creativity and efficiency.

The information content of television commercials in general is at an all-time nadir. There is barely time in a 15-second commercial—and precious little more in a 30-second-spot—to communicate much information, and no time at all when information is out of fashion. And consumers are not altogether happy about it.

Consumers want more product information than they get.

While many of today's commercials are surely appreciated in their own right for what they are, consumers still want and need the "news of the marketplace" that was once contained in David Ogilvy's long copy ads. And because the quality of product information available from the other major source, the retailer, has also deteriorated significantly, the need is even more prevalent. Even if a store is not self-service, it is increasingly rare to find knowledgeable sales help, even for relatively high-ticket durable items.

As a result of these changes, consumers have to work harder to make the brand decision. In a survey conducted by the Roper Organization for *Good Housekeeping* magazine, a representative cross section of a thousand women were interviewed to determine how they were coping with the increasingly complex marketplace and hectic life-style of the nineties. Seventy-nine percent reported reading product labels much more carefully than they used to. "Entertaining, humorous presentation" ranked ninth out of ten attributes in terms of what they said it took for an advertisement to make a good impression on them, saved from the bottom of the barrel only by "celebrity endorsement."[5]

The same report concludes that the consumer of the nineties, "seeks straightforward information in product advertising. And she values advertising which provides information on many of the same factors which influence her purchase decisions—like messages featuring a guarantee-backed promise of quality, along with frank cost and product information."[6]

The Beginning Years, and other information-based brand-loyalty programs, fill these needs admirably. Which is why, as a DFM strategy, they are capable of building the good feelings that lead to loyalty for brands otherwise no more remarkable than their competition. Virtually every piece in these programs revolves around extensive, in-depth "news of the marketplace." They reach precisely those consumers who are likely to be most influenced by the news, those who, because of their buying behavior, have the most interest in the category. And they take advantage of the unique capabilities of a grossly underestimated method of communicating with consumers: the direct mail from which Albert Lasker and John Caples and David Ogilvy once learned so much.

How the direct-mail ugly duckling has once again become a swan is explained in Chapter 8.

CLOSEUP

Ogilvy on the Ancestry of Long Copy

The following quotes are excerpts from a presentation given by David Ogilvy in 1939 to the staff of the London advertising agency, Mather & Crowther, who had sent him to the United States to soak up U.S. advertising techniques. He returned a disciple of the "scientific advertising" tradition of Claude Hopkins and John Caples, as well as the "hard-sell" school of Rosser Reeves. And he remained a disciple throughout his career, despite scoring some of his most noticeable successes, for clients such as Hathaway and Schweppes, with advertising that was influenced as well by the "image" school of Bill Bernbach.

What is fascinating about the presentation, aside from the amount of wisdom it contained, is that at the time, Ogilvy, by his own admission, had yet to write his first ad. Likewise fascinating is that he so clearly recognized the debt owed to direct-marketing techniques by those who would practice good salesmanship in advertising, a debt that would resurface in Differential Marketing more than fifty years later.

> The most important job of an ad is to center all the attention on the merchandise and none on the technique of presenting it. Advertising has got to *sell*.

> In writing ads, act as you would if you met the individual buyer face to face. Don't show off. Don't try to be funny. Don't try to be clever. Don't behave eccentrically. Measure ads by salesmen's standards, not by amusement standards.

> My first basic rule consists in this premise: that the proved principles of mail-order advertising should be applied to all campaigns.

> In mail-order advertising, false theories melt away like snowflakes in the sun. The advertising is profitable or it is not, on the face of the returns.

The copy in mail-order ads is always long. It tells the complete story. The more you tell the more you sell.

You are like a salesman in a busy man's office. You have been trying to get in for several years. You will never be admitted again. This is your one chance to get his order. If you only shoot half your sales story, you are a dope.

Cover every phase of your subject. One fact appeals to some, one to another. Omit any fact and a certain percentage of your prospects will miss the one fact which would have sold them.

In mail-order advertising the illustrations are always to the point. They earn the space they occupy.

Use pictures only to attract real prospects. Use them only when they form a better selling argument than the same amount of space set in type.

Mail-order advertising does not deal in generalities. It is *factual, exact, and specific.*

Platitudes and generalities roll off the human understanding like water off a duck's back. They leave no impression. They suggest a general carelessness of truth. They lead readers to discount all the statements you use.

But actual figures are not discounted. Specific facts, stated in exact terms, are believed.

If a claim is worth making, it is worth making in the most impressive way. A specific, definite statement occupies no more room than a loose platitude.

It is important to realize that building ads for high readership is quite different from building ads on proved mail-order principles of salesmanship. Remember the difference, and whatever you do, do it with your eyes open.

8

INVOLVING THE CONSUMER WITH THE BRAND

Executive Preview

Direct mail is often dismissed as "junk mail," tacky and unwanted. Yet marketers such as Kraft Foods, Unilever, and Procter & Gamble, are increasingly learning that a well-crafted brand-loyalty program delivered through the mail is a powerful way to generate sales and profits because it actively involves the consumer with the brand.

Information is the driver for almost all brand-loyalty programs. It can be either information specifically about the brand or the way it's used, or more general information relevant to the user's lifestyle. Often it is information that is too complex to communicate in television or print, or the kind of information that is only appropriate for high-profit consumers, not the wider target audience.

Involving the consumer with information, and thus with the brand, is a proven method for producing long-term attitude and behavior change. But the opportunities to develop involvement in conventional media are rare. The direct-mail medium can take advantage of its three-dimensional nature and flexibility to provide a range of possibilities for consumer involvement, including samples, demonstrations, requests for reader ideas, and questionnaires.

F or many marketers the mention of direct mail instantly conjures up one of two thoughts: an envelope stuffed full of coupons or the dreaded "J" word, junk mail. The first seems contradictory and the second antithetical to a Differential Marketing (DFM) strategy of building quality perceptions and brand loyalty among high-profit consumers.

Packaged-goods marketers are particularly skeptical about direct mail. In addition to the other concerns, they believe they already have extensive experience with direct mail—as a promotional medium. What they are referring to are cooperative couponing vehicles that are distributed nationally to tens of millions of households, usually saturating middle-and upper-income zip codes. The Carol Wright mailer, marketed by Donnelley Marketing, Inc., is the largest of this type. The Donnelley promotional survey reports that this kind of direct mail is used by over 75 percent of respondents.[1]

Part of the perception problem is marketers' own fortunate station in life. As upper-income households, they're bombarded by more than their fair share of magazine solicitations, special one-time offers, catalogs, and preapproved credit applications. Many of these mailings are broadly targeted, often on the basis of some kind of income measurement. It's purely a hit-or-miss proposition whether the offer is of any interest. But if the recipient is a fly-fisherman, or a model train builder, or a gardener, he or she is likely to have a far different reaction to a new catalog for that special hobby than to one more life insurance solicitation.

It's not junk if it interests you.

The quality of the pieces we often see in the mailbox is far different from that of the typical brand-loyalty program. There are exceptions, but much direct mail is response-driven in the traditional sense. Which is to say, the mailer doesn't care about what recipients *think* or *feel* about the product, only that they plunk down their money for it. And the look and tonality of the package reflects this attitude.

It doesn't look like junk if it's a brand-loyalty program.

Marketers *do* care—desperately—how consumers think and feel about their brands. They take great pains to build that caring into their mail packages. Any perception that all direct mail looks junky has been lapped by reality. At least reality as practiced by such multinational giants as Kraft Foods, Unilever, American Express, Nestlé, Procter & Gamble, Kimberly-Clark, the House of Seagram, and Ralston Purina, as well as by smaller but equally respected marketers like DowBrands, Helene Curtis, Gerber, Ben & Jerry's, and Sandoz. John Cummings, an Armonk, New York, based consultant, established a service called *John Cummings & Partners DBM/scan®* in 1991 to track database marketing activity by consumer marketers. As of early 1995, *DBM/scan* had monitored more than 250 loyalty programs from more than 100 different consumer marketing companies. The Closeup at the end of the chapter lists the 49 new programs that *DBM/scan* monitored in 1994.

It would be a gross overstatement to say that all marketers in all of these companies are implementing DFM strategies through information-driven, direct-mail delivered, brand-loyalty programs. In fact, in several instances, successful programs have fallen victim to management change or the blind pursuit of short-term results via promotion. But to varying degrees, farsighted marketers in all these companies have seen the power of this new communications vehicle. In most cases, their strategies are not yet referred to as "Differential Marketing," but more often than not they clearly meet the definition laid out in this book. And the way the information is presented demonstrates that many marketers have independently rediscovered and absorbed the lessons of David Ogilvy and the sales impact of "the news of the marketplace." In addition, they have apparently learned the secret of building loyalty and sales is actively *involving* the consumer with the brand.

INFORMATION AS THE DRIVER

Virtually all the brand-loyalty programs from leading consumer marketers have one thing in common: relevant and useful information. The information may be *brand-specific*, about the brand itself, or *value-added*, about that aspect of the consumer's life into which the brand fits. Or both.

"The more you tell the more you sell."

That was the advice that David Ogilvy gave to the staff of Mather & Crowther in 1939. And that advice has been taken to heart by those who practice DFM today. One newsletter in a loyalty program for Maxwell House coffee introduced the consumer to a new improvement to keep the coffee fresher, the "Fresh-Lock Packet." The same issue provided ideas and recipes for a festive Sunday brunch. *Everyday Best*, a newsletter for Spray 'n Wash soil and stain remover, explained how the three versions of the product, stick, liquid, and gel, each had a different specialty in the "Spray 'n Wash cleaning system." In the same issue were articles about the best fabrics for staying cool in the summer and a tip for keeping the "pills" on fabric from becoming a nuisance while doing the laundry. (See Figure 8.1.)

The medium is the message.

The choice of information and the way it is presented often take advantage of the uniqueness of direct mail. The manner in which consumers are addressed can acknowledge that the marketer is aware of their *specialness*. "Dear Chocolate Cookie Lover" began a letter from Pepperidge Farm. The recipients of a brand-loyalty program for Martell Cognac were greeted simply, but elegantly, as "Mesdames et Messieurs."

Frequently the information is of a nature that can not be produc-

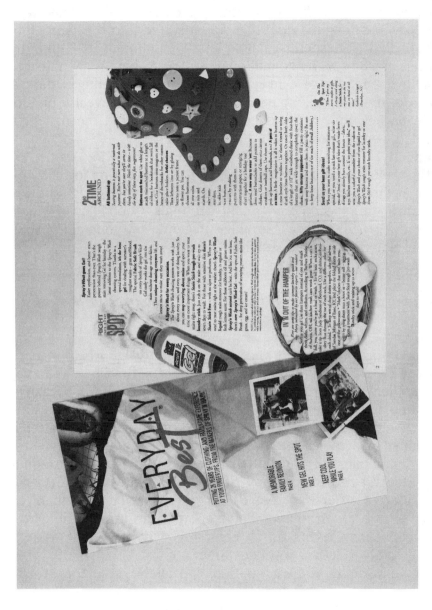

Figure 8.1 An example of *Everyday Best*®, Spray 'n Wash's newsletter. Permission granted by DowBrands L.P.® Trademark of DowBrands.

tively communicated in any other medium. The Fresh-Lock Packet for Maxwell House coffee was actually a small envelope filled with moisture-absorbing material that was inserted into the can before it was sealed. Not exactly a simple idea to communicate within the confines of a 30-second commercial. And probably too technical to draw in the reader of a magazine ad. But by creating a die-cut replica of the Maxwell House can that opened to reveal a picture of the packet, the nature of the improvement and the benefit it provided were telegraphed to the consumer.

Similarly, Good Start Infant Formula from Carnation, owned by Nestlé, touts its extra "gentleness" step in making its formula. An insert in the mailing provides a graphic three-step illustration of how "through a special process, the protein in Good Start is broken down into smaller pieces, to make it gentle on your new baby's still-developing digestive system."

Even though it's information, it's also advertising.

In addition to being relevant and useful, the information must support the positioning and personality of the brand. In a mailing for The Glenlivet scotch whisky, tasting the single-malt is compared to tasting a fine wine. Sandoz created the "Parents Club" for Triaminic cough and cold medicines. The sixteen-page newsletter is dominated by articles about health care for children, as well as an in-depth sales message about the six varieties of the product, all written in a friendly but earnest and authoritative tone. Contrast that with Ben & Jerry's "Chunk Mail," published "now & then" on "recycled paper with soy-based inks" and featuring everything from news about new flavors to the company's charitable activities to lengthy, off-beat letters from customers.

But importantly, the information can also extend the brand's positioning. Just as network television programming is designed with the largest possible audience in mind, a brand's advertising strategy is usually developed and validated against a broadly defined target group, such as "Women 18–49." This makes sense in a mass-media environment, where demographic breaks like that one are among the few means available to better target advertising impres-

Figure 8.2 A sample of a mail-piece for The Glenlivet. Courtesy of the House of Seagram.

145

sions. But it makes much less sense in a DFM brand-loyalty program, where factors other than demographics are the primary distinguishing characteristics of those receiving the mailings.

Clearly, for maximum effectiveness, the differences of the high-profit segment must be considered and catered to. By taking advantage of the privacy of mail, marketers can talk to their high-profit customers in a way that is relevant to them, but not necessarily relevant to the broad target audience.

Ziploc storage bags, for example, are positioned as the best way to keep food fresh in the refrigerator, the freezer, or the lunch box. Straying from that single-minded focus in advertising would run the risk of diffusing the brand's image, and leaving the door open to competitive freshness claims. However, in their newsletter program to heavy zippered-bag buyers, Ziploc also touts other uses for the brand, such as how to use a Ziploc bag to make ice cream or a Caesar salad (see Figure 8.3). Rather than hurting the image, that kind of information helps build brand usage and loyalty because, in many cases, heavy buyers *are* heavy buyers because they have already learned for themselves the many uses of the bags beyond food storage.

The case of Ziploc is a good example of how the information in brand-loyalty programs can and should be geared to high-profit consumers, who often have different needs, habits, or lifestyles than the broad target audience. And who seek different, and often more detailed, information.

The information doesn't have to interest everybody, just high-profit consumers.

This observation should help allay the concerns of those marketers who might fear that their product is too mundane and "low interest" to warrant an information-driven program. Usually that feeling is based on the reported perceptions of *all* users, not those relative few who buy and use the most, or who are actively in the market, and who, by extension, have the most interest in the category.

Virtually every brand has "a story to tell" to high-profit consum-

Involvement makes the message stick.

experiment conducted by behavioral scientists at The Ohio University, funded by the Ogilvy Center for Research & Development, demonstrated how involving consumers with an advertisement can extend that attitude change significantly, even if there is a *single* exposure.[3]

group of consumers in Columbus, Ohio, were given a print ad n unfamiliar low-cholesterol margarine to read. They were told after reading it, they would be asked to pass the information g to someone else in an adjoining room. A similar group of umers was also given the ad to read, but not told about the to relay the information. And a third group was recruited ly to provide a baseline of attitudes toward the margarine. were not shown any advertising.

e attitudes of all cells toward the margarine were then measured. two groups who had been given the ad to read showed equal ases, statistically significant, versus the attitudes of the unex-d, baseline group. At that point the consumers were told that the riment was completed and sent home. Those who had prepared selves to pass on the information never were asked to do so.

ght weeks later, both exposed groups were recontacted by e, and under the guise of an unrelated market-research survey, questioned about the margarine. The attitudes of those con-rs who had simply been asked to read the ad had declined to line levels. But the attitudes of those consumers who were ared to pass the information along, remained at the higher, stically significant level.

hile this exercise was a laboratory situation, real-world experi- has conclusively demonstrated that a single communication an information-driven, direct-mail delivered, brand-loyalty ram can produce this same impact. *Direct mail* as a medium a unique ability to involve the consumer with information about rand, and thus produce long-term attitude change. The com-e evidence about its impact is marshaled in Chapter 9, but how t mail manages this feat first needs explaining.

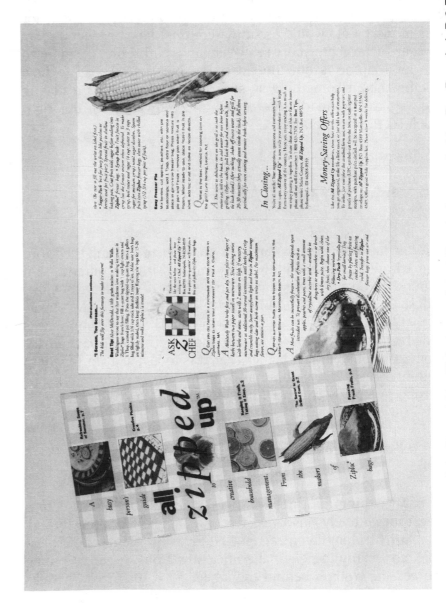

Figure 8.3 An example of *All Zipped Up,* Ziploc's newsletter. Permission granted by DowBrands L.P.® Trademark of DowBrands.

ers. Certainly there are many successful programs for brands in presumably high-interest categories, like cosmetics and premium whiskies and automobiles and food of all types, whether for adults, babies, or pets. But there are a surprising number, as well, for what most marketers would assume were mundane products: soap, dishwasher detergent, stain remover, and bathroom cleaner, to name a few. Ziploc is not the exception but the rule, as to how information about something as simple and common as a plastic storage bag can be made interesting and relevant with the right approach to the right audience.

INVOLVEMENT AS THE CATALYST

As important as information can be to the consumer, and therefore to the marketer, it is absolutely of no value if it goes unread, or if read, found to be uninteresting or irrelevant. It was David Ogilvy himself, in *Confessions of an Advertising Man* who made the observation that "you can't bore people into buying."[2] And that book was published at a time when, arguably, most people's threshold for boredom was considerably higher than it is today, in a world where the unthinkable will probably happen tomorrow. What is true for advertising is equally true for brand-loyalty programs.

You can't bore people into being loyal.

The key to using information successfully is to present it in a manner that actively involves the consumer with the brand. *Involvement* has long been recognized as a key element of salesmanship, especially in personal selling situations. A car salesman tries to get the walk-in behind the wheel for a test drive. A sales clerk in a clothing store encourages the customer to try on the dress. An insurance agent offers a free analysis of the tax impact of a prospect's estate. In the first two instances, the involvement

gives consumers a chance to experience what own the product. In the third, it enables them meaning of the product for them personally rat the abstract.

It follows that involvement might also be a pow tising. Yet rarely is consumer involvement the g team in developing the campaign. Breaking th yes. Memorability, yes. Brand benefits, yes. Bu involvement, in the true sense, seems more th reach.

The nature of most advertising media, and th use those media, work against consumer involv media are one-way. The broadcaster or the publ tiser sends, the consumer receives. The only m ple to follow up on a message that piques th extra step of a phone call or a reply card or a Traditional media also operate within strict ti straints, minimizing the opportunity to engag imagination about the ownership experience. A dia reach everyone, or a wide cross section of e only present the general relevance of the sellin personal one.

Moreover, involvement with brand advertising larly audacious goal when consumers very ofte volved with the medium itself. Magazines or skimmed rather than read. The television is ofte turned on as background diversion while the hou its business. And even when consumers concentr or the programming, it is all too easy to flip the remote control when the ad comes along.

Yet if involvement can be achieved, it can be p studies have demonstrated the long-term effect consumer attitudes toward a brand. But they hav the attitudinal effect of a single exposure to adver rapidly in a real-world environment, usually dec sure levels within a week or two. Hence the tra on frequency in media planning. But frequency is if the advertiser *can* manage to involve the cons

Involvement comes with the territory.

Part of mail's unique ability to involve derives from the tangible nature of an envelope, which needs to be dealt with in some fashion, even if only inspected and discarded. And that envelope can come in a countless variety of sizes and shapes, providing the advertiser great flexibility in terms of its contents. But beyond direct mail's unique physical characteristics, several other techniques of the direct marketer's trade are invaluable in involving the consumer with information about the brand. The first is recognizing consumers as *individuals*.

Traditional media are "public" media. Special needs or interests are singled out at the risk of confusing, boring, or even offending large portions of the audience. Special individuals simply can't be singled out.

But in the private medium of the mail, the advertiser has considerably more latitude. How marketers can and should cater to the mind-sct of high-profit consumers has already been discussed. But with just a minimum of extra effort, it's possible to cater to the characteristics and circumstances of *individual* consumers to heighten their involvement. Personal recognition works as well in the mail as it does in frequent-flier programs, where, as previously mentioned, airlines have learned that special courtesies extended to their best customers, such as greeting them by name, can count for as much as the free trips.

Direct-mail personalization is one of the most obvious ways of increasing the chances that a consumer will become involved in a mailing. People do not usually receive important mail addressed to "Occupant." On the other hand, so-called "personalized" mail is hardly personal if the consumer's name, gender, street name, city, or all of the above are mangled beyond recognition. Accurate data-input is a necessity.

Personalization is so common today that it is basically price-of-entry. People no longer think they are being addressed as an "audience-of-one." Indeed, they probably only notice personalization when it is sloppily done. But other ways of recognizing the importance of good customers in a personalized way have proved to be very effective in enhancing the impact of brand-building mailings.

A shining example is that of the brand-loyalty program for Huggies Disposable Diapers, highlighted in Chapter 7. The mailing date of each issue of *The Beginning Years* for each family was scheduled to coincide with the actual age of the baby, so that each mom and dad read about what to expect in *their* baby's development for the upcoming three months. This approach is marketing to an "audience-of-one-at-a-time."

Jack Daniels bestows the title of "Tennessee Squire" on its best customers, and sends them a deed, suitable for framing, to a small but individually numbered plot of land owned by the distillery. One follow-up mailing merely consisted of a short letter from the County Executive of Moore County, Tennessee, welcoming the new Squire to the county tax rolls and including a snapshot of "the countryside surrounding your piece of land." (Presumably, that letter won't be followed up at a later time with a bill for unpaid taxes.) Similarly, high-profit cardholders of American Express received a four-page, single-spaced letter from the president of the company, thanking them for their use of the card and extending several special offers for use in establishments that accepted the American Express Card, offers available only to the card's best customers.

At the other end of the family pecking order, Club Mighty Dog from Nestlé sent an official membership certificate, also suitable for framing, to the dog of the household, personalized with the pet's name. And promised a birthday card each year, as well.

Sometimes it's enough to simply give consumers the *opportunity* for recognition. Miracle Whip salad dressing publishes one of the many recipes submitted by readers in every issue of its *Miracle Whip Cooks* newsletter, along with the creator's picture (see Figure 8.4). And in its newsletter, Ziploc prints tips from consumers about new and inventive ways of using the bags.

Information is the driver, involvement is the catalyst.

This kind of feedback serves a second purpose as well, irrespective of whether or not the recipe or the tip is accepted. Encouraging

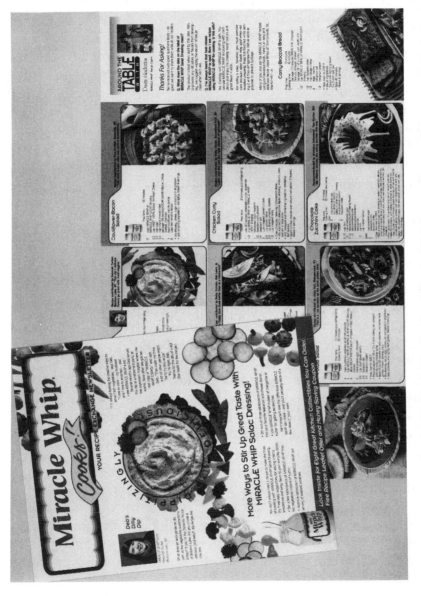

Figure 8.4 An example of *Miracle Whip Cooks*. Miracle Whip's newsletter. Courtesy of Kraft Foods.

153

consumers to communicate back to the marketer, and giving them a reason for doing so, is nothing more than a new spin on another time-honored direct mail technique, the *involvement device.*

That is the two-word answer to anyone who has ever wondered why the gurus of direct mail encourage consumers to waste time fumbling through an envelope full of stamps in order to enter a million dollars sweepstakes. And, by the by, maybe also to subscribe to a few magazines.

These kinds of involvement devices, as commonly used in traditional direct mail, often seem tacky and pointless to consumers. And undoubtedly they do their share to contribute to the widespread popularity of the J-word. But the theory behind them is sound and has repeatedly proved its effectiveness.

Involvement devices make the selling message tangible.

The physical interaction and time spent with the stamps is certainly not wasted from the direct marketer's point of view. Because each stamp represents a different publication, it drives home the point that there are many good offers available. The consumer's decision becomes *which* magazine rather than whether or not to buy.

The same theory has been successfully translated into brand-building direct mail in a way that has no chance of annoying consumers but intrigues them. Involvement devices that are brand-related rather than extraneous substantially increase the impact of brand-loyalty program mailings.

Perhaps the simplest brand-related involvement device is a *sample.* Ziploc enclosed a new kind of vegetable bag in its newsletter; General Foods International Coffees, a foil-packet of a new flavor; Procter and Gamble *two* packets of two different variants of Pert Plus shampoo. Gerber sends an *entire box* of baby food samples to new mothers, nine varieties in all, together with a silver-plated feeding spoon.

Pond's Age Defying Lotion with Alpha Nutrium sent a sample as well, but added a second involvement device—a *demonstration*—to encourage consumers to try the breakthrough, new facial moisturizer. Included in the mailing was a transparent template of a face that could be placed over the bathroom mirror to show the consumer where to look for signs of aging—and to note the improvement produced by Pond's. In effect, this device was a clever updating of the old Procter & Gamble dictum of giving consumers a demonstration they could perform in their own home.

Even if an actual demonstration is not feasible, the brand benefit can often be *visualized* in an involving fashion. In a previous mailing for Pond's Age Defying Complex, the consumer could see how the product removed wrinkles and made skin look younger and healthier by sliding a transparent overlay across the picture of a woman's face printed in the brochure (see Figure 8.5).

And finally, to add impact but not necessarily expense, various kinds of *questionnaires* can be employed. Simple, straightforward questions about how consumers like the brand and what they think are its primary advantages are not always included for database-building purposes but rather to cement the benefits in the consumer's mind.

Or more elaborate response mechanisms can be created. Pepperidge Farm asked consumers to vote whether a new product was more like a chocolate or a cookie by punching out a perforated picture of one or the other and sending it back.

BEYOND INVOLVEMENT: BRAND ADVOCACY

Involvement can be such a powerful marketing tool in brand loyalty programs that consumers actually become unofficial spokespersons for the brand.

Involvement transforms brand buyers into brand advocates.

They tell their neighbors and friends about the program and share the materials, generating the most priceless sales tools of all, personal recommendations and positive word-of-mouth.

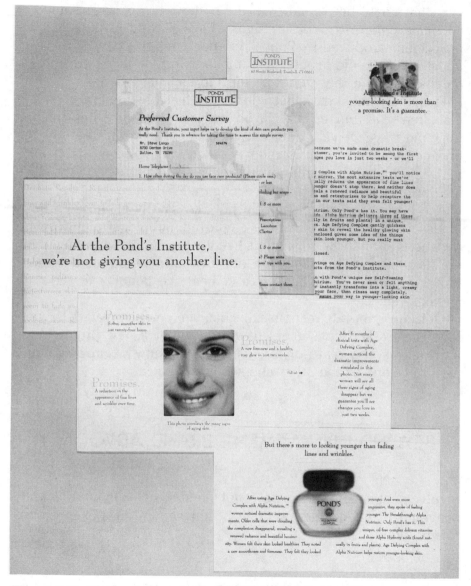

Figure 8.5 The mail-piece for Pond's Age Defying Complex facial moisturizer. Reproduced by courtesy of Chesebrough-Pond's USA Co.

Why would consumers want to talk up advertising? Because it's a special kind of advertising—unique and relevant and helpful. And it's always nice to be first "in the know." That it does happen with astonishing regularity is beyond doubt, if not beyond skepticism. The confessions at focus groups are ubiquitous, and they are confirmed by numerous research studies that have consistently monitored high levels of pass-along of program materials. But the best evidence is the "new recruits," consumers who write or call to get into the program, or whose names are submitted by current recipients.

In one program, over 20 percent of participants were recruited in this manner. And though it helps to have a highly interesting or unusual product, it's not a requirement. One of the highest rates of pass-along recorded in an attitude and usage study—over 50 percent—was for a packaged-goods household product that most marketers wouldn't think twice about characterizing as mundane and low-involvement.

Best of all, these new recruits are likely to be high-profit consumers. Understandably, the recruiters don't want to subject their friends and neighbors to advertising materials for products in which they're not likely to be interested.

In one trial program for an exclusive, premium whisky, for example, consumers were specifically asked for suggestions about friends who might like to know more about the brand. Almost 10 percent of the respondents who took advantage of the trial offer provided the marketer with, on average, between two and three names and addresses. This despite the fact that no additional incentive was promised. And when those names were mailed, they responded more than three times as well as any other group the marketer had solicited.

Brand-advocacy behavior is often cited as proof that the nature of these programs is not merely to build brand equity and loyalty, but to foster the kind of dialogue between the marketer and the consumer that is simply out of the question when only conventional media are used. And even beyond a dialogue, to create an emotional bond or "relationship," as discussed in the next section. But whether brand advocacy is or is not a manifestation of such a phenomenon, it surely is proof positive of the power of actively involving the consumer with the brand.

IS IT RELATIONSHIP MARKETING?

The examples just described demonstrate many of the elements that make a brand loyalty program successful. Yet in the current jargon of the industry, the word that is most commonly applied in describing why these programs are effective is "relationship."

The underlying, and basically unchallengeable, assumption of the proponents of "relationship marketing" is that if a personal, two-way dialogue between the marketer and consumer can be developed, greater brand loyalty will result. And clearly, this kind of communication includes many elements that can foster such a dialogue, such as toll-free telephone numbers, questionnaires, and the like.

Would-be converts from traditional marketing have been quick to adopt the relationship terminology. Undoubtedly it strikes a sympathetic chord with the thinking du jour of mass advertising, that the major purpose of advertising is to forge an emotional bond with the consumer.

The problem with the term, aside from whether or not it is accurate, is that it is easily picked on. In a world where relationships are often one of the more troubling aspects of life, scoffers abound. And because they reject that notion, they reject the concept of using loyalty programs to help build brands, especially in common, everyday categories, like packaged goods.

"Who wants a relationship with a plastic bag?"

The notion that direct mail is a relationship medium originated with the first wave of consumer marketers who moved into direct marketing—financial service providers like American Express, retailers like Sears, airlines like American, even new-breed cataloguers like Lands' End. Most have several things in common, and not much at all in common with the marketers of products like food storage bags.

The importance of what these relationship marketers sell, at least as measured by their customers' cash outlay, is relatively high.

Much if not all of their dealing with customers is done directly, not through middlemen. Communicating regularly by mail is usually an integral part of their business, if for no other reason than to send a monthly billing statement or a recall notice. The communication comes from the company, which after all is made up of *people*, not from a brand that the company markets. And perhaps most important, there is a *service element* in their dealings with their customers. What they are striving to do is to ensure that it is a *good* relationship, and permanent; one based on their *value* to the consumer, not merely habit or inertia.

Classic "relationship marketers" already have a relationship, even if it is only a transactional one.

Not so for marketers of products like packaged goods, which share few factors that make a relationship plausible, much less inevitable. Only a few packaged goods, such as diapers, make a significant dent in a consumer's disposable income over the course of a year. Consumers go to supermarkets, not factories or regional sales offices to buy their mayonnaise or zippered storage bags. In fact, they often have no idea of the company behind the brand, and they certainly don't expect to hear from them, ads and coupons excepted. And the only time service becomes an issue is when they send in proofs-of-purchase for a rebate or a premium.

In truth, when put to the test of reasonableness for the ordinary person, or the ordinary marketer, it's hard to see how these programs could work by building a relationship. And yet, there is incontrovertible evidence that's exactly what these programs do accomplish, at least for some portion of the audience that receives them.

Calls to the DowBrands consumer affairs department increased exponentially after they began testing direct-mail programs for just three brands. And virtually all the additional calls were complimentary. Kraft Foods has received thousands of letters from consumers willing to share their "special moments" with General Foods International Coffees, with no incentive other than the promise that their letters would be read and the possibility that they might be printed in a future mailing. And telephone surveys conducted after mailings have been received show consistent increases in measures of so-called relationship attributes for the brand, like "Thinks its customers are important."

Having acknowledged that for some consumers something exists that has the appearance, if not the intensity, of a relationship, let it be said that in most programs, the overwhelming majority of consumers are never heard from directly. This fact is bad news only for those who cling to the idea that nothing is achieved unless a relationship is created and demonstrated.

It doesn't matter if it's a relationship, as long as it sells.

If a relationship is what the potent combination of information and involvement produces, all the better. Those relationships are only the most proactive manifestation of the brand loyalty that is being built over a much wider base, and, as demonstrated in Chapter 9, that reveals itself in the only place it truly counts, when consumers vote with their wallets at the retail store.

CLOSEUP

New Brand-Loyalty Programs in 1994

The following is a list of the forty-nine new loyalty programs reported by *John Cummings & Partners DBM/scan* during 1994. Some programs may have been initiated in prior years, but not previously monitored. Many, if not most, programs include some form of newsletter which may not be reflected in the program's name. Club Mighty Dog from Nestlé, for example, includes a newsletter called *Wag Times*.

Company	*Brand*	*Program*
AkPharma	Beano	*Beano Bulletin*
American Popcorn	Jolly Time	*Jolly Times Newspaper*
Boston Beer	Samuel Adams	*Boston Beer Newsletter*
Campbell Soup	Campbell Brands	Campbell's Cookbook Club
Carvel	Carvel	Club Carvel
Chesebrough-Pond's	Cutex	Club Cutex
Coffee Discovery	Coffee Discovery	Coffee Discovery Club
ConAgra	Healthy Choice	*Choices for Happier Living*
Coors Brewing	Zima	Tribe Z
Helene Curtis	Suave	*Suave & Savvy Newsletter*
Earth's Best	Baby Foods	Family Program
G. Heileman	Old Style	Territory Merchandise
G. Heileman	Special Export	Excessories Catalog
Growing Healthy	Growing Healthy	New Mother Program
Hallmark	Hallmark Cards	Gold Crown Program

Company	Brand	Program
Hallmark	Hallmark Cards	Keeping in Touch
Hardee's	Hardee's	Frequent Fryer Program
Hershey	Hershey Brands	Hershey's Kids Club
Hiram Walker & Sons	Cutty Sark	Real McCoy Collection
Hiram Walker & Sons	Canadian Club	Connoisseur's Club Collection
Kraft Foods	Macaroni & Cheese	Kraft Treasures Club
Mars	Uncle Ben's	Country Inn Travel Club
Melitta	Melitta	Coffee Bean Counters Club
Merck	Pharmaceutical	*Vital Interests Newsletter*
Nestlé	Mighty Dog	Club Mighty Dog
Pepsico	Pepsi Cola Brands	Pepsi Merchandise Catalog
Pet Inc.	Downyflake	Power Rangers Fan Club
Philip Morris	Marlboro	Marlboro Country Store
Philip Morris	Merit	Merit Awards Program
Pinkerton Tobacco	High Country	Sportsman's Collection
Pinkerton Tobacco	Red Man	*Roundup Newsletter*
Pinkerton Tobacco	Red Man	Outdoorsman Club Rewards
Polaroid	Polaroid	Polaroid Preferred Program
Potato Board	Potatoes	Mom of the '90s Club
Quaker Oats	Kibbles 'n Bits	Good Doggy Club
Ralston Purina	Purina O*N*E	Purina O*N*E Customer Club
Ralston Purina	Eveready Energizer	C.L.U.B. Energizer
R.J. Reynolds	Camel Lights	*Camel Insider VIP Magazine*

Company	Brand	Program
R.J. Reynolds	Winston Select	Select Weekends Catalog
Sara Lee	Sara Lee Meats	Sara Lee Sandwich Club
Schering	Claritin	Allergy Index Program
Scott Paper	ScotTissue	Scott Savers Club
Scott Paper	Baby Fresh	Lucky Duck Club
Seagram	Mumm Cuvee Napa/ DVX	Club DVX
Snyder's of Hanover	Snyder's of Hanover	Creative Pretzel Eaters Club
Starbucks	Starbucks	Encore Membership Program
Taco Bell	Taco Bell	Frequent Rewards Club
Tree Top	Tree Top Juices	Tree Top Birthday Club
Willabee & Ward	Cafe Britt	World's Greatest Coffee Club

9

THE MEASURED IMPACT
OF BRAND-LOYALTY
PROGRAMS

Executive Preview

If the objective of a brand-loyalty program is to increase sales and profits by building brand equity and loyalty like advertising does, then its impact must be measured like that of advertising. And it has been by many marketers who have launched this type of program, particularly research-oriented packaged-goods marketers.

A standard research methodology for measuring changes in brand equity is the attitude and usage study. Such studies, employing matched samples, a test cell that received the loyalty program compared with a control cell that did not, show significant and consistent gains in awareness, attitudes, and claimed purchase behavior.

The most rigorous methodology for measuring advertising's impact on volume over an extended period of time is a matched panel test, based on either scanning or diary data. Both types of panel tests, as well as actual marketplace performance, have demonstrated significant and consistent sales gains driven by brand-loyalty programs.

As impressive as the individual test results are, they are not as impressive as the totality of the tests. Never once has a brand-loyalty program not produced substantial gains in both equity and sales measures.

Moreover, the sales gains compare favorably with those registered in the landmark Information Resources Inc. (IRI) study, "How Adver-

165

tising Works." Gains in volume produced by brand-loyalty programs were essentially the same as those of successful weight and copy tests in the IRI study. But the success rate of the brand-loyalty programs in producing those volume gains was substantially higher. Television weight and copy tests produced statistically significant gains less than half the time. Brand-loyalty programs produced statistically significant gains in virtually every test.

Because of their high degree of targetability, the dramatic increase in spending against high-profit consumers achieved through brand-loyalty programs is far more affordable than comparable increases in conventional media, which essentially impact all consumers equally.

W hile the subject of *how* brand-loyalty programs involve the consumer with the brand is relatively complex, the proof of the impact of that involvement is simple and straightforward—and still largely confidential. Therefore, no specific brand results can be cited. Even so, a necessarily broad and disguised run-through of the research findings ought to be enough to convince all but the most die-hard skeptics.

If brand-loyalty programs work like advertising, they should be measured like advertising.

The key role of these programs in a Differential Marketing (DFM) plan is to drive sales by building brand equity and loyalty, just like advertising, but to a highly targeted rather than a broad audience. Logically their effectiveness in fulfilling that role must be judged by the same standards that advertising effectiveness is measured. And it has been.

Market research studies show consistent and significant gains in brand equity measures and volume among consumers who received brand-loyalty programs compared with similar consumers who did not receive them. Two key words in that statement are *consistent* and *significant*, because what is really striking about the results is not the impact of any single program, as impressive as it might be, but the overall pattern. These kinds of information-driven programs do the job, and do it very well virtually every time.

No advertiser has researched the brand-building power of brand loyalty programs as thoroughly as Kraft Foods. Based on that extensive experience, John Kuendig, vice president of marketing development, has concluded, "If the program is done right, and adheres to brand values, it increases brand loyalty and volume, even for brands that are already spending significant amounts of money in advertising and promotion."[1]

Helene Curtis, Inc., is a marketer who is just beginning to climb the experience curve. They began their first brand-loyalty program in 1994. Their initial learning indicates that these kinds of brand-loyalty programs "can positively impact a brand's image and achieve short-term volume gains simultaneously," says Jon Achenbaum, vice president and regional marketing director for North America. "In other words," he observes, "it can do the jobs of both traditional advertising and promotion."[2]

MEASURING GAINS IN BRAND EQUITY

The technique advertisers most often use to measure the impact of an advertising campaign on brand equity is the *attitude and usage study*, commonly known as an A&U. Several hundred consumers, selected by means of a random sample, are contacted, usually by phone, and asked a series of questions to determine their awareness of the brand, their attitudes about it, and their purchase habits. A&Us are normally conducted at periodic intervals, such as monthly or quarterly, and results from each wave of interviews are compared to previous waves. Or, two A&Us are conducted simultaneously for two different campaigns and evaluated one against the other, *test versus control.*

The latter method has been adapted for testing the equity-building effect of a single contact of a brand-loyalty program. The test cell receives the mailing plus all normal brand activity. The control cell, drawn from the same name source, receives only the on-going advertising and promotion. Thus, A&U levels in the two cells measure the added value contributed by the mailing itself.

Traditional direct marketers do not normally employ an A&U to evaluate effectiveness. They rely on specific measures of response such as applications, subscriptions, or inquiries. While the brand-building effect of mail for these kinds of marketers can be measured, it seldom if ever is. So the dozen or so A&Us that have been conducted by Ogilvy & Mather Direct (the direct marketing agency of Ogilvy & Mather Worldwide) clients since the early 1990s have all been conducted by consumer marketers, specifically packaged-goods marketers, who were new to the discipline, and, importantly, for whom the desired response was more difficult to isolate and measure because it occurred at the retail store rather than by reply card or phone.

Each marketer had their own questions and methods for probing brand equity, but in general, there were three major areas of questioning. First, how aware were consumers of the brand? Second, what were their attitudes about the brand's benefits? And third, where did the brand stand in the hierarchy of the consumer's repertoire? Because every marketer did not question consumers in all three areas, the number of A&U test results vary measure to measure.

The brands ran the gamut from food to spirits to personal care to household products. Virtually all were established brands. About two-thirds of the tests were conducted in North America, the other third in Europe. No pattern was evident in terms of particular categories or sectors performing better than others. Rather, results seem to depend on the interest value of each particular piece.

To provide uniformity in reporting, the range of results are cited on an *index* basis, with the control set at 100. For example, if the level was 40 percent for a particular measurement in the control cell and 52 percent in the test cell, the indexed gain would be 130, that is 52 percent divided by 40 percent multiplied by 100.

Brand-loyalty programs produce substantial and consistent gains in brand awareness.

Gains in awareness ranged from an index of about 110 to about 135 for established, well-known brands, and to well over 250 for new brands and niche brands. The median gain in brand awareness produced an index of 127 and the average gain an index of 141.

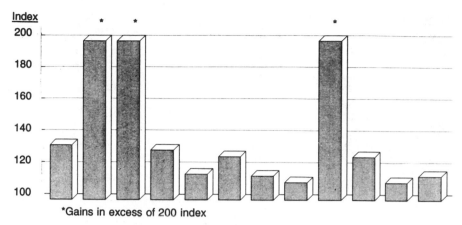

Figure 9.1 Building brands through DFM: gains in brand awareness. (Source: Client A&U studies.)

The A&U results are summarized in Figure 9.1. These levels reflect *unaided* or *spontaneous* awareness; that is, the consumers mentioned the brand without prompting when asked to name the brands they were familiar with in the category, rather than responding to a list provided by the interviewer.

Turning to attitudes, most advertisers probed a battery of attributes about the brand. For purposes of simplicity, the *key* attitude, that is the one that best expressed the main point communicated in the mail piece, is cited. For example, if the piece focused on the skin-softening benefits of the brand, the key attitude would be "Makes skin soft and smooth."

Brand-loyalty programs produce substantial and consistent gains in brand attitudes.

Gains in attitudes ranged from an index of about 105 to about 150 for established, well-known brands, and even higher for niche brands. The median gain in key attitudes produced an index of 119 and the average gain an index of 124. The A&U results are summarized in Figure 9.2.

For brand usage, a variety of questions were asked, ranging from

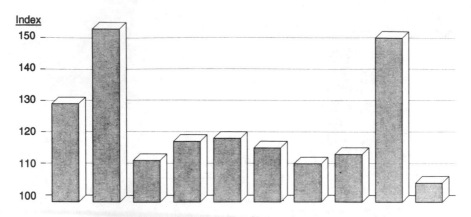

Figure 9.2 Building brands through DFM: gains in key attitudes. (Source: Client A&U studies.)

current behavior, such as "brand bought most often," to future intent-to-buy. Whatever the specific question, its purpose was to help marketers determine where their brand fit into the consumer's repertoire. Was it a favorite brand? Was it used often? When was it last bought?

Brand-loyalty programs produce substantial and consistent gains in claimed usage and purchase.

Gains in claimed usage or purchase ranged from an index of about 110 to about 180, for both new and established brands, irrespective of size. The median gain produced an index of 125 and the average gain an index of 135. The A&U results are summarized in Figure 9.3.

Gains were not only substantial and consistent, but also long-lasting.

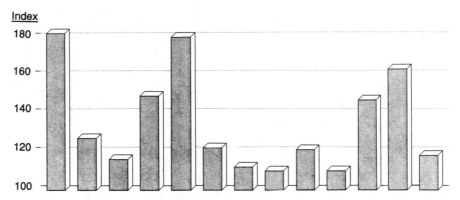

Figure 9.3 Building brands through DFM: gains in usage. (Source: Client A&U studies.)

As remarkable as these results are, even more remarkable is the timing of the surveys, which confirms the depth of the changes produced by these brand loyalty programs. All gains in brand equity were measured six to twelve weeks after the receipt of the communication in the home. In other words, the impact on brand values of a single mailing of the loyalty program was still measurable, and in most cases significantly so, *two to three months* after the consumer's receipt of the mailing. To fully comprehend how dramatic an effect is produced by a single exposure, it is only necessary to compare those results to the dismal record of television copy testing, where on average, about 80 percent of the audience can't even remember seeing the commercial only twenty-four hours later.

MEASURING GAINS IN BRAND VOLUME

Although A&Us provide a relatively simple and economical way of assessing the effectiveness of advertising, they are regarded by most marketers as "soft" measures of performance. They measure how consumers *say* they think and what consumers *say* they do rather than what they *actually* do. To truly understand the influence of any marketing activity on sales, consumer *behavior* must be monitored.

This monitoring can be done in the marketplace, either in a test market or broad-scale as the program is rolled out, or more conservatively in a controlled environment such as a *panel test*. All these methods are lengthy and relatively costly, but they provide marketers with "hard" conclusive evidence on which to base their decisions, usually before making a major commitment.

Loyalty-program panel testing tracks consumer purchases over an extended period of time, most often six months to a year. In almost every instance, it measures the impact of multiple contacts. Either consumer diaries or electronic scanners can be used to capture the data. Sales volume in the test panel is compared with the volume in a control panel from a similar group of consumers who do not receive the mailings.

Brand-loyalty programs produce substantial and consistent gains in sales volume.

The impact on volume of ten programs has been tracked by Ogilvy & Mather Direct clients over the past several years, either through panel testing or national roll-out, where results were compared year to year. Once again, the data reflects experience in both North America and Europe. Gains in volume ranged from an index of about 110 to about 140 for established brands, and to over 250 for a relatively new niche brand. The median volume gain for established brands indexed at 127 and the average gain indexed at 125. Importantly, the increases at the lower end of the range were registered for the largest brands. So although the percentage gain was more modest, the absolute gain was still significant. The panel test results are summarized in Figure 9.4.

Two phases of the Profit Cycle account for these gains: increased usage and increased share of customer from retained buyers, and retention of would-be lapsed buyers. Typically, the majority of gains occurred inside the bucket of retained buyers, although the gains achieved by preventing buyers from deserting the brand franchise

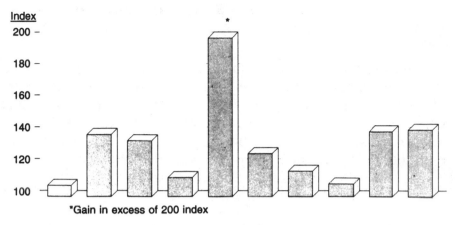

*Gain in excess of 200 index

Figure 9.4 Building brands through DFM: increases in sales volume. (Source: Client research.)

were by no means insignificant, even for high-profit, heavy buyers who lapse at a far lower rate than medium or light buyers.

Figure 9.5 shows a typical pattern of the source of volume gains in the high-profit segment. Again importantly, the gains registered were clearly driven by increases in brand loyalty, not promotional response.

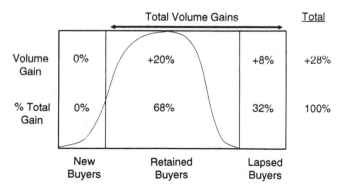

Figure 9.5 Source of gains in high-profit volume: typical brand-loyalty program. (Source: Client panel data.)

Sales go up, percent on deal does not.

In all cases where the amount of purchases made with the aid of a promotional incentive was measured, the increase in percent of volume sold *on deal* was nil or negligible. To the extent that coupons or other promotional incentives were included in the brand-loyalty programs, consumers seemed to use them in place of, rather than in addition to, other promotional incentives.

One point bears reiterating:

No single example is as important as the totality of the examples.

Not once has a brand-loyalty program developed by Ogilvy Direct failed to produce a substantial gain in volume when measured over a six-month or longer period. In other words, the broad range of results cited include all the available results, not just those that were successful.

PUTTING THE RESULTS IN PERSPECTIVE

Nothing works all the time. Undeniably, the first brands to experiment were those that were especially suited for this kind of brand loyalty program. And they had the advantage of operating in a competitive vacuum. Nonetheless, these are substantial gains compared with what most marketers experience when they change their spending level or their advertising campaign. But how substantial? Results like these need to be put into perspective.

Perhaps the most comprehensive study of advertising effectiveness was conducted by Information Resources Inc., or IRI, who is in the business of supplying marketers with panel and retail sales data collected by electronic scanners at the supermarket check-out counter. IRI's "How Advertising Works" project was a landmark in understanding the impact of television advertising on consumer behavior.[3] Sponsored by sixteen major marketers, four leading ad agencies, and the Network Television Association representing ABC, CBS, and NBC, the study analyzed almost four hundred tests conducted over a seven-year period in IRI's BehaviorScan markets during the mid- to late-1980s.

The tests were of two types: *weight tests* where advertising spending was significantly increased behind the same campaign, and *copy tests*, where spending was held constant but the advertising campaign was changed. Results were first presented to an Advertising Research Foundation conference in November, 1991.

A study as complex and massive as "How Advertising Works" yields an enormous amount of data that is subject to differing results based on the analytical methodology. The IRI data has recently been reanalyzed by many of the same team members responsible for the original report. In order to present the most objective basis of comparison for the brand loyalty test results, both the original and new figures are included for review.[4]

The IRI team analyzed more than two hundred weight tests for established brands, using an 80 percent confidence level to judge the statistical significance of success or failure. Significant increases in volume were achieved for 46 percent of weight tests according to the original analysis and for 33 percent of the tests in the new analysis. The average increase in volume was 23 percent in both cases.

The IRI team also analyzed almost one hundred copy tests for established brands. Significant increases in volume were achieved for 31 percent of copy tests in the original analysis and 25 percent of tests in the new analysis. The average increase in volume again indexed at 23 percent in both cases.

Brand-loyalty programs produce comparable gains in volume to successful television weight and copy tests.

These brand-loyalty program results reflect both a change in weight and a change in medium, which to a varying extent necessitates a modification of the advertising strategy. Nonetheless, in comparison to the advertising copy and weight tests the results of the loyalty-program panels are impressive. The median increase in sales for loyalty programs for established brands indexed at 127, representing a 27 percent increase in volume and the average gain indexed at 125.

Brand-loyalty programs produce more consistent gains in volume than television weight and copy tests.

Statistically significant gains were registered in virtually all of the brand-loyalty program tests, versus 25 percent to 46 percent (depending on the stimulus and the analysis) in the "How Advertising Works" study. The validity of this comparison is reinforced by the use of the same kind of data sources in both instances. In fact, about half of the brand-loyalty program tests were actually conducted by means of the IRI panel.

The loyalty program results ought to be impressive, a skeptic might say. After all, the cost of reaching consumers through the mail is many times the cost of conventional media. Multiply spending in television and print by the same amount, and marketers would be likely to see the same results, or better.

The mathematics is true but the logic may not be. An on-going brand-loyalty program can increase brand-building spending eight or ten times against the higher profit segments. But increases in weight in conventional media—even sizable increases—by no means guarantee increases in sales volume, as attested to by the half to two-thirds of weight tests that were unsuccessful according to IRI's analyses. The conclusion of the "How Advertising Works" analytical team was, "We found again and again that *TV advertising weight alone is not enough*."[5] In fact, the *unsuccessful* tests had a higher average increase in weight against the target audience than those that were successful, 88 percent versus 77 percent. The IRI report concluded that, at least in television, "weight increases don't necessarily correspond to higher sales nor do decreases in weight necessarily correspond to decreased sales. We also found no apparent relationship between the size of the weight increase and sales success."[6]

More important, it's not economically feasible to increase weight in conventional media to the extent it can be increased through loyalty programs because of the enormous waste factor.

Significant increases in weight are only affordable when they are highly targeted—as in brand-loyalty programs.

It's one thing to increase advertising pressure by 100 percent or more against a small group of high-profit consumers, but quite another to increase it 100 percent against *everybody*. It is the targetability of direct mail to the relatively small, higher profit segments that permits marketers to take advantage of the medium's ability to involve consumers with the brand, despite the high cost per contact. And to use it to drive incremental profitable volume.

Naturally, the leverage of targetability only exists if the marketer knows whom to target. The issue is complicated by the fact that unlike a broad demographic group in conventional advertising media, high-profit consumers must be reached one name and address at a time. To accomplish this task effectively and efficiently, marketers need help. And help has recently appeared on the scene—in the form of the consumer database and associated data-based tools and techniques, the subjects of Chapter 10.

10

ENABLING DIFFERENTIAL
MARKETING THROUGH
TECHNOLOGY

Executive Preview

The means to implement Differential Marketing have emerged simultaneously with the concept. The ability of the marketer to target brand-loyalty programs and use conventional media and promotion more selectively are enabled by information technology and management, specifically the marketing database and associated statistical tools and techniques for increasing the productivity of marketing data.

Databases are already moving into the mainstream of marketing, used by companies as diverse as automakers, casinos, and packaged-goods marketers. The two largest consumer goods databases have been built by Procter & Gamble and Kraft Foods, both of which are estimated to have more than forty million households on file.

The marketing database plays a central role in Differential Marketing as the driver for brand-loyalty programs and as a key tool in helping adapt traditional marketing practices to Differential Marketing purposes. It is also driven by the same programs and vehicles that it helps drive. On-going advertising and promotion activities are the simplest and most efficient way to build the database.

The marketer's objective should not be to maximize the size of the database but to optimize it by including only those consumers who are likely to be responsive to additional communication. This goal, and other refinements that improve the productivity of the database, can be accomplished by employing statistical modeling

*techniques. Most powerful and versatile of these data-based helpers
are "affinity models." They are used to help create the database by
identifying which consumers in the promotional file or on a rental
list are most likely to be high-profit. Even more important, they are
the key tool for adapting traditional advertising and sales promotion
vehicles to better serve the principles of Differential Marketing.*

D ifferential Marketing (DFM) is an idea that has arrived just in
time, not only in relation to the need for new thinking but
also in terms of the means to implement it. DFM would not
have been actionable for most brands as little as ten years ago.
Very possibly, it will be standard operating procedure ten years
hence.

Technology is on the side of Differential Marketing.

Technological innovations are at the heart of all phases of DFM,
from more efficient data collection to more precise targeting of
high-profit consumers. Several technology-driven tools and techniques, such as "selective binding" in magazines, have been developed and refined in just the last few years and are currently in
active use by forward-thinking marketers. Several more, such as
advanced check-out counter couponing systems, are now emerg-
ing from the conceptual stage into practical communications alternatives. And still others, off the drawing board and into market
testing, such as interactive TV, are real enough to make some
confident predictions about the opportunities they will provide in
the not too distant future.

Underlying all these tools is a fundamental enabling technology:
the marketing database and the associated data-based techniques
for information management and manipulation. It is the database
and its statistical helpers that enable marketers to identify and
target individual high-profit households.

THE MARKETING DATABASE

"Marketers know more about you than ever before ... and they know how to use it." So read the headline of *Business Week*'s recent cover story about database marketing.[1]

Whether that statement, especially the latter part, is completely accurate or not is less important than the fact that the establishment business press has pronounced database marketing mainstream. It is not just catalogs, record clubs, and credit card companies who are using databases, but automakers, casinos, tobacco companies, and, most eye-opening of all, at least to the uninitiated, packaged goods.

Actually, the trend was old news by the time it made the cover. As the *Business Week* article correctly noted, direct marketers have been using databases for many years. But so have some consumer goods companies, like Kraft Foods, Procter & Gamble, and the House of Seagram. R. J. Reynolds, the tobacco company, was the first pioneer. They went from a standing start in the early 1980s to an estimated twenty to twenty-five million names at the time of the Kohlberg Kravis Roberts buy-out in 1987. At that time, maintaining and marketing to those names reportedly represented the largest single line item in the company's marketing budget.

Many other marketers subsequently followed in Reynolds's footsteps. Donnelley Marketing Inc.'s *Survey of Promotional Practices*, which is heavily weighted toward packaged-goods companies, reports that 56 percent of the marketers surveyed in 1993 were building a database, and another 10 percent were planning to do so.[2] And since 1991, *DBM/scan* has monitored more than 800 consumer goods companies that are running the kinds of programs that enable them to collect database information.

Moreover, the size of the databases that are now being built befit the size of the customer base of the companies that are building them. John Cummings, the founder of *DBM/scan*, estimates that the R. J. Reynolds database, currently thirty-five million households, ranks only third among companies who market frequently purchased consumer goods. Procter & Gamble is first, according to Cummings, at forty-four million. Kraft Foods is right behind at forty million, although when combined with the tobacco company data-base of twenty-six million, Philip Morris as a company is clearly the most aggressive consumer-goods database marketer. *DBM/scan's* list of the top consumer goods databases is provided in the Closeup at the end of the chapter.

Clearly, many packaged-goods marketers have gotten over any initial reservations about the wisdom of building a computerized list of names and addresses and relevant marketing information about individual households. To their credit, this is not only foreign but also exotic territory for marketers who are accustomed to think-ing of their target audience as half the men or women in America, and using Gross Rating Points (GRPs) as their scorecard.

Yet despite all this database activity, it would seem that the *Business Week* cover story was not only old news but also premature in concluding that marketers "know how to use it." Different compa-nies and different brands use their databases very differently, from better targeting of promotional offers to a research tool to sending out the kind of brand-loyalty programs that are a hallmark of DFM. And some seem to use it hardly at all, perhaps not quite knowing how it fits in with their on-going marketing efforts. John Cummings observes that "we've picked up only 175 companies using direct mail out of the total of over 700 in the *DBM/scan* file. It appears that many more companies are building the database than ex-ploiting it."[3]

Those marketers who adopt the DFM philosophy will find not only *many* uses for their database, but also many *new* uses.

The database is the engine for Differential Marketing.

First and foremost, the database is the means for targeting brand-loyalty programs directed at high-profit consumers. But beyond that, it plays an important role in tailoring conventional advertising and promotion vehicles to DFM ends. And, as dis-cussed in Chapter 12, it may prove to be a path to that most elusive of goals, closer and mutually beneficial cooperation with the retail trade.

Moreover, those marketers who embrace DFM will know exactly how the database fits into the rest of their marketing activities. It will be found at the very center.

The engine is fueled by the programs it helps drive.

The best and usually the principal source of information for the database is on-going marketing and sales activities. A toll-free number in advertising or on the package, for example, or a few simple questions on the back of a coupon or rebate certificate or a take-one at the point of sale. Or, for durables, a warranty card or other bounce-back device, or the sales slip itself.

The vast majority of large consumer marketing databases have been built in precisely these ways. In 1994, more than 40 percent of data collection efforts monitored by *DBM/scan* were found in magazine ads and more than 30 percent in free-standing inserts. Almost 5 percent consisted of toll-free telephone numbers in television commercials. While small in comparison to other sources, the list of companies using 1-800 numbers in their "image" commercials, fifty in 1994, is growing fast.

Using on-going activities to gather data works because not much information is truly required. Other than name and address, the only *mandatory* questions are those that allow marketers to classify the consumer into the correct profit segment and to determine the brand's position in the consumer's repertoire.

Too much information is as much a problem as too little.

There's an old saying in direct marketing that the fastest way to go broke is to have too much data. For most marketers, trying to create a detailed profile of every consumer is a logistical nightmare and an economic drain. Asking too many questions will also reduce the amount of consumer response by making the process seem onerous or an invasion of privacy.

For a durables marketer, the date of purchase and the model may be the only information that is necessary. For packaged goods, category buying rate and the brand's share of customer are the key requirements. More complex products or services, such as credit cards or insurance, naturally will benefit from more detailed information. But the collection of that information is usually an integral part of the selling process.

As much as it flies in the face of experience, traditional demographic information is purely *optional* for many marketers. Surrogates for targeting are not needed if purchase behavior is known. If demographic data is later found to be required, it can usually be added by matching the marketer's database to compiled household level databases or to census data. The process is explained later in this chapter in the section dealing with data-based tools and techniques.

Marketers who have put off building a database because of the seeming complexity of collecting and storing so much information should take to heart the lesson about keeping things simple. In the final analysis, consumer databases are no more about individual households than GRPs are about individual women 18–49 or magazines are about individual subscribers. It's the aggregates that count.

The function of the database is not to market to individual households but to profit segments, one household at a time.

Ten to twenty years from now, marketers are likely to be tailoring most, if not all, of their communications to the individual, aided by the sweeping technological changes in the media discussed in Chapter 15. Today, that kind of precision is rarely efficient or necessary. Generally, every household in the segment can receive the same basic communication, just as every woman 18–49 watching a particular TV show sees the same commercial. To the extent that there are differences, they can be of a kind that are preprogrammed into a computer, such as a special thank you for joining to new members of the program, or a reminder that an automobile is likely to be nearing its 15,000 mile service visit.

HOW BIG, HOW FAST, AND HOW MUCH?

The efficiency of using on-going marketing activities to bootstrap the database does not address a concern expressed by many marketers: the presumed difficulty and time-consuming nature of recruiting enough high-profit consumers to make a real impact on brand volume and profits. Especially those high-profit consumers who are relatively less loyal to the brand or who never buy it at all. And particularly when the brand commands a market share more befitting a tugboat than a battleship.

In fact, the size of the brand is not that limiting a factor in gathering data from category high-profit consumers, especially for frequently purchased goods and services, where high-profit buyers distribute their purchases across a number of brands.

A brand's penetration of heavy buyers is always significantly greater than its share of market.

Because heavy buyers buy *many* brands, even the smallest brands have a relatively high percentage—or penetration—of total heavy buyers in their franchise. Panel data shows that for packaged-goods brands with market shares below 10 percent, the percentage of category heavy buyers who purchase the brand at least once during the course of the year is 30–40 percent. For brands who "own" the category with 40 percent or more market share, 65 percent to more than 90 percent of heavy buyers make at least one purchase. The same pattern applies to frequently purchased services, like fast food.

Similarly, the time it takes to build a database is not the hurdle it is often thought to be.

Marketers in a hurry can jump-start the database.

For many brands, an "instant database" can be created, large enough for testing or sometimes even for actual use. Consumer service businesses, for example, often have records of customer transactions. And packaged goods marketers usually have what used to be called their "shoebox" but which is now more likely to be a computer file at their promotion fulfillment house containing a complete list of the names and addresses of responders to past promotions.

John Cummings recalls one medium-size packaged-goods company that had promotion responder names tucked away in *eight* different fulfillment houses and promotion agencies. "No one at this company had any idea that they already had the makings of a multi-million household database."[4]

Classifying these raw names into their proper profit segment can be aided by using the statistical modeling techniques discussed later in this chapter in the section, "Beyond the Database." Syndicated data can also be used to help start a database or augment on-going activities. For example, automobile makers can purchase extensive data on car ownership, compiled from automobile registrations in more than thirty states. And marketers of products for young children can obtain lists of 70 percent or more of the mothers of new babies born each year.

Third-party data availability is not limited to high-ticket or high-margin items. As interest in database building has mushroomed, services that collect category and brand-usage information across a wide range of packaged-goods products and services have increased in size and reliability. The sources for this brand-usage information is most often a multicategory questionnaire distributed to consumers through a variety of means, including co-op mail, Sunday newspapers, and mail-order package inserts.

This kind of syndicated data is very helpful in two ways. It speeds up the database building process, and it serves as the principal source for finding high-profit consumers who don't currently use the brand or who haven't responded to the brand's data-gathering efforts. Combining syndicated data with information from on-going marketing activities permits the marketer to achieve critical mass, and to achieve it all the more quickly.

Just how big is "critical mass"? For a marketer just beginning to implement the principles of DFM, it may be as few as a hundred thousand names to initiate the test of a brand-loyalty program. For marketers who are highly dependent on their database efforts, it's as much penetration of high-profit consumers as is achievable. If *DBM/scan's* estimate of the size of the R. J. Reynolds's database is correct, they have on file the names and addresses of more than 60 percent of the smokers in America.

Most marketers operate somewhere between those two extremes. For most brands, 50 percent penetration of the high-profit segment, a reasonable long-term goal, amounts to five to ten million households. The giant databases of Kraft Foods and Procter & Gamble are really an amalgam of much smaller databases for each of their brands. What's more, absolute size is not necessarily the best indicator of success.

A bigger database is not necessarily a better database.

Optimizing, not maximizing, the penetration of high-profit consumers is the real goal of database building. There are high-profit consumers in every category who simply will not be influenced by a marketer's efforts, no matter how special, or who will be influenced only minimally. The key is finding those high-profit consumers who *will* be responsive to greater communications investment, and marketing to them accordingly. The statistical modeling techniques that have been developed to help marketers achieve this goal are discussed in the next section.

No discussion about the database would be complete without a few words about the issue of its perceived expense.

"In terms of the total communications budget, the cost of a database is more like a rounding error."

That statement comes from Lynn Wunderman, president of Marketing Information Technologies (MIT).[5] She is in a good position to know. MIT manages the databases of several key consumer marketers, including the House of Seagram, and acts as a database and statistical modeling consultant for many others, American Express and Kraft Foods among them. Wunderman's estimate is that the first year cost is no more than $.30 to $.35 per name. Moreover, half or more of that expense represents one-time data entry and initialization, which can be cut substantially if the name has already been keypunched on a promotional file. After the first year, the annual maintenance for a large database of ten million or more can be as low as $.03 to $.05 a name.

Before whipping out the calculators, those numbers need to be put in perspective. The useful life of a database name is almost always more than a year. Depending on the category, it can easily be three to five years, and perhaps even longer. So marketers should think of those one-time charges as being prorated over a span of time, even if conservative accounting rules do not permit them to be amortized in such a fashion; and if cross-category information is collected, prorated across brands.

Moreover, whatever the expense of the database is today it will be less tomorrow and still less the day after. The free-fall in data storage and processing costs over the past ten years is not likely to end soon, while the value of the data is going in exactly the opposite direction.

Having said all that, it's understandable why some marketers pause when they hear the price. A $20.00 media cost per thousand (CPM) represents only *two cents* an impression. So building the database is the equivalent of a $300 or $350 CPM, and that's before any messages are delivered.

The simple truth of the matter is that the alternatives in a DFM plan *are* going to be more expensive than conventional media and advertising on a cost-per-contact basis. But the impact per contact is also significantly greater. Cost is never an issue if the return is great enough. Results like those documented in Chapter 9, combined with improvements in targeting of conventional media and promotion, more than justify the use of higher cost vehicles by producing greater returns at a constant budget level. Chapter 14 is devoted to a thorough discussion of the financial aspects of DFM.

BEYOND THE DATABASE

"You don't have to own it to use it."

That's how Lynn Wunderman characterizes her philosophy of using information to improve marketing productivity. "I don't even like to call it database marketing. Database is like the D-word. It's easy for peoples' eyes to glaze over. What we're really talking about is information management, no matter where that information comes from."[6]

What Wunderman is alluding to are the statistical modeling and other data-manipulation techniques that are used to both enhance the power of the database as well as to better target conventional media and sales promotion in DFM. They all revolve around a very simple but powerful proposition.

All high-profit consumers look alike.

Such a sweeping statement may not be true *physically*, but it is not far from the truth *statistically* in any given category.

High-profit households can be described or "modeled" by using statistical analysis to reduce a large number of demographic and geographic characteristics to the small number that truly distinguish the group. The modeling can be accomplished by a variety of analytical procedures, from the familiar multiple-regression to the more exotic neural network techniques. Once a so-called *affinity model* is created, it can then be applied to any list of names and addresses, such as a magazine subscription list, and the probability of any household being high-profit can be determined by how much they "look like" the model.

This process is a twist on the theory underlying familiar clustering systems, such as Claritas Corporation's Prizm and Strategic Mapping, Inc.'s ClusterPlus, that group neighborhoods on the basis of kindred geodemographics and then analyze their buying patterns. The typical custom analysis for DFM purposes begins with known buying patterns, and then analyzes the characteristics of *individual households* rather than neighborhoods to determine which are most important in distinguishing them from other households.

The 250 or more characteristics or *variables* that are used in developing the affinity model are readily available from third-party sources who compile the data for virtually every household in the country. Many of these variables are the same standard demographics used in media targeting, such as age, income, and household size. Others are more unique but powerful indicators of a household's buying habits, such as home value or car ownership. To create the affinity model, the only information the marketer needs to have in hand is a list of names and addresses of households who are positively identified as being high-profit buyers. And even this information can often be obtained from outside sources.

Because affinity models can be developed from third-party household buying data, they are not dependent on the existence of the database. In fact, marketers often create affinity models *before* they build a database.

Affinity models are catalysts for building the database.

Affinity models help marketers both initialize and accelerate the database-building process. They can be used to "score" a brand's historical promotion file and classify those names into their most likely profit segment. Or they can be applied to rental lists to determine which households are the best prospects for database-building surveys.

Importantly, the same statistical techniques used to develop affinity models can be employed to create other kinds of models that improve marketing targeting and productivity. For example, a year-long panel test for a major packaged-goods brand showed a total increase in heavy buyer sales of about 10 percent among those consumers who received an on-going brand-loyalty program. Considering the substantial size of the brand, these results were good but by no means spectacular in comparison with other tests. A *performance model* was developed by MIT to distinguish those households who would respond best to the brand-loyalty program as it rolled out.

Performance models are catalysts for making the database more productive.

MIT's performance model was able to identify the top 50 percent of households who accounted for more than 80 percent of the volume increase. Or to put it another way, the model distinguished the top 50 percent of households who showed a 17 percent increase in volume from the bottom 50 percent whose average volume gain was less than 5 percent. Because of the additional leverage, the mailing quantity could be cut in half with little loss in incremental volume, substantially improving the efficiency of the brand-loyalty program as it expanded nationally.

Most models are second-stage database marketing tools with important but narrow applications, used to refine the database and brand-loyalty program performance. In addition to performance models, *vulnerability models* pinpoint consumers on the database who are especially prone to reducing their purchases—the "declining retained buyers" who were so devastating to Taster's Choice, or who are likely to churn out of the brand franchise entirely. *Cross-selling models* are developed to determine who on the database is a likely high-profit customer for other brands the marketer offers. The exception to these narrow applications is the affinity model.

If the database is the engine, affinity models are the wings.

Not only are affinity models used to help create the database, they are also the vital tool for extending the principles of DFM beyond brand-loyalty programs into traditional media and promotion vehicles. This critical and potentially revolutionary function is discussed at length in Chapters 11 and 12.

CLOSEUP

How Big Is the Database?

Who knows? Or, more important, who will tell?

The inherent confidentiality of database building and database marketing is one of its strengths. It's difficult for competitors to imitate or retaliate if they don't know what's happening. Nonetheless, John Cummings, president of *John Cummings & Partners*, the organization that developed the *DBM/scan* tracking service for consumer marketers, is willing to hazard an estimate.[7] The following projections are based on information gathered at industry meetings and seminars, informed speculation, and the public record.

Company	Size
Procter & Gamble	44 million
Kraft Foods	40 million
R. J. Reynolds	35 million
Philip Morris	26 million
Quaker Oats	20 million +
Ralston Purina	20 million
Walt Disney	19 million
Kellogg	14 million
Mary Kay Cosmetics	13 million
American Tobacco	12 million
House of Seagram	10 million
Warner-Lambert	10 million

Cummings is the first to admit that these are simply estimates. And they do not take into consideration what portion of the database is "active." There may be names on the database to whom the marketer is no longer marketing. Moreover, they do not include companies whose database is a by-product of transactions, such as American Express, Time Incorporated, or Reader's Digest. The Reader's Digest database is reportedly the largest in the world, with more than sixty million names and addresses on file.

Other major consumer companies who have sizable databases, but not large enough to rate inclusion in the top dozen, include American Home Products, Anheuser-Busch, Bausch & Lomb, Burger King, Campbell Soup, Chesebrough-Pond's, Clorox, Coca-Cola, Con-Agra, Coors, DowBrands, Ford, General Mills, General Motors, Gillette, Johnson & Johnson, Kimberly-Clark, Nestlé, Pepsico, Pizza Hut, Polaroid, Sandoz, Sara Lee, Scott Paper, and Upjohn. And many others too numerous to enumerate.

11

ADVERTISING IN THE DIFFERENTIAL MARKETING PLAN

Executive Preview

Advertising will continue to play a pivotal role in Differential Marketing. No other discipline is as effective in building brand equity and interest across all profit segments and preserving the brand's share of voice. Advertising also is instrumental in maintaining sales force and trade enthusiasm. And it serves an important role in attracting new buyers.

But advertising will also be changed by Differential Marketing. The role of advertising will have to be more precisely defined to complement the role of the brand-loyalty program. Effectively communicating with those high-profit consumers not reached by the program is a key objective. Research has proven that advertising works best by generating more sales from current buyers.

The overriding need to reinforce the loyalty of high-profit consumers may lead to changes in creative strategy and execution. The different perspective of high-profit consumers can be highly influential in strategy development. And involvement in advertising may become a more important objective, leading to the use of new advertising vehicles such as infomercials.

The targeting of advertising can also be substantially improved. Statistical modeling techniques can be applied through "selective binding" to target magazines more precisely against a high-profit audience. Moreover, the potential exists for employing similar tech-niques in traditional television planning to create "selective televi-sion" through volumetric targeting.

Traditionalists may breathe easier. Pending the pouring of the concrete for the information superhighway, media advertising will remain a key, and in many instances pivotal, agent in the typical Differential Marketing (DFM) plan. Nothing matches advertising's ability to provide a cost-efficient means of reaching the broad-based audience, creating brand awareness, favorable attitudes, and purchase interest across all profit segments. Defensively, it preserves the brand's share of voice amidst the cacophony of competitive claims. And advertising has an important role in helping create sales force enthusiasm and trade support and distribution.

Business-as-usual doesn't mean that nothing should change.

The discipline of advertising also has much to learn from the brand-loyalty program experience, both in terms of targeting and creative content. In a traditional marketing plan, the target is more often than not defined as a broad demographic group, such as "Women 25–54," with household size and income added as a refinement. And the mission of advertising is generally assumptive, to carpet-bomb everybody in that wide swath of the population for general motivational purposes. It is not customary to attempt to determine just how those higher levels of motivation will alter consumer behavior and thus translate into increased sales and profits.

But when consumer franchises and brand profitability are reevaluated from a DFM perspective, a more surgical strike is called for. First, because the *kind* of behavioral change and *on whom* it is induced are the crucial determinants of any improvement in profitability. And second, because advertising now often shares the task of building the brand with a loyalty program. Thus, the initial step in integrating DFM thinking into the advertising planning process is to determine the precise target and mission for all brand-building activity, and how advertising and loyalty programs interrelate, not only in terms of who they reach, but also what they say.

THE ROLE OF ADVERTISING

The Profit Opportunity Matrix is a useful framework for strategizing how media advertising and brand loyalty programs can work together most productively. Chapter 5 demonstrates how for many brands, especially in mature categories, consumer buying behavior trends within the bucket of retained buyers are critical to brand profitability. Thus, any discussion of the role of advertising must begin with an examination of its potential impact on that group.

High-profit retained buyers are the target of choice for brand-loyalty programs. But no program will reach all consumers in this important group. In fact, when the program is first implemented, the loyalty program is likely to reach only a small portion. Advertising clearly needs to play a dominant role in sustaining and building brand interest and purchase among those high-profit retained buyers not reached by the program. Targeting issues aside, this is a role for which advertising is well-suited, as demonstrated by "How Advertising Works," the IRI study cited extensively in Chapter 9.

Advertising works best by getting current buyers to buy more.

As revealed by the IRI study, the principal source of increased sales in successful copy or media tests for established brands was more purchases by current brand buyers, not additional volume from new buyers. In the actual test year, about two-thirds of the volume increase was accounted for by increases in buying rate. In the two years after the test was complete, increased purchases from current buyers accounted for over 80 percent of the residual gains. Moreover, those buying rate differences in the second and third year were almost *double* the incremental sales in the test year.[1] This important finding has significant implications for the creative strategy and execution as well, which is discussed in the next section.

An analysis of the Profit Opportunity Matrix will also lead most marketers to conclude that new buyers do not need to be a priority target for a special DFM program. Yet clearly every brand requires a constant supply of new buyers to thrive. Thus, it would logically seem that advertising's role will be critical in the first phase of the Profit Cycle for all profit segments, particularly for new brands or brands in dynamically growing categories.

Advertising is a key tool for attracting new buyers into the franchise.

The fact that the "How Advertising Works" study found attracting new buyers to be a less productive role than building business from current consumers in no way diminishes its importance. Undoubtedly, one reason for the seemingly smaller impact is that new buyers tend to be low-profit buyers, as shown in the analysis of the Profit Cycle in Chapter 5. Another reason may be that current levels of advertising were more than enough to attract those new buyers who were willing to be attracted. In other words, advertising spending in the control cell may have already reached the point of diminishing returns in terms of new buyer acquisition. As the Profit Cycle demonstrates, if advertising, together with sales promotion, had *not* been effective in recruiting an adequate supply of new buyers, volume gains might never have been achieved because of losses from buyers churning out of the franchise.

Advertising is a key tool for funnelling buyers into the brand-loyalty program.

What's more, advertising's role need not stop with introducing new buyers to the *brand*. The inclusion of a response mechanism, such as a toll-free telephone number, in *all* brand advertising is a simple and economical database-building technique. An offer for more information about the brand, or for enrollment in the brand-loyalty program, attracts those consumers who are most interested in the benefits of the brand, not just in promotional offers.

Within these broad guidelines, there is obviously much room for the marketer to adjust the relative roles of advertising and brand-loyalty programs to the brand's specific circumstances. The only mandatory strategy is to make sure that these two loyalty-building vehicles do interrelate productively. And the need for doing so goes beyond targeting. How the role of advertising is *defined* has a fundamental influence not only on media planning but also on creative strategy and execution. In fact, it's difficult to conceive how the proper copy strategy can be developed in the absence of a clear understanding of advertising's mission.

DIFFERENTIAL CREATIVE

The notion that *what* advertisers have to say is dependent on to *whom* they are saying it and *how* they wish them to respond should not be especially startling. But the degree of precision called for in DFM does suggest that special attention be paid to this interrelationship.

Mission impacts message.

A good example of the impact of the role of advertising on the creative work comes from Miracle Whip salad dressing, marketed by Kraft Foods. The mission of both the advertising and the brand-loyalty program for Miracle Whip was to stimulate current high-profit buyers to extend their usage of the product. A typical television commercial began with a husband questioning his wife about why she was using Miracle Whip to prepare a casserole. This gave her the opportunity to explain that Miracle Whip was good for cooking too, not just for salads and sandwiches. An 800 phone number at the end of the spot allowed interested viewers to identify themselves by calling for a recipe booklet. Those that qualified as high-profit could then be enrolled in the ongoing program.

The Miracle Whip example is typical of how advertising strategy and execution need to be tailored to produce the specific behavioral change that is desired. This is particularly true as the primary role of advertising shifts from attracting new buyers to reinforcing and building the usage of current buyers. The Miracle Whip commercials clearly talk to current Miracle Whip users. The jar is on display on the kitchen countertop from the opening. This kind of approach may also attract nonusers, but when it does it's a bonus. Moreover, advertising's shift in role must manifest itself not in just what current users *do* but how they *think* and *feel*.

All benefits are not created equal.

The product usage and brand choice of high-profit consumers are very often characterized and motivated by different factors and circumstances and desired benefits than those of the broad, target audience. The example of zippered food storage bags is cited in Chapter 8. The average buyer uses them the way they are advertised, solely as a means of storing food in the refrigerator, freezer, or lunch box. But high-profit buyers have found the easily sealed plastic bags to have dozens of non-food-related uses that help them to be better organized and efficient in their lives.

Even though zippered plastic bags are ordinary, everyday products, high-profit consumers clearly see a benefit that is far more important and central to their sense of self than mere food protection. They are more involved and have much deeper and richer feelings about them than buyers in general. As DFM shifts the focus of marketing from broad demographic targets to the high-profit segment, advertisers must learn to recognize the *unique perspective* that characterizes that segment and leverage it on behalf of the brand.

To continue with the zippered plastic bag example, the sense of satisfaction gained from being organized and efficient is clearly evident in the brand-loyalty program for Ziploc, directed at high-profit buyers. And if the media advertising were directed solely at this segment, it should be similarly evident. But even if the advertising campaign is directed at a wider audience, which it currently seems to be, there are some good reasons to incorporate this emotional satisfaction into the creative execution without diluting or contradicting the functional superior food-protection message.

What's good for high-profit buyers can be good for the broader target audience.

The unique perspective of high-profit consumers can often serve as a way to enrich the brand's selling message by tapping into the needs and feelings of those consumers who are or who are most likely to become high-profit. Without doubt, this line of thinking has significant implications for the way in which marketers and their agencies approach the creative process. Too often, strategy development, and the market research that supports it, focuses on product benefits as perceived and rated by the broad demographic audience. The "winning" positioning is then layered on to the brand, like a label pasted to a jar, and the resulting executions are then exposed to the same broad audience to be evaluated.

This approach has several obvious drawbacks. Since all consumers are not created equal, even all women 25–54, giving them all the same right to vote is self-limiting. The perceptions of the small group of best customers and prospects are likely to be drowned out by the chorus of the uninvolved. And in real life, product benefits and brand attributes, as perceived by those high-profit consumers, are intertwined, if not inseparable. If Ziploc has done its job properly, heavy buyers are not simply passionate about zippered plastic bags as organizing and efficiency tools. They are passionate about Ziploc, *the brand*.

To maximize effectiveness, the DFM creative process must recognize these distinctions. Ogilvy & Mather incorporates this thinking in its Brand Stewardship philosophy, particularly in the development of the BrandPrint™, which is meant to supplement and add dimension to the more traditional copy strategy. The BrandPrint is designed to be a concise and insightful articulation of the role that the brand plays or might play in the consumer's life. The BrandPrint for Ziploc, for example, would be likely to include the satisfaction that consumers feel about being organized and efficient.

Advertising is not always targeted solely to high-profit consumers. But often, the feelings expressed in the BrandPrint are best gleaned from involved, high-profit consumers because they have the deepest and richest understanding of the brand. They are, therefore, best suited to help marketers determine how to tailor their messages in a way that doesn't just sell their *products* but rather advertises their *brands*.

INVOLVEMENT IN ADVERTISING

Just as the message may change as advertising's role shifts, so may the way the message *works*. The sine qua non of conventional marketing communications in a cluttered media environment is "stopping power." If it's not noticed, it will never have an impact. Getting consumers' attention will always be critical, but the lesson from brand-loyalty programs is that involvement with the message, if it can be produced, is a powerful motivator.

If it doesn't involve, it won't sell.

Admittedly, involving a consumer with an advertising message in today's cluttered media environment seems like a formidable challenge, given the typical time and space constraints. The balance between attention and involvement is surely far easier to achieve in a brand-loyalty program where the recipients are expecting the communication, often even looking forward to it. Yet, a few innovative advertisers are attempting, and succeeding, in achieving that balance in their broader-based advertising.

What works for attention may also work for involvement.

Many marketers have long admired the Christmas season "spectaculars" from Absolut vodka, where some sort of unique device, such as a computer chip programmed to play "Jingle Bells," is affixed to the page of advertising. Many have also assumed that the purpose was to stand out in the fat, ad-filled issues typical of holiday season magazines. Even the trade press has referred to them as "attention-getting gimmicks." These ads certainly do grab the attention, but most of them also go on to involve the consumer with the devices, if in no other way than by "playing" with them. For a category where most brands have about as much to say about themselves as the Sphinx, this is a breakthrough way of focusing the reader on the product for an extended period of time.

The House of Seagram, which markets Absolut in the United States, has also employed involvement as a strategy in ads that do not have the benefit of an on-page device. A good example are the Father's Day ads for The Glenlivet single malt Scotch whisky, which for several years appeared in newspapers such as *USA Today* and the *Wall Street Journal.* Several weeks before Father's Day, the brand ran a full-page ad inviting readers to submit their "Dad's uncommon words of wisdom" and promising to publish the best of them in time for the big day. They also told readers how to order a bottle of The Glenlivet for Dad by phone. (See Figure 11.1.)

Thousands of interesting and often witty quotations were submitted. But just as important, thousands more were undoubtedly thought about by readers, involving them for a few seconds or even minutes with the unique offer from The Glenlivet and with the brand. And when the winners were published just before Father's Day, they made for irresistible reading. Using this involvement technique, a single ad was able to drive home brand equity, sell bottles directly off the page, and add names of interested—and likely high-profit—consumers to the database.

In television, the potential for involvement may be best realized through "infomercials." These long-form extravaganzas have something of a raffish reputation in traditional advertising circles, not only

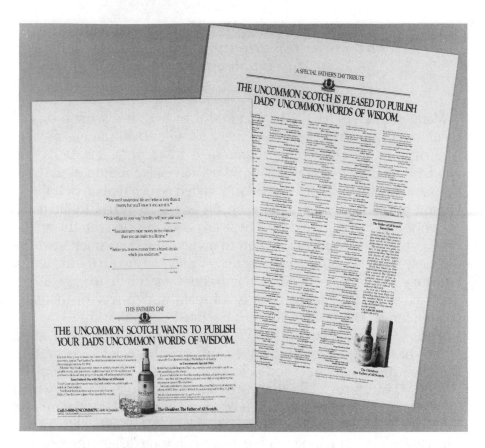

Figure 11.1   The House of Seagram's Father's Day ad for The Glenlivet. Photo courtesy of the House of Seagram.

for the products they offer—everything from cosmetics to faux diamonds to videotapes and training paraphernalia for the golfing impaired—but also for the style, or lack thereof, with which the products are hawked. Many advertising people find it difficult to believe that something so obviously devoted to salesmanship can actually sell.

But spurred by the billion dollar plus volumes of Home Shopping Network and QVC, conventional advertisers, as well as direct marketers, are giving infomercials the proverbial long look. They customarily run in the time periods where historically the predominant type of advertising has been public service announcements; in other words, unsold or basically unsalable time. Sophisticated targeting techniques are hardly necessary when the marketer has little choice but to pay a cut-rate price for remnant time. Nonetheless, infomercials are *highly* targeted—by consumers rather than media experts or modelers.

Infomercials find their own high-profit audience.

Infomercials are the ultimate tool for "Field of Dreams" style self-selection, that is, "Run it and they will come." "They" being the high-profit buyers. After all, who else would watch? Moreover, infomercials provide the marketer with the opportunity to translate the learning from brand-loyalty programs into television and involve the consumer with the brand.

Relevant and involving information sells— whatever the medium.

And it's not only $75,000 worth of cubic zirconia a minute that sells, but *brands*. Everything from cold cuts to car insurance, jeans to pick-up trucks to condensed soups. All this was proved in the early 1980s by what at the time was such a well-publicized venture in the brave new world of 50 + channel cable television that it became a Harvard Business School case. "The CableShop" was tested in Peabody, Massachusetts, jointly sponsored by Adams-Russell Inc., the local cable company, and the J. Walter Thompson advertising agency, together with seventeen leading national advertisers, including Kraft, Kodak, Levi-Strauss, Campbell Soup, Sears, Merrill Lynch, and Ford.

An extensive research program in Peabody, as well as in a subsequent and much larger test, revealed consistent gains in brand awareness, attitudes, and purchase by consumers who had seen an infomercial for the brand. Importantly, this positive effect was not limited to some lunatic fringe of cable viewers. During the nine-month Peabody trial, 60 percent of all cable households claimed to have viewed infomercials on The CableShop. This compared with 63 percent claimed viewing of CNN, 60 percent for ESPN, and 51 percent for the USA network. Between 25 percent and 50 percent of all cable subscribers viewed The CableShop each month, the figure varying with the number of new infomercials that appeared.[2] More startling findings of the comprehensive research program are contained in the Closeup at the end of the chapter.

The primary lessons of The CableShop are that information-driven video can be an effective selling tool for a wide variety of brands. And that many, if not most, consumers are willing to take the time to learn about products in this fashion, as long as the products are relevant to their interests and needs.

A secondary, but nonetheless important finding, is that marketers will not rush to embrace the new and improved while the tried and true is still readily, and cheaply, available. The CableShop closed its doors in 1985 after two years of successful market tests. Its epitaph was provided by a smug Madison Avenue guru who characterized it as "not good communications theory or practice. It's like using frogs to see if they fly."

Today, in a decidedly more brand-hostile environment, flying frogs no longer seem like such an outrageous idea. Since 1993, *DBM/scan* has monitored almost a dozen *thirty minute* infomercials from national advertisers, including Fixodent denture adhesive (Procter & Gamble), Sominex sleep aid (SmithKline Beecham), Weight Watchers diet foods (H. J. Heinz), Barbie dolls (Mattel), Avon beauty products, and Toyota cars.

Infomercials are clearly anything but bad communications theory and practice. Nonetheless, whether any of these efforts, most of them monitored while still in test, ultimately survive a rigorous cost-benefit analysis and become an integral part of the brand marketing program is difficult to predict. Certainly, like any embryonic idea, they face long odds. But if they are thought of as part of a well-orchestrated DFM plan rather than as a one-off experiment, they may yet prove their considerable worth for building brands.

SELECTIVE BINDING

Incorporating DFM thinking and learning into the strategic planning and creative processes are steps one and two for improving the effectiveness of the advertising program. Step three is achieving better targeting by adapting traditional advertising media to DFM targeting techniques.

The most widespread, current application of the extension of DFM principles into traditional media is in magazines, which can now be used to reach individual high-profit households more effectively by harnessing the power of statistical modeling. By developing an affinity model that identifies high-profit households, and capitalizing on advanced printing and binding technologies, virtually any marketer, even those without an up-and-running database, can turn magazines into a highly targeted DFM vehicle.

Selective binding gives magazines the targetability of mail.

Selective binding is the term generally used in the publishing industry to denote a variety of techniques that exploit the power of the computer in the binding process to individualize the makeup of a magazine. It can be used to customize an issue for a subscriber by providing different editorial or advertising, by inserting bind-in cards or targeted inserts to select copies, and by ink-jetting personalized messages, either on-page or on the bind-in card. Publishers routinely use the technique to ink-jet the subscriber's name and address on a blank label printed on the magazine cover.

The process was pioneered by R.R. Donnelley & Sons Company, the world's largest commercial printers, in the early 1980s. But the thinking had to fall in place before the technology had value for advertisers. As a result, the first widespread advertising use of selective binding was delayed until 1992, when Richard Shaw, vice president of media and direct marketing at the House of Seagram, saw the opportunity to create a competitive advantage by reducing wasted circulation to the large number of magazine subscribers who do not drink distilled spirits. Working with Marketing Information Technologies (MIT), the first models for foreign bottled Scotch drinkers were developed and applied.

This pioneering use of models by Shaw and Seagram and MIT led the way to a better understanding by publishers of the potential benefits, both to advertisers and to space sales. More than fifty publications from publishers such as Time, Inc., Hearst, and Times-Mirror, subsequently announced they were able to provide selective binding. The list includes both broadly targeted magazines such as *Newsweek*, *Ladies Home Journal*, and *Sports Illustrated*, and special interest publications such as *Golf*, *Popular Science*, and *Working Mother*. The technique has now been picked up by several other major advertisers, including Philip Morris and Chrysler.

Critical to the process is an affinity model that can provide enough improvement in the composition of the plan to more than offset the data processing charges and the cost per thousand (CPM) premium that publishers demand for buying only a portion of the circulation. Currently, that premium averages about 25–30 percent, although it's likely to fall as publishers increasingly understand that rather than creating a remnant space problem, the process substantially enhances the attractiveness of the print medium. In fact, some enlightened publishers now waive the premium as an added incentive to generate additional business. The data processing can be as little as $1.00 a thousand when the cost is spread over several brands.

The key issue, of course, is whether the added expense is more than compensated for by the improvement in targeting that can be achieved. For highly targeted niche brands, key buyer group composition can typically be increased by 75–100 percent at 25 percent penetration of the circulation. That means that for the top 25 percent of the magazine circulation that is selectively bought, the incidence of the target group is essentially *doubled*, from, for example, 10 percent incidence of high-profit buyers in the overall circulation to 20 percent in the selective buy.

Selective binding can be like increasing the magazine budget by half.

The balance between the lift in target audience and the price premium determines the increase in efficiency. If the total premium is in the 30 percent range, the number of high-profit consumers reached per dollar of expenditure can be increased from between 30 percent and 50 percent, depending on the lift provided by the model. Experienced media planners are surprised and delighted with gains of that size. It allows them to expand the magazine list, and thus increase reach, or to trade off untargeted reach for targeted frequency by increasing the number of insertions. It may even allow them to add magazines that they would never consider buying nonselectively.

For brands with larger high-profit segments, where gains are not likely to be as large, or for companies with a stable of brands, a *portfolio buying* strategy often makes the most sense. Portfolio buying is when marketers purchase the entire circulation but target different ads for different brands to different subscribers. By buying the run-of-book, marketers can eliminate a major reason for the CPM premium, the publisher's fear of not being able to sell the remnant space. Thus, the marketer should be able to negotiate a minimal upcharge. Unfortunately, reports from several marketers indicate that some publishers see a portfolio buy as just another way for an advertiser to cut spending, rather than as a way of making their medium more valuable to advertisers. So negotiations will continue, as publishers, like marketers, struggle to balance their traditional way of doing business with the changing needs of their customers.

Another approach to selective binding is an *enhanced impact* strategy, where the marketer buys the entire circulation for a regular ad but selectively incorporates a bind-in card or other form of insert adjacent to the ad in copies of likely high-profit consumers. Publishers are very amenable to this use of the technique because they perceive it as adding to revenue rather than diminishing it. And there is no remnant space problem. Thus, in this case, advertisers do have increased negotiating leverage.

Enhanced impact is a useful strategy for advertisers who have a great deal of information to communicate, such as an automotive manufacturer who wants to preview the entire fall line of new cars and list local dealers, or a cosmetics brand with numerous line-extensions to cross-sell.

Both these situations could be handled with a selectively inserted mini-brochure. For some brands, the brochure might even include a sample or some form of involvement device, such as a scent strip. Used in this fashion, the magazine serves as a more economical delivery vehicle for what is essentially a direct-mail piece. The insert also helps to "break the book," causing it to fall open to the advertiser's page, thus increasing the likelihood of being noticed.

Enhanced impact is also particularly fruitful and cost-efficient for advertisers who are seeking to build their database rapidly. This can be accomplished by the addition of a postage-paid bind-in card with the consumer's name and address already ink-jetted on it. A subscriber can respond by simply tearing it out and answering a few key questions. Only those consumers who are most likely to be high-profit have the opportunity to reply, thus making the data-gathering process highly efficient. This technique is frequently employed by cigarette marketers, who are among the most aggressive database builders.

SELECTIVE TELEVISION?

The challenge now facing marketers and advertising agencies is translating the principles of selective binding into the critical and dominant medium of television. A key hurdle is that in magazines the message can be varied *household to household*, but with the current state of technology in television, the message can only be varied *daypart to daypart* or *program to program*. Thus, rather than identifying high-profit households, it is necessary to identify which dayparts or programs high-profit households are watching.

The difficulty of skewing television impressions to high-profit consumers with conventional demographic targeting is demonstrated in Chapter 6 and Figure 6.3. Even if some modest skews are achieved, their effectiveness is blunted by the fact that competitive advertisers achieve the same modest skew.

High-profit consumers don't get a higher share of advertising impressions.

In the early 1990s, when NPD/Nielsen, Inc., was attempting to sell TV viewing and product purchase data collected from the same households, they studied forty-nine brands across ten categories, comparing the share of voice for heavy category buyers to the share of voice for all households. The results obtained from this *single-source panel* are shown in Figure 11.2. NPD/Nielsen's conclusion was that "the picture was incredibly flat. Essentially, those households who offered the most potential because they account for almost all the category sales did not see any more advertising relative to competition than did the average household.... It follows that one of advertising's key challenges is to find ways to outperform competition by reaching more target households, thus wasting less advertising."[3]

However, NPD/Nielsen's data also demonstrated that if greater than average skews against heavy buying households are achieved, more sales are produced. They used their single-source panel to analyze the effect of different schedules on two competitive brands that had a clear difference in sales produced by advertising, despite comparable advertising weight and, presumably, the same demographic target. Brand A had "relatively more incremental sales effects from advertising than did Brand B. This difference could not be totally explained by greater weight or more persuasive copy. Something else was going on, and that was a difference in delivery

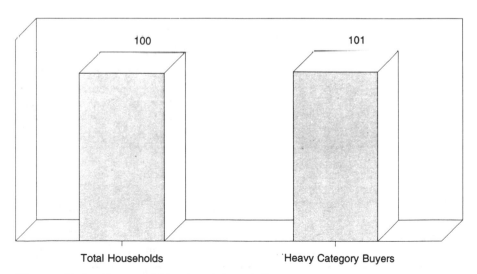

                100   101

        Total Households   Heavy Category Buyers

Figure 11.2 Current TV advertising delivery for forty-nine brands in ten categories. Index of share of voice. (Source: NPD/Nielsen, Inc.)

against a key target group, heavy category buyers."[4] Although apparently accidental, the difference was significant.

Advertising works—more impressions produce more sales.

As shown in Table 11.1, 52 percent of Brand A's commercials went against a weekday audience, which had a 116 index of heavy category buyers. Only 26 percent of Brand B's commercials were found in weekday. Conversely, 34 percent of Brand A's commercials were run in prime time, a daypart with a 93 index against high-profit consumers, versus 60 percent of Brand B's. As measured by NPD/Nielsen, the short-term effect of the advertising, after factoring out other variables, was 20 percent greater for Brand A than it was for Brand B.[5]

This 20 percent improvement in Brand A's sales was achieved by a stronger schedule in a daypart that overdelivered category heavy buyers by 16 percent and a weaker schedule in a daypart that underdelivered those same high-profit buyers by 7 percent.

TABLE 11.1 COMPETITIVE BRAND
TV DELIVERY AGAINST TARGET

	Heavy Category Buyer Target Index	Percent of Commercial Exposures	
		Brand A	*Brand B*
Weekday	116	52%	26%
Fringe	100	10	5
Prime	93	34	60
Late night	90	1	7
Weekend	100	3	2
		100%	100%

Source: NPD/Nielsen, Inc., 1991.

But these viewing skews may be modest in comparison with differences in impression delivery on a *program* basis. A comparison of heavy buyer program viewing habits versus those of a broader but relevant demographic target audience can be made using data collected by Simmons Market Research Bureau, Inc. (SMRB) in their annual Study of Media and Markets. While SMRB reports claimed viewing in the past two weeks, rather than the metered ratings provided by Nielsen, the substantial differences between *volumetric* and demographic target audiences found in SMRB data strongly suggest that wide variations do indeed exist.

Table 11.2 shows the program "ratings," based on claimed viewing, of a dozen popular prime-time programs for both a volumetric target—heavy yogurt buyers—and a logical demographic target, Women 18–49.[6] The greater the rating, the higher percentage of the group watch the particular program. For example, 13.1 percent of all Women 18–49 reported watching "Beverly Hills, 90210" in the past two weeks, in comparison with only 7.6 percent of heavy yogurt buyers. Or to put in media terms, the show has a program rating of 13.1 among the demographic target, but only 7.6 against the volumetric target.

Undoubtedly, one reason for the substantial differences in program ratings between the two groups is the simple fact that about a third of heavy yogurt buyers are men, so shows that have a higher proportion of male viewers, such as "60 Minutes" or "Law and Order," have an advantage for achieving higher ratings against the volumetric target group. But the inclusion of men in the volumetric target only explains part of the difference. The remainder must be driven by attitudinal or lifestyle differences that are reflected in program selection, or by demographic factors that are not customarily given great weight in media planning and buying. Whatever the underlying cause, the magnitude of these differences, if confirmed by *actual* viewing data, throw open the door to the possibility of a revamped—and more productive—program selection buying and negotiating process.

The existing evidence from Nielsen and SMRB certainly does not guarantee that any targeting improvements that can be achieved through *volumetric targeting*, rather than demographic targeting, will be as dramatic as those produced by selective binding. But the

TABLE 11.2 COMPARISON OF VOLUMETRIC AND DEMOGRAPHIC
PROGRAM RATINGS

Program	Women 18–49	Heavy Yogurt Buyers
America's Funniest Home Videos	7.6	6.0
Beverly Hills, 90210	13.1	7.6
Coach	13.5	10.1
Dr. Quinn, Medicine Woman	7.9	9.7
Full House	10.3	7.8
L.A. Law	7.8	9.3
Law and Order	4.8	7.0
Melrose Place	11.8	6.5
Murder She Wrote	7.3	12.4
Roseanne	16.3	11.3
Simpsons	10.1	7.6
60 Minutes	7.0	9.3

Source: Simmons Study of Media and Markets, 1993–94, Courtesy of
Marketing Information Technologies

opportunity for any targeting improvement in television should not
be undervalued.

Even small improvements can have a big impact.

Media negotiators fight tooth and nail for a 5–10 percent improvement in coverage against the target audience. And, based on the data
cited in Tables 11.1 and 11.2, a 5–10 percent increase in impressions
against high-profit consumers would certainly seem achievable for
brands whose demographic targeting strategies place them in the
position of "Brand B." Chapter 14 demonstrates how such a relatively minor increase in television impression delivery against the

high-profit segment can have major implications for the reduction of waste against other segments, and thus free up budget for more targeted efforts like a brand loyalty program.

Moreover, the selectivity by daypart, or even by program, could conceivably be enhanced by employing the same kind of affinity models used for selective binding against television viewing audiences. Using a model of high-profit buyers, rather than reported purchase behavior, would help counteract any instability in viewing patterns caused by small sample sizes, especially at the program level. The model also has the advantage of targeting consumers who demographically *look like* high-profit consumers, not just those who already are. The modeling approach dovetails more closely with the dual role of media advertising in a DFM plan, to both build share of customer of existing buyers and attract new buyers, especially high-profit new buyers.

In fact, in the short term, any marketer interested in volumetric targeting is likely to have to use a model to determine the dayparts and programs with the highest concentrations of current and potential high-profit buyers. Nielsen's Scantrack service, which linked product consumption and viewing habits directly, was discontinued, reportedly for lack of support by marketers, who were concerned about the smaller sample size used for television ratings in the panel and the higher cost necessitated by the collection of buying data. The same is true for volumetric targeting as for selective binding, and for so many other developments that will aid DFM.

The thinking has to fall in place before the technology has value.

"Selective television" through volumetric targeting is certainly less proven than selective binding in the marketplace, but its conceptual foundation, from a DFM perspective, is every bit as solid. If buying behavior and viewing behavior are both linked and projectable, it has the potential for being one of the most powerful of DFM tools. How volumetric targeting might be combined with other approaches as part of a fully orchestrated DFM plan, and why it is likely to flourish on the information superhighway, are discussed in Chapters 13 and 15, respectively. But first, it is necessary to understand how DFM thinking and tools can be productively applied to the other majors sectors of the traditional marketing communications mix: sales promotion and trade relations.

CLOSEUP

The Brand-Building Power of Long-Form Infomercials

The ability of information and involvement to significantly build brand values through the direct-mail medium was thoroughly documented in Chapter 9. The same combination seems equally potent when translated into a video environment.

Unlike most of the current crop of infomercials, those that ran on The CableShop, ranging from about five to fifteen minutes in length, were not primarily intended to get the viewer to call a toll-free number and purchase the product at that moment. Rather, they were designed to persuade viewers about the brand's benefits so that they would buy it on their next shopping trip. In that respect, they resembled conventional television advertising.

Another similarity to conventional 30-second commercials was that the brands featured were already well known to viewers and widely distributed through normal retail channels. Their average brand awareness level was about 70 percent. Most of today's infomercials sell little-known brand names, or brands exclusively distributed through television sales.

Where the infomercials on The CableShop parted ways with convention other than in length, was in the scope and depth of the information they conveyed. Eighty-five percent of viewers found the infomercials "useful." Only 15 percent found them "not very useful," as compared with the 58 percent who characterized broadcast commercials in that fashion. Another major difference was that the infomercials did not interrupt and intrude on regular program viewing. Consumers switched over to The CableShop channel and chose to watch or not to. Because of this self-selection process, viewing of a particular infomercial was not random but highly purposeful.

Not unexpectedly, the highest viewership levels were registered for brands with broad appeal, such as food and clothing. The lowest were for narrow-interest products, such as financial services. This selectivity, together with an interesting presentation of the brand-

TABLE 11.3   ADVERTISING IMPACT OF THE CABLESHOP
INFOMERCIALS

	Saw Infomercial	Didn't See	Index
Awareness	83%	70%	119
Overall positive attitude	63	43	147
Past-month purchase	37	28	132
Intent-to-buy	50	38	132

selling message, guaranteed a high level of involvement. Fifty-one percent of viewers expressed some degree of agreement with the statement that the infomercials were more interesting than network *programs*.

The resulting positive changes in brand equity, as measured by a telephone tracking study, should come as no surprise. Table 11.3. documents the striking increases.

An article in the August/September 1983 issue of the *Journal of Advertising Research*, written by the late Sonia Yuspeh, of J. Walter Thompson, and this author, who at the time was the General Manager of The CableShop, summarized the results of the initial Peabody test. "The success of The CableShop concept seems due in large measure to its ability to satisfy consumers' real need and desire for product information without intruding on their enjoyment of entertainment programming. Moreover, the longer form permits advertisers to include a wide array of information that is useful to consumers in making a buying decision.... Undoubtedly, other delivery systems for informational advertising will develop over time as the benefits of this form of advertising become more widely known."[7]

12

SALES PROMOTION AND TRADE RELATIONS IN THE DIFFERENTIAL MARKETING PLAN

Executive Review

Generating trade support and short-term volume spikes continue to be important roles for sales promotion in a Differential Marketing Plan, as is promotion's contribution to bringing new buyers into the franchise. Sales promotion efforts are also a primary means of identifying high-profit buyers for the database.

The same kinds of statistical modeling techniques that are applied to media can be employed to improve the targetability of sales promotion. However, improving sales promotion delivery against the high-profit segment runs the risk of making a bad Brand Loyalty Equation worse. Therefore, the Differential Marketing goal must be to generate the promotional volume the brand needs to achieve its objectives, while increasing short-term profitability and minimizing additional damage to brand loyalty. This is accomplished through promotional targeting which increases the level of incremental volume for the brand.

Other applications of Differential Marketing thinking to consumer promotion include using offers strategically in on-going brand-loyalty programs and altering the nature of the incentive to be more attractive to high-profit buyers. New technological advances allow coupons to be dispensed at the retail check-out counter based on

historical purchase patterns, not just on the current purchase. As
these systems expand, they hold out the promise of using promotion
as a way of building the share of customer of high-profit consumers.

Retailers are discovering that the Pareto principle applies to their
own customer bases. As a result, they are exhibiting a surge of
interest in database building and relationship marketing. Retailers'
relative lack of experience and skills offers marketers an opportunity
to forge an improved relationship through the sharing of databases
and loyalty building techniques.

T he roles of consumer promotion, trade promotion, and trade
relations are so intertwined that it is often difficult to discern
where one leaves off and the other begins. In current marketing
practice they share a common objective: to push more volume
through the retailer, most often by reducing the price of the brand.
Consumer promotion is no exception, despite the outward appearance of "pulling" the brand through the system by means of an
offer delivered directly to the consumer. Rare is the brand manager
that does not use consumer promotion efforts as an incentive for
the trade to provide merchandising and advertising support, or who
does not believe that much, if not most, of the volume spike comes
as a result of those trade actions.

The by-product of these three activities is also depressingly similar. Greater volumes are achieved at the expense of significantly
lower profit margins. And as a group, they create the kind of marketing environment that sensitizes consumers to price and helps desen-
sitize them to the value of brands. The latter is particularly injurious
to brand loyalty because consumer and trade promotion spending
now accounts for as much as 75 percent of total marketing spending
for many brands.[1] And the bulk of the impact of that spending falls
on the high-profit segment.

Although volumetric targeting is currently more potential than
reality, the impact of statistical modeling can still be substantial in
better targeting conventional advertising to the high-profit segment.
These same modeling techniques can be even more powerful when
applied to traditional sales promotion practices, particularly the
targeting of bread-and-butter consumer promotions now delivered

via FSIs, free-standing inserts. But there is one thorny, fundamental problem.

Better targeting could actually make things worse.

Sales promotion productivity, in the traditional sense, depends on more redemption from the high-profit segment. Any greater pressure against this segment can only further imbalance the Brand Loyalty Equation and slice deeper into the profitability of the very group that accounts for almost all of the brand's profits.

Thus, introducing Differential Marketing (DFM) thinking into the planning and implementation of sales promotion and trade strategies is more complex than it might initially seem. The overriding objective must not be simply generate more promotional volume. Rather, it must be to generate the volume the brand needs to achieve its objectives, while increasing short-term profitability and building long-term brand loyalty, or at the very least not undermining it.

THE ROLE OF SALES PROMOTION

After many years of escalating promotion spending, and a widespread feeling that massive couponing and rich trade allowances are "a cost of doing business," it would take a healthy dose of wishful thinking to believe that the situation could be reversed overnight. A saner strategy is clearly called for in a DFM world: more loyalty-building and less price-sensitizing marketing activity. Nonetheless, the speed with which any change is implemented must reflect the realities of the marketplace.

One of those realities is that the volume spikes generated by price-off promotional events cannot be instantly replaced by a sudden infusion of brand loyalty, even if it is not particularly profitable volume. And especially if the spending is critical to staying in the good graces of the retailer. So, like advertising, promotion retains a traditional role in a DFM plan. Sales promotion continues to gain trade support while stimulating volume across all profit segments through *short-term purchase incentives.*

But while performing this generalized role, sales promotion can also begin to fulfill the more targeted objectives of DFM. An obvious application is in the first phase of the Profit Cycle. Along with advertising, sales promotion continues to be an important vehicle for bringing *new buyers* into the franchise, particularly high-profit new buyers.

Stimulating brand trial is frequently offered up as one of the primary justifications for sales promotion. And just as frequently it is debunked with statements to the effect that "studies show that 80 percent of the consumers who use a coupon would have bought the brand anyway."

Both are true, but one is truer than the other.

The ratio of new buyers to retained buyers who take advantage of a promotion varies from category to category and from offer to offer. It is also dependent on how a "new buyer" is defined. But the evidence is clear that retained buyers always account for the majority of promotional *volume.* The Closeup at the end of the chapter examines the issue in greater detail.

The pattern of heavy promotional buying by current buyers obviously can raise havoc with brand profitability. Therefore applying DFM thinking, sales promotion must strive to bring new consumers into the franchise *without* excessively subsidizing current buyers. The way to accomplish that objective is turn the purchases of current buyers into a positive influence on brand growth.

Subsidies can be kept down by driving share of customer up.

As demonstrated by Information Resources Inc.'s (IRI) "How Advertising Works" study, a major problem with much of sales promotion is that the incremental profit is less than the cost. The surest way to overcome this problem is to tailor promotional efforts to drive more *incremental* purchases from current buyers; in other words, to increase the brand's share of customer in the high-profit segment.

This strategy will also contribute to building the long-term brand loyalty of these high-profit consumers. The sales promotion itself does not necessarily produce brand loyalty, but repeat buying stimulated by sales promotion certainly contributes to a consumer's *feeling* of loyalty. To argue otherwise would be to say that consumers are continually conscious of the fact that they have succumbed to bribery rather than exercised their right to choose, and to deny them the power of rationalization for which they (and we) are so justly famous.

Finally, just as with advertising, there must be a mechanism for sales promotion to funnel new *high-profit* buyers into the brand-loyalty program. Consumer sales promotion can help build the database by providing a simple and efficient way for high-profit consumers to identify themselves. Most of the consumer goods companies monitored by *DBM/scan* that have collected database-type information, have collected it by including a few simple questions along with the promotion offer.

LEVERAGING MASS CONSUMER PROMOTION

Free-standing inserts (FSIs) have long been the default consumer promotion delivery vehicle for packaged-goods brands. And other kinds of advertisers, from retailers to telephone companies, have followed the packaged-goods lead. Great gobs of colorful coupons and fliers fall out of the Sunday newspaper into consumers' eager hands. Their very abundance is, without doubt, a major contributor to the increased price sensitivity manifest in consumer buying habits.

When they were first introduced in the early 1970s, FSIs were embraced as an effective new way to drive consumer trial and purchase. They had a low absolute cost and a low cost per redemption. But as the number of FSI-delivered coupons grew, redemptions fell. At the same time, marketers and retailers became increasingly conscious of the volume that could be driven by trade events, such as feature prices and store displays.

Over time, FSIs began to be seen more as an adjunct to trade promotion spending, a way of assuring the retailer that the marketer would support the trade event by driving consumers into the store. But as scanning data confirmed that the majority of volume sold during a promotional event was the result of the trade support, not the coupon, retailers took an increasingly jaundiced view. Marketers had to up the FSI ante continuously, both in terms of distribution and coupon value, to make an impression on the retailer. And even then, the retailer preferred to take the money in allowances or other price adjustments. Hence, the dramatic shift within the promotional budget to trade promotion.

Clearly, any attempt to reform mass consumer sales promotion practices along DFM lines must start with elevating the capabilities of FSIs or finding a suitable alternative. The key to either approach is more selective targeting. The issue is not how to find the target. Statistical affinity models can be brought to bear in the same manner as in magazines or television. Rather, the issue is *who* the appropriate target is, and *what* delivery vehicles are used to reach them.

FSIs are customarily targeted to high *Brand Development Index*— BDI—markets, where the brand's sales are above average. This targeting strategy produces the greatest volume of redemptions— because it reaches the largest number of current buyers! A simple and less profit-depleting alternative, already employed by some brands, is to target markets with a high *BOI*, or *Brand Opportunity Index*. The BOI is the difference between the *Category Development Index* (CDI), which measures the strength of category sales in the market relative to the national average, and the BDI. A market with a high CDI and a low BDI would have a high Brand Opportunity Index because it logically offers the brand the greatest opportunity for growth. Redemption in high BOI markets may not be as great as in high BDI markets, but there is less likelihood of subsidizing current high-profit buyers and more chance of drawing new buyers into the franchise.

All zip-codes are not created equal.

The principles of DFM can be even better served by targeting promotions to smaller units of geography *within* markets. Within virtually every market, there are great variations in demography and lifestyle that have a significant impact on consumer buying habits. Unfortunately, the kind of co-op FSIs used by most marketers usually cannot be distributed to geographical units any smaller than *form breaks*, large sections of a metro area, such as Long Island in the New York market.

But promotion performance can often be improved by combining retail scanning data with statistical modeling to identify smaller high-profit units of geography, zip-codes or even block groups, units of about 400 or so households. These smaller areas can then be reached by employing a door-to-door delivery company, such as ADVO, or a co-op mailer such as Donnelley Marketing's Carol Wright. In fact, the use of mail, either solo or co-op, allows the marketer to target even more precisely, at the individual household level.

Alternate delivery vehicles have cost-per-thousands significantly higher than that of FSIs. However, because of their greater target-ability and impact, marketers have often found that they can outper-form FSIs on the basis of DFM productivity.

An exciting new possibility is measuring that productivity on the basis of PPI, or the *Promotion Profitability Index*. The PPI factors in the proportion of sales on deal that are *incremental* as opposed to those that would have been made anyway in the absence of the promotion. The higher the PPI, the higher percentage of incremental profit driven by promotion.

The PPI measures value, not just volume.

While not as easy to calculate as either BDI or BOI, the PPI on a market level can be derived from an in-depth analysis of scanner data. Targeting FSIs on the basis of the market's Promotion Profit-ability Index has the advantage of allowing the marketer to continue to distribute a large quantity of coupons to support trade events while reducing the penalty to the bottom line. Moreover, through either cluster models or proprietary modeling, the concept of the

PPI can conceivably be extended to smaller units of geography, or possibly even to individual households.

While still in the early stages of development, the use of the PPI as the basis for promotional targeting holds out the possibility for producing sales on deal that change the buying behavior of the target group in a way that fully supports the brand's *marketing* objectives rather than just creating a temporary bump in volume, thus allowing sales promotion to play a greater strategic role in the marketing mix.

DATABASE PROMOTIONS

A database-driven brand-loyalty program can further enhance the strategic aspect of consumer promotion. The same communications that build the loyalty of high-profit consumers can also be employed for exercising more control over the target, timing, amount, and nature of incentives. The power of the database can be used to vary the promotional offer consumer to consumer, thus producing the maximum return in sales and profits while minimizing any unnecessary subsidies.

There is absolutely *nothing* contradictory about mentioning promotion and loyalty-building in the same breath. Given the current promotional climate, it is unrealistic to assume that even the brand's most loyal customers will never take advantage of an incentive— to buy either the brand or a competitor. And not offering high-profit customers a reward for their loyalty is a fruitless attempt to deprive them of what any consumer, including those same high-profit customers, can find every Sunday in the newspaper.

In fact, promotional incentives positioned as a "thank you" or a "special benefit" in the context of an on-going loyalty program are likely to further reinforce that loyalty. The evidence from the brand-loyalty program tests cited in Chapter 9 demonstrates that when these kinds of offers were included, the results were not an increase in promoted volume but rather an increase in *overall* volume.

"You don't have to pat yourself or your brand on the back when you're talking to your best customers," observed John Kuendig, of Kraft Foods. "You should take the opportunity to pat *them* on the back."[2]

Rewards are always better than bribes.

The reward can be something as simple as a coupon. Or it can be special merchandise that reflects the brand's value, like the gadgets offered by Ziploc to help keep the consumer organized. Crystal Light, the artificially sweetened powdered soft drink marketed by Kraft Foods, found a unique way of rewarding the loyalty of high-profit consumers by *selling* them single-serving packets that were not available through ordinary retail channels.

Clearly, in any program of this type some consumers are more promotionally sensitive than others. The loyalty programs from cigarette companies have reached the stage where the recipients can be segmented on the basis of that sensitivity and placed on different "promotional tracks" with different coupon values and different promotional frequencies to maximize their profitable volume. This segmentation can be based on consumers' answers to questions collected during the database-building process. Or a statistical model of "promotionally sensitive" consumers can be developed and applied to the households on the database.

In addition to including promotional offers in an on-going loyalty program, the database can be used to drive highly targeted promotions, either for one brand or many. An example of a successful multibrand program that combines offers with brand reinforcement is *We're Right for You* from Kraft Foods (see Figure 12.1). For four consecutive years, Kraft has sent out this multipage booklet with coupons, editorial, and brand sell, to millions of households on their database that have demonstrated an interest in health-conscious or diet-conscious products. By combining twenty-five brands under a single thematic umbrella, a high degree of efficiency and effectiveness can be achieved.

Winter 1994

We're Right For You

From Kraft General Foods

A Commitment To A Healthy Lifestyle.

Dear Valued Consumer,

The new year is the perfect time to commit yourself to a healthier lifestyle. That's why this issue of *We're Right For You* focuses on ways to keep your Healthy New Year's Resolutions.

For example, we've included helpful tips from our nutritionists on diet and exercise, and some delicious and nutritious recipes using "We're Right For You" products from Kraft General Foods. In addition, "Resolution Resource" on page 7 is full of information to help you keep your resolutions, including the USDA's Food Guide Pyramid. Why not put it up on your refrigerator door for easy reference?

I hope you enjoy this issue of *We're Right For You* and that you'll find it helpful in achieving your goals.

Sincerely,

Stephanie Williams

Stephanie Williams
Consumer Representative

P.S. To help us better understand your tastes and nutrition goals, please be sure to fill out the survey on page 7.

You Can Do It!
Keeping Your '94 Resolutions.

Like noisemakers, funny hats, and the ball dropping over Times Square, making resolutions is a New Year's tradition. This year, if your resolution is to eat better and get more exercise, here are a few tips to help you succeed:

• *Exercise your right to lose weight.* Weight control specialist John Foreyt, Ph.D. says a commitment to exercise is the number one predictor of weight-loss success. Even moderate regular exercise over the year can add up to weight loss. The key word is *regular.*

• *There are no forbidden foods.* Nutritionally speaking, there are no "good" or "bad" foods. All foods can be part of a balanced diet in moderate amounts.

• *Words to live by:* broiled, boiled, baked, steamed, and poached.

• *Two bodies are better than one.* A workout partner may be just what you need to stick to your exercise program.

• *Don't ride when you can walk.* Walking is an increasingly popular activity in the U.S., and for good reason: it can burn stored body fat, it's low-impact, and you can do it practically anywhere.

• *Snack smart. Look smart.* Snacking can fit into a healthful diet. So snack smart. Put crunchy fruits and vegetables on the top shelf of your refrigerator so they're easier to reach and harder to forget.

Here are other ideas using "We're Right For You" products from Kraft General Foods

• Think "hot cereal" for breakfast, lunch or a late night snack. Place ½ cup GRAPE-NUTS® Cereal and ½ cup skim milk in microwaveable bowl. Microwave on HIGH 1½ minutes. Stir. Add fresh fruit or honey, if desired. Makes 1 serving.

• Microwave CHEEZ WHIZ LIGHT Pasteurized Process Cheese Product as directed on label. Serve over hot cooked vegetables or baked potatoes.

Figure 12.1 Sample of Kraft Foods' *We're Right for You* booklet combining offers and brand reinforcement. Courtesy Kraft Foods.

LEVERAGING INCENTIVES

The incentive itself can be another tool to help bring consumer sales promotion more into line with DFM thinking. The value or the nature of the incentive can be varied in a way to attract the right target or to produce the desired change in buying behavior. For example, simply making a coupon contingent on multiple purchases will skew redemption towards heavy buyers.

Make the offer fit the objective.

A favorite tactic of cigarette marketers is the "time-release coupon." This is a series of coupons, each good for a limited period of time, designed to encourage a repeat buying habit. They can be sent to new members of a loyalty program to cement their relationship or to all members as a way of counteracting heavy competitive activity or a new brand introduction.

Any promotion that rewards continuity of purchase will attract heavier category buyers and encourage repeat buying. Some of the recent examples from the cigarette category have combined purchase continuity with strong brand imagery. The Marlboro Adventure Team, from Philip Morris, was a sweepstakes for a wilderness vacation combined with a continuity program. Proofs of purchase could be redeemed for items such as outdoor clothing and recreational equipment featuring the Marlboro logo. As a follow-up, the brand launched the Marlboro "Country Store."

"Camel Cash" is "cool" green stamps, delivered right on the pack. The award structure is a wide variety of "Joe Camel" merchandise suitable for every variety of party animal. The "Camel Cash" promotion actually does double duty, in that R. J. Reynolds uses it as an incentive to recruit high-profit consumers into the loyalty program.

IN-STORE CONSUMER PROMOTION

In-store couponing systems have been nibbling away at the entrance to the information superhighway since the mid-1980s. Catalina Marketing, based in St. Petersburg, Florida, was the pioneer in linking a computer to the laser scanner at the check-out counter to dispense coupons based on what products the consumer had just purchased. For example, the computer can be programmed to issue a coupon for a six-pack of Diet Pepsi to anyone who buys Diet Coke. Catalina's system can be found in almost 10,000 supermarkets, reaching more than 100 million shoppers each week.

In Donnelley Inc.'s *16th Annual Survey of Promotional Practices*, 60 percent of marketers reported using electronic couponing. In comparison, only 53 percent of marketers claimed to have used magazine coupons, and only 48 percent newspaper coupons other than FSIs. But in terms of its share of the couponing budget, electronic couponing ranked seventh out of seven alternatives.[3] This disparity points to experimentation rather than commitment on the part of marketers. But that tentative approach should change rapidly for marketers who adopt the DFM philosophy.

In-store couponing is a revolution lying in wait.

Catalina, and its major competitor, Advanced Promotion Technologies, or APT, have both recently introduced a second-stage system that is a significant improvement over the earlier model. Instead of merely responding to a consumer's current purchase, it responds to a consumer's purchase *history*. With this advanced system, not every consumer purchasing a six-pack of Diet Coke would necessarily receive a Diet Pepsi coupon. The Diet Pepsi brand manager might choose to issue the coupon only if the consumer was a heavy cola buyer. Or only if Diet Coke had 50 percent or more of the consumer's share of customer. Or only if Diet Pepsi had not been purchased in any of the last three purchase occasions. Or any combination of the above.

With a system like this in place, the potential for implementing

DFM promotion strategies is endless. It will be particularly helpful in achieving the objective of a greater share of customer from high-profit consumers. It should also prove to be an effective new way of building the database. The same machine that prints out a coupon can also print out an application for enrollment in the brand-loyalty program. And because the computer can be programmed to dispense the form only to high-profit buyers, the consumer is already prequalified.

Like the alternatives to FSIs, the cost per coupon distributed will be more expensive. But even if marketers choose to put on their accountant's hats, most should quickly discover that the incremental profit, both short-term and long-term, is greater as well. Like so many other technological developments, once DFM thinking is in place the value is readily apparent, as it seemingly is to Procter & Gamble, which owns a 14 percent stake in Advanced Promotions Technologies. And to Kraft Foods, which has entered into a multi-year strategic alliance with APT to help develop new opportunities for collecting and using the consumer data produced by the system. It should be no surprise that these are the same two companies that head *DBM/scan's* list of consumer database marketers.

LEVERAGING TRADE PROMOTION
AND RELATIONS

Marketers, at least those marketers who have not read this book, may be *uneasy* about overwhelming consumers with coupons and other promotional incentives, but they don't seem overly *distraught*. Yet to a brand manager, they are indignant, aggravated, sometimes even *volcanic* about the share of the marketing budget that goes to trade promotion. In the latest Donnelley Marketing survey of promotional practices, the number was hovering around 45 percent.[4] To add insult to injury, many marketers feel double-crossed. As they see it, while the retailer's left hand collects the money, the right hand aggressively pushes more private label product onto the shelf. Although packaged-goods marketers may have the most intense feelings in this regard, the struggle between marketer and retailer can be found in virtually every sector of consumer goods and services.

"How's it going to help me with the trade?"

That's the burning question about any new idea or concept, not just DFM. One answer, of course, is that by strengthening consumer loyalty, DFM should relieve the pressure to push volume, low or no-profit volume, through the features and displays that the trade promotion dollars buy. But that clearly is a long-term payoff. And as one marketer observed, loyalty is of little use if the brand is no longer on the shelf.

Another answer is that the wrong question is being asked. What marketers really ought to be wondering about is what might happen to their trade relations if they *don't* start adopting DFM practices.

Retailers have the inside track for Differential Marketing.

Retailers in all channels currently have as much, if not more, interest than marketers in the fundamental conceptual underpinning of DFM—the critical importance of heavy buyer loyalty—and a key tool to build it—database-driven "relationship" programs. And in the battle to collect the necessary information, retailers possess the doomsday weapon: the ability to pick up data *transactionally* at the cash register.

The reason for the trade's surge of interest is not difficult to fathom. Store expansion has significantly outpaced population growth. Retail floor space ballooned from 8 square feet per person in the early seventies to almost 20 by the early nineties.[5] Sales have had a hard time keeping up. During the same period, retail sales in constant dollars dropped from over $200 per square foot to about $130.[6] In contrast, the growth of sales through mail order catalogs has consistently outpaced store-based sales growth. Excluding food stores, catalogs now account for about 10 percent of retail sales.[7] Significantly, this fast-growing competitor relies on the very database and relationship marketing techniques that have captured the interest of retailers.

What's more, the Pareto principle is no longer news to retailers. Trade journals and industry studies are full of examples like the one from the nationally known retailer who determined that the top 7 percent of customers accounted for 40 percent of annual sales.[8] Even the grocery trade, who arguably were in denial for many years, has been made aware of the extreme leverage exerted by a relative handful of customers by reports like the one sponsored by Coca Cola, cited in Chapter 3. Equally well understood is the fact that these heavy buyers distribute their purchases over a range of competitive retailers, and that the name of the game in a sluggish economy with low population growth must be to build the store's share of customer among these high-profit shoppers. The result is predictable.

Retailers are the eager new recruits of the database revolution.

A survey conducted by Deloitte & Touche for the Direct Marketing Association among a cross section of retailers reports that fully two-thirds of them have relationship or database programs in place, and that 40 percent of those who don't are planning such a program.[9] The survey respondents represented virtually every type of retailer: apparel, food, drug, home entertainment, toys, sporting goods, books, automotive, hardware, appliances, and home improvement.

The figures may be inflated somewhat by a tendency to overrepresent Direct Marketing Association members. But there is no denying that there is a massive sea change underway in the trade's thinking about the source of their profits and how to increase them. Major national retailers, such as Sears, have frequent-buyer programs up and running. And numerous tests are underway in food stores, where retailers controlling 50 percent of the all-commodity volume are believed to have the equipment to collect universal product code data at the individual household level.

Most critically, retailers do not face the same obstacles as marketers in collecting the information vital for a database. It is essentially there for the taking as a by-product of everyday business transactions. Data collection is often simply a matter of scanning an individual's "preferred customer" or check-cashing or store credit card, or just asking for and entering the customer's telephone number.

At the present time, the purpose of all this database building has little to do with marketers, and everything to do with building the retailer's own business. One apparent danger for marketers is that retailers will further strengthen their grip on customer ownership and gain added negotiating leverage. Another is that they will attempt to accelerate the trend to private label through their programs. A third, and perhaps most ominous, is that they will use database programs to try to extract additional funds from marketers.

In many instances, particularly in the grocery trade, electronic marketing is set up as a separate profit center. And it is a profit center that has some heavy up-front costs. As a result, the pressure to develop revenue is intense. An executive of one food chain told a major marketer that they were expected to participate in that chain's new database marketing program and gave him the price. More pointedly, the marketer was also told that the chain did not expect the marketer to cut any of his other trade spending. But the need to develop revenue for these new database efforts may also present an opportunity to marketers who have gained experience with databases of their own.

Retailers may be in the best position to collect the data, but they are not necessarily in the best position to use it.

Retailers are merchants before they are marketers. According to the Deloitte & Touche study, two-thirds of the retailers who had relationship programs up and operating had no relationship marketing *plan* in place.[10] Clearly many of them could benefit greatly from the marketing experience and wisdom, as well as the funds, that marketers can bring to an alliance. Working together, rather than at cross-purposes, may be the short-cut to realizing the full potential of their programs.

Food retailers would seem to be in particular need of counsel. Insiders report that the availability of data has temporarily outstripped the grocery trade's ability to interpret and utilize the data. Retailers have barely had a chance to digest the operational changes brought about by laser scanning before marketing changes are being thrust upon them. They are not generally willing to turn over this data to marketers, or even to third parties, and they are concerned in the extreme about preserving their customers' privacy. But they are nonetheless eager to find ways to use the data productively, with a minimum of cost and effort.

Sensing opportunity, a few leading packaged-goods marketers with large databases, notably Procter & Gamble, Kraft Foods, the House of Seagram, and Quaker have been aggressively attempting to align their efforts with those of retailers. P&G has been working with Publix for several years to produce a newsletter that features its brands, and has developed numerous cooperative mail pieces with other chains, such as Shop Rite. Quaker has helped produce a program directed at African Americans for Safeway. And *DBM/scan* has picked up joint efforts of Kraft Foods with Wegman's, Big Bear, Safeway, and Sam's Clubs. Seagram has been particularly successful in working with the trade, because the high margins on their products encourage retailers to experiment.

"Our database has been a tremendous asset in building retailer relations."

So states Richard Shaw, vice president of media and direct marketing for the House of Seagram.[11] "When retailers produce mailings for the database customers that live within their trading areas, they see real gains in store traffic and profits." Interestingly, many of the retailers who are taking advantage of the Seagram database are the grocery chains in those states where it is legal for supermarkets to sell distilled spirits. As they see the positive impact in that category, their interest is likely to broaden to the many other kinds of products they carry.

What marketers have to offer retailers is marketing expertise, a revenue stream that hopefully can be diverted from trade promotion budgets, and access to a database of names that can be combined with those of retailers for purposes of consumer communication. But it is not generalized marketing knowledge that retailers need as much as the specialized know-how gained by breaking new ground with database-driven brand-loyalty programs, and the new perspective on consumer buying behavior and ways of altering it in the retailer's favor offered by the DFM concept.

Specifically, marketers can bring experience in profit segmentation, information-driven communications, predictive modeling, selective binding and printing techniques, financial justification, and basic database management and operations. The dance floor is virtually empty. Two-thirds of the retailers with up and running databases are not using any analytical techniques more sophisticated than simple list-selects and the stand-by of old-fashioned direct marketers, Recency/Frequency/Monetary Value analysis.[12]

To return to the original question asked by most marketers about helping with the trade, DFM can be of enormous help if marketers use it to forge a cooperative working relationship to implement its ideas and principles in a mutually beneficial manner. Each party has the ability to bring unique and complementary skills and assets. And with some planning and initiative on the part of marketers, it is possible that many, if not most, of the dollars now being poured into purely price-oriented events can be redirected to building not just volume but profitable volume and loyalty from both the brand's and the store's customer base.

MICROMARKETING

Micromarketing, like infomercials and relationship marketing, is one of the many "solutions" floating around the industry. Sometimes referred to as "database marketing for the sales force," it is a potentially important piece of the overarching DFM concept.

Micromarketing is Differential Marketing for trade promotion.

The objective of micromarketing is to direct a marketer's trade dollars to the stores and programs where they will provide the greatest return. For converts to DFM, that means stores and programs with the greatest profit opportunity.

Micromarketing is effective because the Pareto principle is pervasive in retailing, just as it is in consumer buying. Not all retailers that marketers deal with are able or willing to offer the same level of current profitability or profit opportunity. Many factors, including trade actions, consumer demographics and lifestyles, geographic preferences, advertising effectiveness, and promotion and merchandising responsiveness, help produce broad swings at the store level. The net effect is that not only which brands sell varies widely store to store, but also which "stockkeeping units" (SKUs), sizes, and varieties of the *same* brand.

All accounts, all stores, and all SKUs are not created equal.

A study by "efficient market services, inc." of Deerfield Illinois, analyzed eight categories in the supermarkets of a Midwest market during a four-week period. On average, less than one sale per day was made in nearly two-thirds of the SKUs in each category. The remaining third accounted for the overwhelming majority of category sales. For example, in the coffee category, only 51 of the 448 SKUs sold more than one item a day in the average supermarket, and they accounted for 75 percent of category dollar sales.

The same study tracked the sales of one brand of vanilla ice cream in ten different stores. The brand's category rank ranged from number one to number twenty-seven, out of about fifty vanilla ice cream SKUs carried by each store.[13]

The dilemma is that retailers don't yet appreciate these differences as much as marketers. Although they have access to very accurate data about brand and SKU movement at the store level, they tend not to use it. Marketers, on the other hand, have no access to the scanner information, but they could use it very productively to improve the overall performance of their marketing programs.

To bridge this gap, statistical modeling can be brought to bear to predict the incidence of high-profit customers by chain and by store trading area. And appropriate, selectively targeted programs can be developed to leverage these areas. Firms such as Spectra Marketing Systems, of Chicago, Illinois, or Market Metrics, of Lancaster, Pennsylvania, have developed proprietary modeling systems that can be adapted for this purpose and applied over a wide range of brands. Or fully customized models can be created as they are for selective binding.

Armed with an account-specific analysis, a marketer can present to the trade buyer a customized proposal for promotion and merchandising support that will maximize performance for the brand. Importantly, it should also demonstrate how it will benefit the retailer, who is indifferent to whether he sells Coke or Pepsi as long as he moves more cases of cola. The ideal situation is a program that provides incremental volume to both the brand and the store; in other words, a high PPI for the brand and a high "retailer profitability index" for the retailer.

Although this kind of "micromarketing" is still in its early stages, and entails significantly more time and effort and expense, the payoff becomes clearer when evaluated from a DFM perspective and incorporated as part of an integrated DFM plan. What such a plan might look like for a representative brand, and how the marketer might harmonize the pieces in the common cause of greater brand profitability, is the subject of the Chapter 13.

CLOSEUP

Does Sale Promotion Promote Trial?

At one time or another, almost every marketer has written a marketing plan with a strategy that went something like . . .

Use sales promotion to generate brand trial.

And no sooner was it written, then the fear took hold that the net effect was actually going to be more like . . .

Use sales promotion to subsidize current buyers.

Happily, marketers no longer need to question their judgment. They are right—in both instances.

Analysis of MRCA panel data reveals that new buyers of a brand are indeed more likely to purchase because of a promotional offer. The yogurt category provides a good example. In 1992, 42 percent of Dannon volume bought by new buyers was purchased "on deal." This compared with only 34 percent of deal volume for the other brands in their repertoire. It seems inescapable that promotion helped stimulate their trial of Dannon. Similarly, 52 percent of Yoplait new buyer volume was purchased on deal. Conversely, only 34 percent of their volume of other brands was purchased with the aid of a promotional incentive.

But the same analysis demonstrates that retained buyers are not shy about taking advantage of promotional offers as well. Retained buyers of Dannon bought 34 percent of their volume on deal, a somewhat lower percentage than the 42 percent of new buyers but still enough to account for more than half of all Dannon promotional volume sold—56 percent to be precise.

Yoplait retained buyers took advantage of the promotional offers even *more* than new buyers. Retained buyers bought 56 percent of their volume on deal, compared to only 52 percent for new buyers. This resulted in 54 percent of deal volume purchased by retained buyers.

Another cautionary signal is that the foregoing analysis may over-state the impact of promotion on trial. Because of the way MRCA defines buyer groups, it assumes that a "new buyer" remains "new" for an entire year. This is a practical definition which helps simplify analysis of the flow of groups of consumers through the Profit Cycle, but it does not always accurately reflect the status of any individual consumer. Arguably, new buyers are only new until they make their second purchase, at which point they become "repeat buyers." Using this narrower definition, the impact of promotion on bringing new buyers into the franchise seems relatively small indeed.

A study of panel data for 12 packaged-goods categories in the United States, Germany, and Japan revealed that on average, 80 percent of the buyers during a promotional sales peak had pur-chased the brand at least once before during the previous year. And that almost 95 percent had purchased it during the previous 2½ years. The study concludes that "when a brand is available at a reduced price (or with a coupon), some consumers respond if the bargain is for a brand already in their portfolio, but seldom, if ever, if it is for an untried brand."[14]

Moreover, the high proportion of promotional volume purchased by "repeat" or "retained" buyers begs the question of how much of that volume is incremental. The answer would seem to be "not much," based on the overwhelming lack of bottom-line promotion profitability revealed by the IRI findings cited in Chapter 4.

The lesson seems clear. Offer it and they will buy—"they" being whoever is in the market.

13

PUTTING DIFFERENTIAL MARKETING TO WORK

Executive Preview

Many new concepts and techniques have been introduced in the preceding chapters. Now it is necessary to demonstrate how they are pulled together and used in the Differential Marketing planning process for a typical brand.

In order to maintain confidentiality, but to provide an example firmly grounded in reality, the brand that is analyzed is YopleX, a hypothetical brand of yogurt based on Yoplait sales data from the MRCA panel and marketing spending and profitability data from industry sources and general norms.

In the past year, YopleX has increased its market share by one and a half points through aggressive new product introduction and promotional spending. The Profit Cycle shows the effect of this strategy on consumer buying dynamics. Significant gains in new buyers were counterbalanced by severe heavy buyer losses. The Profit Opportunity Matrix reveals that if lapsed buyers and declining retained buyers together had maintained their purchasing levels, they would have increased YopleX's volume by more than 60 percent, far greater than the 24 percent actually achieved. Thus, the central challenges facing YopleX are to consolidate new-buyer gains without upping the promotional ante and to cut down on the opportunity loss from lapsed and declining retained buyers, particularly high-profit buyers.

To meet these challenges, YopleX's primary marketing objective must be to build volume and profits by increasing the brand loyalty of current high-profit buyers. Key strategies include improved tar-

geting of advertising and sales promotion through the application of statistical modeling, as well as the implementation of a brand-loyalty program.

Differential Marketing (DFM) is a simple idea. But its implementation spells change for many aspects of the marketing plan. And change is never simple.

Many new concepts and ideas have been introduced in the preceding chapters, as well as many new techniques and tools. But several questions remain. How do all these new elements fit in the communications planning process? How are all the possible improvements pulled together into a cohesive whole? Just how are new initiatives such as a brand-loyalty program or infomercial funded without incremental spending? And the acid test of DFM: despite the sacrifice of some mass marketing *efficiency*, does the increase in *effectiveness* make it worthwhile to upset the old apple cart quite so dramatically? Or, to boil it down to the essence of the DFM business proposition, does targeting more spending against the greatest profit opportunity actually produce more profits for the brand?

To help the reader address these issues, this chapter and Chapter 14 are devoted to examining how DFM thinking might be incorporated in the marketing communications planning process of a representative brand, and to evaluating how it might perform versus a more conventional approach. The example is meant to be illustrative rather than prescriptive. What is important is not the details of an actual plan, but the thought process that gives it birth.

To remain firmly grounded in reality, but to avoid compromising confidentiality, the brand that is analyzed is YopleX, first introduced in Chapter 6. YopleX is hypothetical but *real*. It is a simulated brand of yogurt based on Yoplait yogurt sales data obtained from MRCA and marketing spending and profitability data from industry sources and general norms. The data used may not be identical to data available from other sources, but the differences are unlikely to be great enough to change significantly any conclusions that are drawn.

Obviously, there are many factors that impact marketing plans and strategies that must remain unknown to an outsider looking in. Therefore, YopleX should be considered to be an independent brand of yogurt, quite distinct from Yoplait, similar only in terms of market position, consumer buying dynamics, and, perhaps, marketing spending and media choice. YopleX's target audience is not necessarily Yoplait's. Neither are the reasons offered for the consumer buying behavior observed in the MRCA panel data. Nor are the DFM strategies that seem right for YopleX automatically correct for Yoplait. Like YopleX itself, they are only meant to illustrate a new way of thinking.

In fact, these strategies would probably not be implemented in precisely this fashion for Yoplait or for any brand. To demonstrate the impact of a fully functioning plan, the assumption is made that there is a minimal "ramp-up" period for any of the DFM improvements and that all of them can be implemented immediately. It is also assumed that no testing of programs is required, a distinct departure from experience, and that the latest conceptual and technological developments contained in this book were available to YopleX as it embarked on its 1993 planning cycle.

The marketing communications planning process typically begins with a detailed *situation analysis* of the brand and the category, which is well-understood by marketers. In trying to understand how YopleX might improve brand profitability, the analysis contained here only covers the highlights, particularly those pertaining to tools developed specifically for DFM purposes. The issue of the advertising creative strategy and execution, essential to any full-blown DFM analysis, has been omitted because of its complexity. Once the marketing objectives and strategies are defined, and the role of advertising established, most marketers readily understand how to make any necessary adjustments to the creative work, including adapting it to gather additional names for the database.

YOPLEX DFM SITUATION ANALYSIS

YopleX provides an interesting case study because it is a dynamically growing brand in the rapidly evolving $800 million nonfrozen-yogurt category. Currently, YopleX is in the number two position with a 14 percent volume share and 19 percent dollar share of market. It has aggressive growth ambitions. The brand group's sights are set on Dannon, the market leader with a 24 percent volume share.

Most yogurt brands market a line of different types of yogurt including regular, low-fat, fat-free, and recently, specialty yogurt products for children such as yogurt sprinkles. In addition, there are a variety of flavors within each type. The complex distribution system needed to maintain all these SKUs—stock-keeping units—in the dairy case helps keep gross margins down to around 55 percent. The product proliferation also increases the burden on the brand name and imagery to provide the unifying element.

Yogurt, in its various forms, has become a mainstream food product, with a little less than 50 percent of all households making at least one purchase over the course of the year. Heavy buying, high-profit consumers are especially dominant. The top third of yogurt buying households account for 83 percent of annual sales volume, buying 48 pounds of yogurt per year, or about two containers of yogurt every week. They typically spread their purchase over three to four brands, giving each about a 30 percent share of purchases, and make almost 40 percent of their purchases "on deal," somewhat lower than most packaged-goods categories.

Heavy users are primarily women, 18–54, but men are also surprisingly well represented, accounting for approximately one-third of total adult consumption. Heavy users are distinctly upper income, $30,000 and above, and skew geographically to the east and west coasts. Fully half the heavy using households have school-age children.

Yogurt is a dynamically growing category.

The yogurt market grew by about 11 percent in 1992, both in terms of pounds and dollars, thanks in part to aggressive marketing of the new children-oriented products. YopleX was a pioneer in these new forms and enjoyed particularly strong growth, increasing its market share by one and one-half share points, while Dannon's share declined by a similar amount. YopleX also increased its household penetration marginally, from 14 percent to 15 percent, while category penetration remained static.

Figure 13.1 is the YopleX Net Profit Matrix for 1993. (Although the brand forecasts a growth of 10 percent in 1993, to sales of $165 million, 1992 volume and spending figures have been used to develop the 1993 Matrix. This will allow the reader to follow along more closely, by referring back to the development of the various matrices in Chapter 6, which also use 1992 figures. This substitution does not materially affect the analysis or the conclusions.)

The brand group has budgeted $47 million for total marketing spending in 1993, $2 million of which is allocated to production. Of the remaining $45 million, $12 million is earmarked for media advertising, $13 million for consumer promotion, and $20 million for trade promotion and trade relations. The percentage of spending in each discipline conforms closely to industry averages as reported in the Donnelley, Inc., *16th Annual Survey of Promotional Practices* based on 1993 survey data. If historical purchasing patterns hold true, only the top two segments are projected to produce meaningful profits for YopleX.

The high-profit segment is especially dominant.

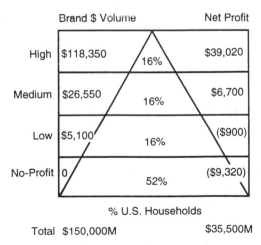

Figure 13.1   YopleX 1993 Net Profit Matrix.

In fact, the profit delivered by the heavy category buyers alone exceeds total profits by more than $3 million. The low-profit segment will be essentially break-even, and the no-profit segment will produce, as it always does, a substantial loss. The lost profit is the mass-media tax, caused by the lack of productivity of the marketing budget against the bottom two segments. Reducing this waste is one of the brand group's chief motivations for investigating DFM.

Translated into percentages, the high-profit segment is expected to deliver almost 80 percent of the volume, and almost 110 percent of total brand profitability. The medium-profit segment will deliver an additional 19 percent of profit. More than 20 percent of the profits the brand will actually earn will go to the mass-media tax collector. (See the Closeup, "Why Excessive Promotion Can Be Hazardous to the Profitability of Your Brand," at the end of Chapter 6 for a complete analysis.)

The proposed media plan for 1993, summarized in Table 13.1, makes use of a wide range of vehicles to better reach the two YopleX target audiences: children for specialty yogurts, and for the main portion of the line, adults 18–54 with a 2:1 female:male skew, household income of $25,000 +, living in A and B counties. Magazines are planned to receive almost 30 percent of the media spending,

TABLE 13.1   YopleX Preliminary 1993 Media Plan

	Sales (in thousands of dollars)	Percent
Television		
Network	3,000	25
Spot	1,500	13
Syndicated	1,000	8
Cable	3,000	25
Magazines	3,500	29
Total Media	12,000	100

with network TV and cable each budgeted to receive about 25 percent. The remainder is divided between spot and syndicated TV. The agency's preliminary analysis of the proposed plan indicates that YopleX will achieve about a 115 index of impressions against the heavy category buying, high-profit households, an above average skew when only mass vehicles are used, targeting efforts notwithstanding.

The preliminary promotion plan for YopleX in 1993 continues to support higher than average couponing and trade deal levels, most of which is concentrated in the high-profit segment. Figure 13.2 illustrates the expected Brand Loyalty Equation for YopleX for 1993 brand buyers. The calculations assume that traditional advertising and promotion planning prevails. The YopleX Brand Loyalty Equation is grossly out of balance. Against the critical group of current high-profit buyers the imbalance is greater than *twenty to one*. This, too, is a situation that the brand group would like to rectify.

Such above average reliance on promotional volume not only threatens brand loyalty but cuts into profitability. YopleX buyers made more than 50 percent of all their YopleX purchases on deal, in comparison with only about 30 percent of their purchases of other brands of yogurt. It was previously noted (see the Closeup about excessive promotion at the end of Chapter 6) that YopleX's margin on promoted volume is only 11 percent, compared with a 40 percent margin on nonpromoted volume.

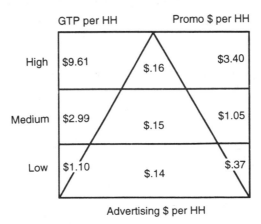

Figure 13.2 YopleX Brand Loyalty Equation, Current Brand Buyers.

High levels of promotion have increased the velocity of consumers through the Profit Cycle.

With a combination of heavy promotion and appealing new products, the brand group did an outstanding job of bringing new buyers into the franchise in 1992, as shown in Figure 13.3. The numbers in each box represent the percentage of total 1992 buyers accounted for by each buying group. More than 50 percent of total 1992 buyers were new buyers. More than 40 percent of these new buyers were high profit buyers.[1]

But YopleX also suffered some severe heavy buyer losses. The equivalent of 45 percent of 1992 buyers churned out of the franchise, and 40 percent of that 45 percent were high-profit buyers.[2] What's more, over a third of retained high-profit consumers made fewer purchases of YopleX in 1992 than they had in 1991.[3]

Churn and evaporation exacted a heavy price on profitability.

Yogurt, in general, is a more volatile category than many packaged goods products. Even so, the turnover in the YopleX franchise was high and the toll on profitability was heavy. This is demon-

	New	Growing	Declining	Total	Lapsed
High	21%	16%	9%	46%	18%
Medium	20%	7%	9%	36%	18%
Low	10%	2%	6%	18%	9%
Total	51%	25%	24%	100%	45%

Figure 13.3 The YopleX Profit Cycle: Total 1992 buying households.

strated by the Profit Opportunity Matrix, illustrated in Figure 13.4. The figures in each box show the percentage change in total volume between 1991 and 1992 contributed by each buyer group, using 1991 as the base.

Year-to-year, YopleX achieved a highly creditable 24 percent increase in volume. The purchases of new buyers alone in 1992 would have increased sales by 54 percent over 1991 totals. And increased purchases by growing retained buyers would have increased them by an additional 32 percent. But these gains were offset by volume losses from declining retained buyers and lapsed buyers. The decreased purchases of the former group would have accounted for a 28 percent volume loss from total 1991 volume. The lost sales from the latter were the equivalent of 34 percent of 1991 volume. This "opportunity loss" was not only severe in the high-profit segment, but also among medium-profit buyers, who had been much more loyal purchasers of YopleX in 1991.

A central challenge for the YopleX brand group in 1993 is to consolidate gains made in 1992 and cut down this opportunity loss, particularly in the high-profit segment. Despite the greater than average tendency of consumers to churn out of the category, the brand must retain as many high-profit buyers as possible. And if it is ever going to wrest category leadership away from Dannon, it must strive to maintain or grow the share of customer of those it does retain.

	New	Growing	Declining	Lapsed	Total
High	+41%	+28%	−10%	−16%	+43%
Medium	+11%	+ 4%	−13%	−11%	− 9%
Low	+ 2%	+ 0%	− 5%	− 7%	−10%
Total	+54%	+32%	−28%	−34%	+24%

Figure 13.4 The YopleX Opportunity Matrix: Contribution to volume change—1991 to 1992.

YOPLEX 1993 OBJECTIVES AND STRATEGIES

Achieving greater stability in the high-profit segment would seem key to YopleX's continued growth. It will be difficult for YopleX to repeat its outstanding 1992 performance in attracting new brand buyers in the face of expected aggressive retaliatory spending and new products from Dannon in 1993. Attempting to do so would undoubtedly mean upping the promotional ante, which would threaten to make a bad Brand Loyalty Equation catastrophic. The mantra of DFM was never more appropriate.

The brand with the most high-profit buyers—and the most loyal—always wins.

YopleX's overriding marketing objective for 1993 must be:

Build volume and profits by increasing the share of customer and reducing churn of current high-profit buyers . . .

. . . while not neglecting the continuing need to attract new buyers into the franchise, especially high-profit buyers.

The crucial mission for the DFM plan seems equally clear: to place more brand-loyalty-building efforts against the sizeable group of high-profit buyers that YopleX has attracted into the franchise, while simultaneously weaning them from the high levels of promotion to which they have become accustomed.

This strategy of shoring up the high-profit franchise does not mean that the need for new buyers should be downplayed. It merely recognizes that traditional marketing practices do not penalize the marketer's ability to influence potential new buyers to the same extent as they do current high-profit buyers. It also recognizes that even in a growing category, a dollar in retained buyer volume is equal to a dollar in new buyer volume, and very often easier to earn and more profitable for the marketer.

YopleX's strategies for 1993 would thus be:

1. Improve targeting of media advertising to high-profit buyers and high-profit potential *new* buyers.
2. Implement a brand-loyalty program to current high-profit buyers.
3. Reorient consumer and trade promotion spending to drive more incremental profitable volume.
4. Fund the brand-loyalty program, to the extent possible, from consumer and trade promotion budgets to improve the balance of loyalty-building and price-cutting communication.

What follows is a brief discussion of how these strategies might be implemented.

IMPROVING HIGH-PROFIT SEGMENT ADVERTISING DELIVERY

A key strategy for accomplishing the DFM mission is to examine current advertising vehicles with an eye to improving their delivery against the high-profit segment. YopleX's preliminary TV and magazine schedules both offer the opportunity to direct more impressions against heavy buyers without radically altering the current media planning philosophy.

The list of fifteen magazines under consideration, many of which the brand has used in the past, is provided in Table 13.2. They range from broad women's service books, such as *Family Circle*, to health- and diet-conscious publications, such as *Prevention*. YopleX uses Simmons Market Research Bureau (SMRB) data to evaluate print audiences. According to SMRB data, the indexes of heavy category buyer readership range from a high of 198 for *Weight Watchers Magazine* to a low of 96 for *Working Mother*. The weighted average is 124.[4]

SMRB also reports that 8.6 percent of all adults are heavy yogurt buyers.[5] (This number is appreciably lower than the 16 percent of high-profit *households* reported by MRCA because it is based on total *adults*, and every person in a household is not a heavy user.

TABLE 13.2　YOPLEX PRELIMINARY 1993
MAGAZINE LIST

Magazine	High-Profit Index
Weight Watchers	198
Shape	179
Sunset	142
Prevention	139
American Health	139
Family Circle	131
Good Housekeeping	123
BH&G	123
People	116
McCalls	116
Woman's Day	114
Sesame Street	111
Parenting	108
Parents	105
Working Mother	96

SMRB also uses a slightly more stringent definition of heavy usage.) Thus, with a weighted average index of 124, the percentage of total high-profit readers of all the magazines in the preliminary schedule is projected to be 10.7 percent.

A low incidence of heavy buyers increases the leverage of selective binding.

Typically, a statistical model of high-profit buyers would be likely to increase composition 75–100 percent in the top quarter of the circulation and about 50 percent in the top half. Eight of the current fifteen publications, including most of the larger and more expensive ones, offer either selective binding or selective insertion capabilities, and others are considering it. Thus, the schedule would not need to be radically overhauled to implement the process. With aggressive negotiating with the publications, overall high-profit segment delivery should be able to be increased by at least a third at a constant budget level.

All eyeballs are not created equal.

A similar modification of YopleX's preliminary TV schedule would also appear beneficial, because even the "eyeballs" (read "viewing habits") of upper income women, aged 18–54, differ. The differences are very evident both in terms of yogurt consumption and television viewing habits. Historically, the brand has had a strong presence in early morning news and upscale cable networks. While the brand uses Nielsen Television Index data to evaluate audience size and composition, a cursory inspection of SMRB data suggests that there may be significant variations in heavy-buyer viewing between programs and networks. For example, SMRB reports a heavy-buyer index of 104 for claimed viewers of "The Today Show," versus a 118 index for "Good Morning America" and a 116 for "ABC News This Morning." Similarly, the top five shows on TBS, USA, and TNT, all cable networks the brand has used extensively in the past, are reported by SMRB to have a 122 index against heavy buyers. The top five shows on A&E, which the brand has used only sparingly, index at 143.[6]

The brand has two alternatives, both of which it will explore because of the experimental nature of "volumetric targeting." The first is entering into discussions with the various suppliers of TV viewing data about working cooperatively to apply a high-profit affinity model against their respondents or panelists to more precisely identify high-profit viewing patterns. The second is to ask agency planners and negotiators to use claimed viewing of high-profit buyers from SMRB as additional input in making their daypart, program, and cable network choices. Even if on closer inspection some program data looks to be unstable, more selective planning and buying by daypart and cable network should improve targeting against high-profit buyers because in the past this factor has never been taken into consideration.

Additionally, spot and syndicated TV markets will be reranked and purchased on the basis of the high-profit affinity model used for selective binding. Given the dynamically growing nature of the category, it is felt that the highest clusters of consumers who demographically "look like" high-profit buyers will give the brand the best combination of current and future business potential against which to place advertising.

Because these volumetric targeting steps are unproven, albeit conceptually sound, the total impact in improvements in TV delivery against the high-profit segment are conservatively projected at 10 percent. Table 13.3 summarizes the projected levels of increase through selective binding and volumetric targeting.

IMPLEMENTING A BRAND-LOYALTY PROGRAM

The second key strategy for building loyalty of high-profit consumers is to implement a targeted program delivered via direct mail. A series of newsletters, containing both product-related and value-added information, has proven to be an effective vehicle for many marketers. The yogurt category in general, and YopleX in particular, seem well suited for this kind of information-driven effort.

TABLE 13.3   YOPLEX 1993 MEDIA PLAN; INCREASES IN
DELIVERY TO HIGH-PROFIT SEGMENT

	Sales (in thousands of dollars)	Percent	Increase
Television			
Network	3,000	25	
Spot	1,500	13	
Syndicated	1,000	8	+10%
Cable	3,000	25	
Magazines	3,500	29	+35%
Total Media	12,000	100	+17%

YopleX has more than one "story to tell."

Yogurt is seen as the kind of food product that fits into a health-oriented lifestyle. And it often is used as part of a weight-loss regimen. Moreover, the uses of yogurt go far beyond its traditional function as a snack or light meal. Cooking with yogurt would seem to offer great potential, not only in terms of consumer interest but also in substantially increasing the absolute volume of yogurt consumed by the household.

The development of new yogurt products for children might also be the basis for a kind of all-family program. Sales data supports the commonsense inference that the children who eat yogurt snacks have yogurt eating moms and dads. Despite a significant overall jump in category volume, largely driven by these new products, there was no increase in category household penetration. And the surprisingly high incidence of heavy usage by men may reflect their wives' encouragement to eat the product.

The brand group decides to reserve judgment on precisely how one or more of these elements might be blended into a brand-loyalty program until research results from high-profit consumers are received. A series of focus groups will be the starting point. Listening to high-profit buyers talk about their experience with the brand is often all that is necessary to zero in on the kind of information that would be most relevant to their habits and needs.

The resulting brand-loyalty program will not necessarily need to restrict itself to a single area of interest. The flexibility of the direct-mail medium allows the marketer to incorporate several different topics in each issue of a newsletter. Or to provide some information only to part of the audience, such as a special insert on healthy snacking for families with school-age children. The development of video material, like a "YopleX Diet and Fitness Routine," will also be considered. It could be used both as a premium for loyalty program participants as well as a test for an infomercial.

The sword of promotion can be beaten into the plowshare of a database.

YopleX is also fortunate in that their heavy promotion has provided them with a list of potential high-profit buyers. The brand's fulfillment house already has a computer file of five million names and addresses of consumers who have responded to rebates and other offers. Using a high-profit affinity model, the top two million households will be selected for inclusion in the program. An additional two million names of claimed heavy buyers are available from third-party sources. Thus, the size of the program in the first year will be four million households.

IMPROVING SALES PROMOTION INCREMENTAL VOLUME

The key to improved sales promotion performance in 1993 is better targeting of offers to drive more *incremental profitable* volume. Currently, the portion of YopleX's consumer promotion that is distributed via FSIs is placed in markets with high Category Development Indexes (CDIs). The brand group's first step will be to rerank the markets on the basis of the Brand Opportunity Index (BOI), which reflects the difference in category sales and brand sales, and thus holds out the possibility of producing more incremental volume. In fact, YopleX has already recognized that efficient mass-market delivery is not the only relevant criteria for choosing promotional vehicles.

All neighborhoods are not created equal.

Because of the upscale skew of yogurt buyers, the category has substantially differing appeal in the wide variety of neighborhoods and towns that make up the large urban markets with high CDIs. For that reason, co-op direct mail, targeted by zip code affluence, is already a significant part of YopleX's consumer promotion plan.

But household income is not the only characteristic that distinguishes heavy yogurt buyers. By applying the heavy-buyer affinity model to the supplier's circulation list, in the same way that it is applied to the subscriber list for selective binding, the brand group hopes to improve further the performance of this vehicle. Alternatives for door-to-door delivery will be investigated as well.

An analysis to determine incremental promotional profitability by market will also be conducted. If markets with the greatest incremental promotional profitability prove to be different than markets with a high BOI, adjustments to the market list will be made and a model will be commissioned to rank *smaller* units of geography on the basis of their Promotion Profitability Index (PPI). A successful PPI model could be used to enhance targeted coupon delivery even further. And it could also be cross-referenced with retail trading areas, for micromarketing purposes. In fact, whether the basis is PPI or BOI, the brand group plans to implement a micromarketing initiative to improve the productivity of the trade budget.

These are all steps that the YopleX brand group can take to produce an immediate improvement of sales promotion productivity. There are several additional actions that will lay the groundwork for future gains. First and foremost is the inclusion on all sales promotion offers, including coupons, of questions that will allow the brand to capture key consumer information for the database—name and address, yogurt consumption, and YopleX share of customer. Second is establishing a priority position on the new checkout couponing systems so that the brand may maintain category exclusivity as they increase in importance as a key promotional driver for increasing share of customer. And third is exploring and testing joint retail-brand database-driven programs, funded by the trade promotion budget.

Obviously, a brief listing of the possibilities for DFM, whether in advertising, sales promotion, or brand-loyalty programs, cannot do justice to all the complexities and uncertainties that marketers will encounter in an actual planning process. Nor can it include all the other ideas that marketers who are intimate with their brands will uncover. What such a run-through can do is demonstrate that there are many options available for moving from a traditional to a DFM philosophy. Chapter 14 focuses on the likely impact on brand loyalty and profitability for brands who avail themselves of some or all of these options.

14

MAKING DIFFERENTIAL MARKETING PAY

Executive Preview

Differential Marketing improvements to the marketing plan must usually be funded within current budgets. Many changes, such as the implementation of selective binding, are budget neutral, or virtually so. Others, such as a brand-loyalty program, require substantial investment, and consequent reallocation of funds from other parts of the marketing budget.

Incremental funding with a "payback" scenario is usually not appropriate because of the difficulty in separating out the impact of the improvements from the impact of the total mix, as well as the extended period of time over which many of the improvements produce returns. A better standard for evaluating the effectiveness of alternative plans is DROCI—Differential Return on Communications Investment. DROCI measures the total return in volume and profit of the alternative plans at equal spending levels. Underlying DROCI is the concept of marginal utility of spending, which reflects the impact of the last dollar spent, or the last million, rather than the average million. In sorting out the various options, the marketer must decide whether a shift of funding of that last million from one budget to another will produce more return in sales and profit in the new vehicle than it did in the old. The continuation of the YopleX example shows how DROCI can be used to analyze the potential of a Differential Marketing plan.

259

F lash back to the CEO in the first chapter who prodded his marketing director to question if brand loyalty were dead, and the Differential Marketing (DFM) effort that so convincingly answered "No." What is the first question the CEO asks the marketer when presented with the results of the loyalty program, showing that brand volume in the test cell was almost 30 percent greater than the control over a twelve-month period?

Correct. "How are we going to fund it?" And then, peering owlishly over the top of his glasses, as though he were staring down the tooth fairy, the CEO delivers the second half of his one-two punch:

"There's no such animal as an incremental budget."

Not for brand-loyalty programs. Or retailer co-op mailings. Or infomercials. Or statistical modeling. Maybe, just maybe, there might be funding for a database that covers all the brands the company markets, presuming the CEO has the necessary foresight to recognize that brand management can't effectively compete without it, no more than they could make do with an inefficient and outmoded manufacturing plant.

In this fundamental truth of the post-mass-market world lies both a challenge and a blessing for DFM. When the marketing pie is sliced into smaller pieces, the vested interests don't just dig in with their heels. They haul out the entrenching tools. But, conversely, they are not able to employ one of their other favorite weapons, that hoary old diversionary tactic, "But will it pay out?"

It's "payoff" that counts, not "payout."

Payout or payback, the point where return is equal to investment, is a reasonable standard for assessing marketing spending decisions where the time frame is relatively short and the results can be completely and accurately measured. As such, it is often applied to direct-mail selling or even to sales promotion, but rarely to advertising. The reason for not doing so is the difficulty in precisely separating out the impact of advertising on sales from all the other factors in the marketplace, as well as the protracted period over which advertising produces results.

Payout is equally inappropriate for a DFM program for two reasons. First, the major new items of expense, such as the brand-loyalty program, function as a supplement to traditional advertising, with the same kind of extended impact and interrelationship with other marketing elements as advertising. And second, the question is not whether to spend or not to spend, but, rather, how to spend most wisely.

DIFFERENTIAL RETURN ON COMMUNICATIONS INVESTMENT

Some marketers are relieved, while others are concerned, that there is no "black box" or simplistic formula for reallocating the marketing budget. The intent of DFM is not to slavishly match marketing spending to profit opportunity, but to match it *better* than it has been traditionally, given the realities of the marketplace. So the reallocation is best accomplished in much the same fashion as the media planning process, and with much the same objective in mind.

The marketing budget is allocated on the basis of which combination of disciplines and vehicles, in the judgment of the decision maker, will produce the greatest return in volume and profit at the agreed-to spending level. This evaluative standard is called *DROCI*, or *Differential Return on Communications Investment*.

DROCI measures the payoff of total marketing spending.

Importantly, DROCI doesn't attempt to isolate the impact of any single discipline. Rather, it recognizes that in the marketplace all disciplines work together, and that the impact of the whole is what is ultimately important, not just the impact of one of the parts. So if the addition of a brand-loyalty program, at the expense of some of the advertising and promotion budget, produces more total volume and profit, then the DFM plan wins. If it does not, then the traditional plan remains in place, shortcomings notwithstanding, until the development of a better long-term solution.

Underlying DROCI is a concept borrowed from microeconomics, the *marginal utility of spending*. Marginal utility is like marginal tax rate. It refers to the impact of the last dollar spent, or the last million dollars, rather than the average million. When assessing marginal utility, the relevant question is not how much return there is from a $10 million promotion budget, but, rather, how much *incremental* return there is from a budget of $9 million versus a budget of $10 million.

In sorting out the various combinations, the decision maker must determine whether the volume and profit loss caused by decreasing one budget by a certain amount is more than offset by the volume and profit gain derived from increasing another budget by that same amount. If it is, then the adjustment should be made. If it isn't, then the budget should remain as it is, because it does not improve the DROCI.

As usual, the real-world application is a little messier than the theory. Measuring marginal utility after the fact is difficult enough. Predicting it is even more so. More often than not, marketers will have to exercise a considerable degree of judgment, while taking into consideration both the short-term and long-term goals of the brand.

FUNDING THE DFM PLAN FOR YOPLEX

Based on the analysis in Chapter 13, the only element in the YopleX marketing plan that will require new funding is the brand-loyalty program. Improvements in advertising and promotion are adjustments, not additions, to spending. Decision on an infomercial will be postponed until the second year, when the brand-loyalty program is up and running.

The estimated cost for the brand-loyalty program is $6 million. This is based on the availability of about four million likely high-profit names and addresses from both the modeled YopleX promotional file and third-party name sources. Each household will be contacted two or three times, at a total annual cost of $1.50 per household, including a $.10 charge for amortization of the cost of the database.

To maximize the correction of the imbalance in the Brand Loyalty Equation, the ideal solution would be to fund this $6 million entirely from the promotion budget, but the brand group fears the consequences of such a drastic step. On the other hand, they do not want to reduce advertising pressure against the high-profit segment. Therefore it is agreed to reanalyze the advertising plan based on the improved targeting afforded by selective binding and more volumetrically targeted television. The objective is straightforward:

Reallocation should not make a bad Brand Loyalty Equation even worse.

Based on the projected improvement factors shown in Table 13.3—35 percent for magazines and 10 percent for television—YopleX will be able to deliver essentially the same amount of advertising against the high-profit segment at a media budget of only $10.5 million, a $1.5 million reduction that can be applied to the brand-loyalty program. Importantly, this cutback will not adversely effect either volume or profit.

As Table 14.1 shows, net spending against the high-profit segment, which controls more than 80 percent of category sales, is equalized to precutback levels through better targeting. The slight reduction in advertising against the medium-profit segment is not significant enough to appreciably alter nonpromoted volume. The larger cut against the low-profit segment will also have little, if any, impact, because the segment contributes less than 4 percent of brand volume. The biggest, and most startling, impact is on the no-profit segment.

TABLE 14.1   ADVERTISING DOLLARS BY PROFIT SEGMENT
BEFORE AND AFTER REDUCTION (in thousands of dollars)

	Before	After	+/−	Index
High	$ 2,217	$ 2,217	NC	100
Medium	1,951	1,842	($ 109)	94
Low	1,858	1,633	(225)	88
No-Profit	5,974	4,857	(1,117)	81
Total	$12,000	$10,549	($1,451)	88

NC = no change.

What's reduced most is waste.

More than $1.1 million, or more than 75 percent of the cutback, is funded from the no-profit segment, which received almost 50 percent of the total budget prior to the adjustment. In other words, most of the reduction comes from the elimination of waste, because by definition the no-profit segment will not make any yogurt purchases in 1993. Any longer-term effect on the no-profit segment is also likely to be minimal. If a category nonbuyer does decide to buy in future years, the stimulus will almost certainly be more immediate. (For a quick run-through of the mathematics, see endnote 1.)

To complete the funding of the brand-loyalty program, the promotion budget must be reduced by about $4.5 million. The sales force argues strenuously that cuts in trade promotion will result in comparable cuts in volume.

Trade promotion is a "fixed variable cost."

Micromarketing or cooperative database efforts notwithstanding, they believe the absolute dollar amount cannot be reduced without also reducing the number of cases trade promotion supports. After much discussion, the trade budget is reduced $1 million, or 5 percent.

These negotiations complete, the only place to find the remaining $3.5 million is in the consumer promotion budget. This sum represents a decrease of about 25 percent, which the brand group accepts, although not without some trepidation. The trade will have to be convinced that the new brand-loyalty program and other initiatives will more than make up for this decrease in terms of pulling volume through the store. One piece of good news is that several salespeople have reported being questioned recently by their retail buyers about the company's commitment to database efforts.

But there is another piece of good news as well. Just because volume is not sold on deal does not mean it will not be sold.

All promoted volume is not incremental.

In fact, based on common sense and experience, as well as the IRI information first cited in Chapter 4, the brand group believes that at least half the promoted volume that is "lost" will still be purchased by consumers *but at full price.* In other words, the promotional cutbacks may cut promoted volume, but they also will cut the subsidies to consumers who would have purchased the brand anyway, even in the absence of the promotion.

Moreover, by targeting promotions using either the Brand Opportunity Index (BOI) or a Promotion Profitability Index (PPI), the portion of the remaining promoted volume that is *incremental* can be increased. The brand group estimates that better targeting will provide them with promoted volume that is 55 percent incremental, rather than the current estimate of 50 percent. This decided, they sit down with sharpened pencils to calculate the estimated DROCI of the DFM plan versus the conventional plan.

DROCI FOR THE YOPLEX DFM PLAN

The major sources of incremental volume in the proposed DFM plan is the brand-loyalty program and the changes in promotional targeting. They are obviously also a major source of incremental profit. A less obvious source of profit is the incremental full price sales derived from a *reduction* in promotion spending. Equally surprising are the profit gains turned up by reducing waste against the no-profit and low-profit segments. This section examines the impact of all of these factors.

As explained earlier, the $1.5 million reduction in the advertising budget does not result in a decrease in non-promoted volume because there is no change in spending against the high-profit segment, which accounts for 80 percent of brand volume. There is, however, a change in profit. The brand's profit *increases* by $1.5 million.

As counterintuitive as it may first seem, the fact that the money will be reallocated to the brand-loyalty program is of no consequence, as long as it is charged as a cost against that program so that profits are not double-counted. Alternatively, the $1.5 million could be treated as a reduction in cost of the brand-loyalty program, so that only $4.5 million in costs would be charged against any profits generated by the program. The net effect is identical.

Calculating the likely incremental volume and profit of the brand-loyalty program is a far more straightforward process. Of the four million recipients, it is estimated that about two-thirds will actually be high-profit consumers. The remaining third will be medium-profit, either those selected by the affinity model because they look demographically very much like high-profit consumers, or consumers who exaggerated their consumption on third-party questionnaires. It is assumed that the amount of volume these households currently account for is in proportion to their percentage of brand buyers in the segment. Thus, the 2.6 million high-profit customers represent 38 percent of the brand's current high-profit customers and 38 percent of the high-profit sales.

It is a simple matter to increase this volume by the projected lift of the program, multiply it by the margin, and subtract incremental marketing expenses to arrive at incremental profit. The calculations are summarized in Table 14.2. The brand-loyalty program is projected to increase volume among recipients by 25 percent, the average increase for established brands in the tests documented in Chapter 9. This gain is the equivalent of increasing the share of customer of current high-profit buyers from 29 percent to 36 percent, a seemingly reasonable goal. Under these assumptions, the brand-loyalty program is projected to deliver an incremental $13.3 million in volume and $1.3 million in profit to the brand.

Importantly, profitability gains are found solely in the high-profit segment. Those medium-profit consumers who inadvertently became part of the program are unable to produce enough sales improvement in the first year to cover the increase in marketing expenditures. In fact, they actually depress the profitability of the loyalty program in the first year by about $1 million. But if the long view is taken, the money spent against them is not wasted.

The impact of the brand-loyalty program lasts well beyond the life of the program.

The "How Advertising Works" study of Information Resources Inc. (IRI) demonstrated that successful advertising tests not only had an effect in the year in which the advertising appeared, but also in the two subsequent years. In fact, the combined buying rate gains in Year II and Year III for established brands almost doubled

TABLE 14.2 BRAND-LOYALTY PROGRAM
IMPACT ON VOLUME AND PROFIT (in thousands of dollars)

	Current Volume	% Lift	Volume Increase	Incremental GTP	Cost	Net Profit Gain
High	$45,440	+25%	$11,360	$6,250	$3,900	$2,350
Medium	7,615	+25%	1,905	1,045	2,100	(1,055)
Total	$53,055	+25%	$13,265	$7,295	$6,000	$1,295

the gains of Year I.[2] If recipients are asked to "resubscribe" to the program after a year, which is customary, many of these non-high-profit buyers will be weeded out. But the impact of the program, which is like that of advertising, is likely to continue and will produce significant benefits for the brand.

It's also important to note that this particular brand-loyalty program will "pay back" if the 25 percent increase is achieved. Nonetheless, it would be shortsighted to attempt to fund it incrementally rather than applying the DROCI concept. The one-year "break-even" point for the program is about a 20 percent increase. But an increase of less than 20 percent, combined with other targeting improvements, will still provide a more favorable volume and profit return for the brand than the conventional plan because the marginal return from the brand-loyalty program, even at that level, is superior to other alternatives. And the program is likely to continue to pay substantial dividends in the future because of the long-term effect of loyalty-building communications. Ignoring DROCI and setting 20 percent as a "hurdle level" for implementation of a DFM plan would deprive the brand of these advantages.

The increases produced by the loyalty program must be offset by the losses in promotional volume due to budget cutbacks. As shown in Table 14.3, trade promoted volume was originally projected to be $54.7 million. A straight 5 percent reduction in budget and projection results in 5 percent lost volume of $2.7 million, but something less than a 5 percent loss in profit. There is actually a modest *profit gain* rather than a loss in the low-profit segment because of the cutback.

Decreasing promotion increases profits in segments where promotion is unprofitable.

Trade volume, like all promoted volume, is normally *unprofitable* for YopleX in the low-profit segment because the cost of the trade allowance and the allocated share of advertising expenses exceed the brand's margin. (The Closeup on excessive promotion at the end of Chapter 6 provides the detailed mathematics about why promotion is unprofitable in the low-profit segment.) Moreover, as shown in Table 14.3, 50 percent of the "lost" volume, or $1.4 million, is still purchased by consumers, but at *full price*. This highly profitable volume more than compensates for the lost trade promoted volume. The net effect on brand profitability of the trade promotion cut is a *gain* of $365 thousand.

How can a reduction of spending lead to an increase in profitability? The simple answer is IRI's conclusion that only 16 percent of trade events are profitable to the brand.[3] Like most trade promotions for most brands, YopleX's trade spending decreases bottom-line profitability because the margin on the *incremental* sales do not cover the cost of the promotion. To achieve breakeven, about 75 percent of YopleX's trade promoted volume would have to be incremental.

Decreasing promotion increases profits when promotion is unprofitable on an incremental basis.

A similar situation is operative for consumer promotion. As shown in Table 14.4, the $3.5 million reduction in promotional spending produces a $7.8 million decline in consumer promoted volume, but a $1.3 million *gain* in profits. In fact, almost $700,000 was saved simply by reducing the distribution of promotional offers to the no-profit segment. The combined effect of cutting back on waste and generating full-price volume in place of half of the "lost" promoted volume turns what initially looked like a troublesome situation into a moneymaker for the brand. What's more, if PPI targeting can indeed increase the percentage of incremental consumer promotion volume by five percentage points, from 50 percent to 55 percent, $1.1 million more full price sales are produced, delivering an additional profit of $600,000.

Short-term profits may increase by cutting promotional spending, but volume doesn't.

TABLE 14.3 REDUCTIONS IN TRADE PROMOTION
IMPACT ON VOLUME AND PROFIT (in thousands of dollars)

	Current Volume	Volume Loss	Current Profit	Profit Loss	Full-Price Incremental Volume	Incremental Profit	Revised Volume	Revised Profit
High	$43,705	($2,185)	$7,125	($355)	$1,090	$600	$42,610	$7,370
Medium	9,390	(470)	950	(45)	235	130	9,155	1,035
Low	1,560	(80)	(350)	15	40	20	1,520	(315)
Total	$54,655	($2,735)	$7,725	($385)	$1,365	$750	$53,285	$8,090

TABLE 14.4 REDUCTIONS IN CONSUMER PROMOTION
IMPACT ON VOLUME AND PROFIT (in thousands of dollars)

	Current Volume	Volume Loss	Current Profit	Profit Loss	Full-Price Incremental Volume	Incremental Profit	Revised Volume	Revised Profit
High	$23,635	($6,215)	$4,915	($1,470)	$3,105	$1,710	$20,525	$5,155
Medium	5,080	(1,335)	105	(175)	670	365	4,415	295
Low	845	(220)	(925)	120	110	60	735	(745)
No	0	0	(2,600)	685	0	0	0	(1,915)
Total	$29,560	($7,770)	$1,495	($ 840)	$3,885	$2,135	$25,675	$2,790

Before avarice triumphs over disbelief, marketers need to remind themselves that they can slash their way to victory through the promotion budget for only so long. In fact, the same actions that produce a net increase in profitability of almost $1.7 million result in a $10.5 million drop in promotional volume and $5.3 million volume loss overall. And as volume losses mount, they are certain to have a highly adverse effect on shelf presence, retailer attitudes, and economies of scale.

The *only* reason that promotion budgets can be cut is that the alternate use of the funds, the brand-loyalty program, produces volume gains that more than offset the losses and even greater profit gains because of the higher margin on those sales. In fact, when all the gains and losses are toted up, as shown in Table 14.5, the net effect of better targeting of conventional advertising and promotion vehicles, plus the addition of the brand-loyalty program, is to produce an increased return on communications investment of $9.1 million in volume and $5.0 million in profit, gains of 6 percent and 14 percent, respectively. In other words, if the assumptions are correct, the DFM plan will significantly outperform the conventional plan on the basis of DROCI.

As a double check, the brand group did a "worst-case" estimate as well. The projected increase of the brand-loyalty program was cut to 15 percent, and incremental volume was assumed to be 75 percent

TABLE 14.5   DROCI WORKSHEET FOR
NET IMPACT ON VOLUME AND PROFIT (in thousands of dollars)

	Volume	Profit
Advertising	NC	$1,450
Brand-Loyalty Program	$13,260	1,295
Trade Promotion Cutback	(1,365)	365
Consumer Promotion Cut	(3,885)	1,295
PPI	1,090	600
Total	$ 9,100	$5,005
	+6.1%	+14.1%

NC = no change.

rather than 50 percent. Even given these pessimistic assumptions, volume increases $1.2 million, and profit $600,000. And these calculations do not take into consideration the effect of the brand-loyalty program beyond the first year, or the pronounced shift in the Brand Loyalty Equation against a large proportion of the high-profit segment, laying a more secure foundation for future growth.

IN SEARCH OF CAVEATS

Is it true that there's "no free lunch"? By now, many readers may be asking themselves that question. If the preceding analysis is to be believed, DFM would seem to have the ability to produce substantial gains in volume and profit with no increase in marketing spending. And, moreover, to set up the brand for a healthier and more profitable future by making a dramatic shift in the Brand Loyalty Equation for the substantial number of high-profit buyers receiving the loyalty program.

And indeed, DFM should be able to do these things. The marginal utility of the brand-loyalty programs that are at the heart of typical DFM plans has been proven beyond any reasonable doubt. For established brands with reasonable marketing support, the spending for these kinds of programs produces more return in volume and profit than the equivalent amount would produce if invested in conventional vehicles. The improvements in media and sales promotion targeting rely largely on existing and proven techniques, and in many cases are already practiced by a limited number of early adopters. And the projections regarding volume and profit changes resulting from promotional cutbacks are based on an objective analysis of the facts as they are best known and understood. In sum, the YopleX example, although hypothetical, should be highly representative of a full-fledged DFM effort in its mature phase. Nonetheless, some caveats are in order.

First, every loyalty program undertaken has not produced a 25 percent annual volume increase among those who received it. About half have done better, the other half not as well. A performance at the low end of the range, about an 8 percent increase, would essentially produce no change in overall volume and profit in the first year, if all other assumptions remained as stated. Although, as an aside, many of those assumptions are likely to be conservative.

Second, it will usually take a marketer more time to build a database to the level where almost 40 percent of current high-profit households can be reached. For many brands, these are not Year I results, but Year III or even later.

Third, it's uncertain how many successive years new volume and profit gains can be achieved. The early adopters are still climbing the database curve. And clearly, as long as new high-profit buyers are added to the database, proportional increases in volume and profitability are within reach. But at some point the law of diminishing returns will set in. Either there will be no more high-profit buyers accessible to the marketer, or the brand's share of customer of those high-profit buyers on the database will have reached its natural ceiling, whatever that might be, but certainly a number considerably lower than 100 percent. The good news is that this new equilibrium level will be considerably higher than the one attainable by traditional marketing means.

Fourth, although the brand-loyalty programs by themselves can have a significant positive impact on volume and profits, the totality of the improvements brought about by a DFM plan depend on saner spending of the rest of the marketing communications budget, specifically on a more rational approach to sales promotion. If competition reacts aggressively to promotional cutbacks by increasing their own promotional spending, there are likely to be some severe short-term dislocations in market share and volume that will put a premium on a longer-term perspective. In other words, there is no guarantee that it will not be painful to be first. The remedy is to thoroughly test all the elements of the plan so that the ultimate rewards can be kept firmly in sight.

And finally, the brand-loyalty program results are those of marketers operating in what is largely a virgin environment. In many ways it is comparable to the early days of television, when a product advertised in the evening was often cleaned out at the shelf the next day. If what could be done *today* from a DFM perspective was all that could *ever* be done, then it is likely it would just be a matter of time before clutter in the mailbox became as pronounced as clutter on the tube and competition reached a new stage of equilibrium. Happily, that is not even close to the case.

Direct mail is a transitional medium for loyalty building.

It's productive for marketers to cut their teeth on mail as they relearn their trade, build their databases, and acclimate their organizations to a new way of marketing thinking. Important and profitable as that will be, the real payoff may be ahead, on the much ballyhooed but also much maligned information superhighway. The problem with the superhighway is like that of the blind men with the elephant. The impression one gets depends on where one grabs hold. The only thing that everyone should be able to agree on is that it is *very large*, and when it throws its weight around, it likely to have a *very large* impact.

But even the enormity of the potential impact seems to have been lost in the recent spate of claims and counterclaims about what shape the highway will take. The irony is that for most marketers, which technology triumphs doesn't matter. What does matter are the changes in consumer benefits, attitudes, and viewing behavior that virtually any technology is destined to produce, and how marketers can best deal with those changes and find new opportunities within them.

All that might ever be done in terms of marketing on the superhighway is impossible to imagine, much less predict, although Chapter 15 does take a cautious stab at doing just that. But by this stage of the book, the goal for *everything that should be attempted* ought to be crystal clear. Differential Marketing is the conceptual on-ramp to this brave, not grave, new world of marketing.

15

DIFFERENTIAL
MARKETING: THE
CONCEPTUAL ON-RAMP
TO THE INFORMATION
SUPERHIGHWAY

Executive Preview

The Chairman-CEO of Procter & Gamble shocked the marketing and advertising world by declaring that the coming revolution in information and entertainment technology, popularly known as the information superhighway, threatened a fundamental underpinning of conventional marketing: "the reach and frequency we need to support our brands." He urged advertisers to take charge as they had in previous media revolutions and create ad-driven programming that would preserve their ability to effectively communicate with their target audiences.

But the circumstances surrounding prior media revolutions are very different from those found today. The technology is far more complex and expensive than that of radio or television. There are many more contenders attempting to shape the content of the superhighway, most of whom have greater entertainment expertise and financial resources than marketers. And consumers have demonstrated their willingness to pay for quality entertainment, which often means commercial-free.

Consequently, overlaying Differential Marketing thinking on this new media environment would seem to be the most productive course of action. Prices for whatever conventional advertising opportunities that continue to exist are certain to rise as audiences shrink. Thus it will be important to target as selectively as possible, preferably high-profit consumers. What's more, the technology itself will provide both greater selectivity and interactivity, enabling marketers to gather data and involve consumers with the advertising message, as is done in brand-loyalty programs. And importantly, there will be ample room in cyberspace to direct consumers to in-depth selling messages, descendants of today's infomercials.

The information superhighway will also change the retailing business dramatically, especially the supermarket trade. On-line grocery shopping is already a successful business in several major markets. Marketers will have a new opportunity to partner with retailers to create mutually beneficial programs in a digital world, where data is money.

For readers who missed the reference, "Advertising's grave new world" was *Advertising Age*'s front page banner headline the Monday morning after the 1994 annual meeting of the American Association of Advertising Agencies. "P & G chief Artzt rocks 4As with specter of TV without ads," proclaimed the subhead.[1]

And indeed, Edwin Artzt, chairman-CEO of Procter & Gamble, the perennial spending leader among America's marketing companies and arguably the most respected, had "dropped a bomb on ad agency leaders," as the lead sentence of the article put it. The explosive device was a rousing speech that was intended as a wake-up call to agencies and marketers alike about the threat to traditional advertising practices posed by the coming changes in technology. Said Artzt:

> "From where we stand today, we can't be sure that ad-supported TV programming will have a future in the world being created—a world of video-on-demand, pay-per-view, and subscription television ... if advertising is no longer needed to pay most of the cost of home entertainment, then advertisers like us will have a hard time achiev-

ing the reach and frequency we need to support our brands."

Of the many notable things about this warning, one of the most notable was the timing.

The speech was like the ringing of an alarm clock—at ten or eleven in the morning.

The major industries that plan to drive the technological and programming change—cable, telecommunications, computing, entertainment—are in constant flux, even turmoil as the various players maneuver to position themselves for leadership roles. And even though there has been much disagreement and debate about the *structure* of the coming information superhighway—how it will enter the home and who will control it—there has been precious little argument about its overall content and direction. It will deliver all the services, and more, that the CEO of Procter & Gamble predicted.

Meanwhile, until Artzt delivered his speech, the industries that had grown fat feeding off the current technology—advertising and consumer marketing—had been conducting business as usual. Perhaps the memory of how the last predicted technological cataclysm—cable TV—had so easily been brought into the mainstream served as a soporific. Artzt chided them for oversleeping this time, quoting Sumner Redstone, chairman of Viacom, one of the more active players in the race to redefine how consumers will receive information and entertainment in the home. Redstone had told Artzt:

> "I've been surprised actually, considering the enormous changes that are in the making right now, and will take place over the next several years, that the advertising agents and indeed the advertisers have not sought to play a different and bigger role in what's going to take place in the multimedia future."

And playing a big role was exactly what the chairman and CEO of Procter & Gamble had in mind, right from his opening words:

"So here's my point: the advertising business may be heading for trouble—or it may be heading for a new age of
glory. Believe it or not, the direction—up or down—is in
our hands."

At last, someone was asking the right question. Not which technology was going to win, but when the winner emerges, just exactly what
are we going to do about it? Where's the on-ramp to the highway?
Coming from an acknowledged leader of the pack, this call to action
was in its own way every bit as galvanizing as Marlboro Friday.

Moreover, Artzt wasn't just declaring that the sky was falling. He
had a plan. The marketing and advertising industries needed to join
together to exert their considerable influence, to take control of the
media environment as they had in the past, to grab "technology change
in its teeth" and make it "the greatest selling tool ever conceived."
This strategy harkened back to the historical response of advertisers
to prior revolutions, as he made clear to the *Advertising Age* reporter:

"The absolute key is to create ad-driven programming that
suits the many new forms of media that are evolving."[2]

Creating ad-driven programming is exactly what the industry in
general, and P&G in particular, had done when radio, and later TV,
appeared on the scene, even giving its name to a new genre of
entertainment, "soap operas."

Taking issue with the chairman and CEO of Procter & Gamble is
not a course to be embarked on without very good reason, particularly because the concerns he raised and the action he urged were
not only well-intentioned but long overdue. And there can be no
argument from marketing and advertising professionals with his
stated objective of turning the information superhighway into "the
greatest selling tool ever conceived."

Where there needs to be debate, however, is the means to this
end. The evidence points to the conclusion that the coming media
revolution is very different from prior ones. And that very different
solutions will be called for in order to capitalize on it—including
overlaying or even substituting Differential Marketing (DFM) thinking for the traditional concerns of reach and frequency. Hence the
perspective of this chapter, a necessary excursion backwards and

forwards in time. Without such a perspective, with all due apologies to the philosopher George Santayana, those of us in the marketing and advertising business who remember the past are condemned to attempt to repeat it.

MEDIA REVOLUTION BEGETS ADVERTISING REVOLUTION

One key lesson from the past is not in question:

Media revolution is advertising revolution.

Every fundamental change in the advertising business has been driven by a fundamental change in the media that deliver the advertising. The eventual acceptance of advertising by the new, "genteel" magazines of the late eighteenth century gave birth to the modern advertising agency. Radio changed the rules dramatically by adding sound and immediacy, freeing advertisers and audiences from the printed page. Television added sight and motion, opening up a vast new array of creative possibilities.

Past revolutions have been "good" revolutions.

Moreover, it's not just that the revolutions happened. Every advertising revolution increased advertisers' ability to efficiently and effectively reach and persuade their target audiences. Magazines provided the first national advertising medium, albeit to a highly select audience. Radio and television democratized advertising, increasing its audience size while lowering its cost, an advertiser's dream. And the practice of interrupting programming for commercials made advertising more difficult to ignore.

And why shouldn't these revolutions have been advantageous to advertising, considering the advertisers' role? That, after all, was Artzt's point.

Advertisers were the revolutionaries.

The upscale magazines of the late eighteenth century just didn't have a sudden change of heart about accepting advertising. They were persuaded by the missionary zeal of J. Walter Thompson, *the man*, who proved advertising's effectiveness to would-be national advertisers and then delivered the contracts to publishers' doors in return for exclusive representation by his fledgling agency.[3]

Similarly, until the economics got out of hand, and the networks strong enough to rebel, the first name of the hit shows in radio and television tended to be that of the sponsor, such as Lucky Strike ("Hit Parade"), Colgate ("Comedy Hour"), and Hallmark ("Hall of Fame"). And even with advertisers largely out of programming, broadcast television is nothing if not ad-driven. The networks now make the decision of what to produce, and when to schedule it, based on only one criterion: the size and composition of the audience that the show will attract, a.k.a. the "eyeballs" that can be sold to the highest bidder.

A DIFFERENT KIND OF REVOLUTION?

In the radio and television revolutions, marketers were able to become programmers because there were few other kinds of companies with both the financial means and the understanding of what the consumer wanted. But in the upcoming revolution, there doesn't seem to be a vacuum to fill.

Entertainment has become not just a business but a megabusiness. Many of the most successful companies have substantial interests in more than one of its numerous sectors: movie production, movie distribution, television production, broadcast television, cable TV, home video, video games, music, professional sports, publishing. Extending that expertise onto the information superhighway is a natural for an industry that thrives on a high risk, high reward philosophy.

Moreover, there is a whole other group of companies interested in participating, technology providers who foresee the potential profits to be made and who are anxious to shape the programming to suit their own skills and capabilities. Chief among them are the various telephone companies, the regional Bell operating companies as well as the long-distance carriers such as AT&T and MCI. Another contender is Microsoft, perhaps the most innovative and certainly one of the fastest growing companies of the late twentieth century. The common links between all of these would-be programming moguls are ambition and extraordinarily deep pockets.

In this kind of league, the financial resources that an advertiser can bring to the party are of relatively minor consequence. As for having a finger on the public pulse, what advertising *reflects*, the entertainment business *creates*. A telling indication, if it is needed, comes from Coca-Cola, who, when seeking an advertising breakthrough, turned from its long-time ad agency to Michael Ovitz, Hollywood dealmaker extraordinaire and head of talent agency CAA, to oversee the development of the brand's new campaign by movie industry writers and directors.

Clearly, the would-be architects of the superhighway don't necessarily *need* Madison Avenue, or its clients. They might *like* to have them, and their advertising money, as Sumner Redstone implied in his remarks. But that will depend on the trade-off with what they view as an even more important revenue stream, the consumer. And the early indications are that consumers can do without advertising. Or more precisely, they can do without the predominant form of advertising on the predominant medium: short, rapid-fire television commercials that interrupt programming.

In this revolution, it may be the consumers who rebel.

In a survey conducted in September, 1994, for *Advertising Age* by Market Facts Telemation research service, two-thirds of U.S. adults flat out said "No" to the question, "Should interactive media include advertising?" In terms of advertising's acceptability, the survey found that nearly half of all respondents felt that advertising was "not at all acceptable" on home interactive services. And another 44 percent stated that it would only be "somewhat acceptable."[4]

Consumers have always groused about commercials, haven't they? So why should the superhighway architects listen? The reason is simple: economic self-interest. On the superhighway, the kind of affluent consumers who are likely to sign on are expected to pay more for television than advertisers. In fact, "free television" has been a thing of the past for quite some time.

Pay-TV subscribers pay as much per year for television as advertisers do.

Bottom line, if the roughly $34 billion total annual spending for all television advertising by all national and local advertisers in all forms of television—network, spot TV, cable, and syndicated shows—is divided by the total number of U.S. television households, the resulting figure is about $350 per year per household, or a little less than $30.00 a month. On most local cable systems, that's about the cost of basic service plus one or two of the pay-TV packages, delivering commercial-free movies, live entertainment, and other original programming.

That kind of outlay gives the builders of the superhighway hope that these homes will pay more for more choice. Somebody will certainly have to pay more to make the staggering up-front cost attractive as an investment. Basically, there are not that many "somebodies" to choose from. It's likely that either marketers or consumers or both will have to increase their spending substantially in order to satisfy the economic expectations of investors in the superhighway. Any of the choices spells increased pressure on advertisers.

The economics of the information superhighway are not on the side of marketers.

How advertiser-friendly the system ultimately is will depend on the source of the additional revenue. The P&G chairman recognized that in his speech to the Four A's:

> "Maybe our involvement means that a pay-per-view movie can be pulled down for half the price—or even free—if it includes commercials. Or maybe it means that the ten-dollar monthly fee for a game channel can be reduced to two or three dollars if we can integrate advertising."[5]

But is it realistic to think in terms of a five dollar subsidy for a movie or an eight dollar subsidy for a game channel? At that price, there aren't many movies or game channels that can be advertiser supported by the $30 a month currently spent by *all* advertisers.

In fact, at current spending levels, P&G's *total advertising budget*, not just its television budget, is only $2 a month per household. And the total budget of Crest, P&G's most heavily advertised brand, is only $.08 per month per household. How much programming can that subsidize? Where's additional money going to come from?

On the other hand, is it realistic to ask consumers to pay those prices and not give them uninterrupted, commercial-free entertainment? If the pay-cable experience is any guide, advertisers will be shunted aside. Despite much talk in the early days of cable TV about pay services such as Home Box Office and Showtime ultimately accepting advertising, it never happened. Even if the pay channels had been able to attract 15 percent of total cable spending, or roughly $600 million in advertising revenue, a very ambitious goal which would necessitate the pay service being as cluttered with commercials as any other cable channel, a subscriber decline of less than 10 percent would have wiped out the entire revenue gain. And given the unequivocal results of consumer research, and the propensity of consumers to "churn" in the absence of such a provocation, a 10 percent cancellation rate would be an astonishingly mild reaction from subscribers.

Programmers on the superhighway are likely to be no more willing to accept the risk of subscriber cancellations than pay-TV services. Their plans call for consumers paying as much as $50 a month or even more for interactivity. Even if some of that $50 comes from non-entertainment revenue, such as home banking or retailing, the revenue stream from consumers is critical. For marketers to be equally important they would have to match that revenue stream, a goal that is not within the reach of current advertising budgets. Ultimately, it comes down to a very basic proposition:

Advertisers can't afford to pay for advertising if consumers are willing to pay more for no advertising.

A DIFFERENT KIND OF SOLUTION

The information superhighway promises to spawn the first advertising revolution that does not expand audiences, increase efficiencies, or make advertising harder to ignore. And also the first one that consumers will have a real say in because they, not advertisers, are expected to bear the brunt of financing the underlying media revolution.

Although consumers may initially express strong reservations about advertising on the superhighway, as in the *Advertising Age* survey cited earlier, their response seems to be less about freedom from ads and more about freedom to enjoy the entertainment that they are paying for. It's safe to say that advertising of a kind and in a place that is generally helpful and useful will not only be tolerated, but even welcomed.

Consumers want advertising—they just don't want "commercials."

The *Advertising Age* survey went on to ask if advertising on interactive media would be more acceptable if certain conditions were met. It would be if it lowered monthly fees, said 60 percent. It would be if they were allowed to choose what ads they wanted to see and when, agreed 57 percent. And 59 percent said "yes" to the question if the ads gave them more in-depth information.[6]

The significance of these results is that consumers gave essentially the same vote of confidence to advertising-on-demand and advertising-in-depth as they did to putting money in their pockets. There's no difference, statistically or intuitively, in the level of response to the three "what-ifs." That doesn't mean that consumers will raise the flag and cheer as soon as they catch sight of the first ad rolling down the superhighway. But it does strongly suggest that there is a perceived level of real value for the benefits that advertising can offer.

This suggestion should come as no surprise after reading this far. It is identical to the reaction of consumers to the infomercials on The CableShop discussed in Chapter 11. And completely consistent with the answers to the *Good Housekeeping* survey cited in Chapter 7. Not to mention the only possible reason for the startling success of the brand-loyalty efforts recounted in Chapter 9.

Advertising itself is not under attack, but rather the model of advertising that worked so well for so long for advertisers, but not so well for consumers, in a world which is rapidly being passed by. A world where advertisers assume, as Ed Artzt did in his speech, that to sell "400 million boxes of Tide . . . we have to reach consumers over and over throughout the year."[7]

Therein lies the heart of the problem, and the soul of the opportunity. As long as marketers cling to an outdated model of communication that depends on constant pressure and repetition to a generally uninterested and distracted audience, their dreams of seizing "technology change in its teeth" are certain to be frustrated. The only choices are to adapt or find another line of work.

Differential Marketing is the conceptual on-ramp to the information superhighway.

What then should the new model be? No surprise here either: DFM is uniquely suited to help marketers build stronger, more profitable brands in a radically altered media environment. There are three key reasons. First, DFM offers the only rational economic strategy for competing in what, under any technological scenario, will be a more expensive advertising medium. Second, the requirements for implementing the DFM concept are facilitated rather than stymied by the likely capabilities of interactive media. And, third, the impact of the superhighway on the *retailing business* will present a whole new set of challenges and opportunities for marketers, which can best be addressed by employing DFM strategies. Each of these points is discussed in more detail in the sections that follow.

THE INFORMATION TOLL ROAD

No matter how the medium develops, the costs are certain to increase. In its most likely incarnation, a combination of both old-style TV and new-style interactivity and on-demand programming, advertisers will have not one but two opportunities to play and pay.

The information superhighway will be a toll road for advertisers.

The current advertiser-supported programming emanating from the four commercial broadcast networks is almost certain to continue in its present form for some time, with only some modest evolutions. It will be the major source of entertainment for households who do not have the money or the desire to hook up to interactive services. And it will be an important component of the programming on those new interactive services. It may even become interactive in some fashion of its own. One idea already in test allows viewers to play along with the contestants on game shows.

The real issue is commercial effectiveness, not commercials.

The fact that ad-supported programming will not vanish does not necessarily conflict with the P&G chairman's warning to the industry. Ad-supported programming in the new media environment is sure to command a smaller audience and thus a higher price from advertisers. What is likely to happen as competitive alternatives increase exponentially is the same pattern that occurred as cable TV siphoned off network viewers. In 1980, the average prime-time share of audience of the three major networks was almost 90 percent. Today it's barely more than 50 percent on average, and less than 50 percent in cable households.[8] During the same period, the average prime-time network cost per thousand soared. Advertisers either paid more for or got less of this increasingly scarce commodity.

How much more network viewing will decline, and prices increase, is difficult to predict. But one thing is certain: The novelty and number of new choices that will be offered by the coming technology will dwarf those brought by cable TV. What's more, there is a second, related problem that advertisers will face:

Quality of audience will be as much a problem as size.

Ad-supported programming is likely to deliver an audience that is increasingly less attractive demographically to advertisers. The people who do not participate in the new media, or who are only marginal users, are likely to be the old and the less affluent. They will rely more on ad-supported programming for their entertainment, and thus constitute a disproportionate percentage of the audience. This, too, is a trend that cable TV foreshadows. For example, in just the five year period from 1987 through 1992, the average prime-time broadcast network rating for women 18–49, perhaps the most prized demographic group for advertisers, declined by a third, from 10.4 percent to 7.0 percent.[9]

Ironically, the very bleakness of the prospects of ad-supported TV may provide a small ray of hope for advertisers taking back the programming reins. In such an environment the networks may be more willing to turn over some of the programming responsibilities, as a cost and risk reduction measure if nothing else. And faced with the inherent difficulty of attracting a large *quantity* of viewers, advertisers who accept the programming responsibility may be more attuned to the *quality* of audience they can attract, as they were in the 1950s, when the advertiser's reputation was as important as the show's ratings. That was the attitude that produced the "Kraft Television Theater," the "Goodyear TV Playhouse," "See It Now," and "I Remember Mama," all mainstays of the so-called Golden Age of Television.

In the DFM model, high quality translates into high profit. And given advertiser control, there very well may be opportunities to tailor the programming to disproportionately attract the high-profit segment. For example, a sneak preview of "Home Alone VI" (or whatever roman numeral) could be an ideal vehicle for the many packaged-goods products where the presence of children under 12 is a key indicator of heavy usage.

But even if those kinds of opportunities are given to advertisers, the solution is likely to be only a partial one. The sheer amount of viewing that will undoubtedly be siphoned off by new entertainment options will mean that there are not enough affordable conventional advertising opportunities to allow most brands to pursue an effective reach-and-frequency-based advertising strategy. By necessity, advertisers will have to seek out new ways of persuading consumers. And that will almost certainly mean turning to some form of extended length and, quite possibly, interactive communication to supplement the commercials on ad-supported programming.

This new kind of commercial might resemble a contemporary infomercial or a CD-ROM disk or something in between. But whatever it looks like, it is most surely going to be far more expensive on a per contact basis than advertisers have grown accustomed to paying, perhaps even as expensive as direct mail is today. The only way to rationalize on an economic basis the higher cost of in-depth selling will be to target, as exclusively as possible, high-profit consumers and to minimize waste to underproductive or nonproductive segments. In other words, to adhere to a DFM philosophy.

If Differential Marketing didn't already exist, it would have to be invented.

THE INFORMATION SUPERHYPEWAY OR THE MARKETING SUPERHIGHWAY?

Before it was the information superhighway it was the new media or 500-channel cable or interactive television or multimedia or the digital pipeline or the wired nation. Semantic consensus was reached sometime in 1994, just as the dates for some of the more extravagant claims and promises came due. It was at this point that the unfortunate pun began to circulate, undoubtedly coined and circulated by those whose apprehension about change was matched only by their inaction.

Characterizing the inevitable convergence of television, telecommunications, and computing as the information super*hype*way is no more useful than whistling past the graveyard. Any idea this complicated and costly, fought over by so many competing interests, is bound to have a long and unpredictable gestation period. There are too many powerful forces driving it to fantasize that it will never be born. Although it's impossible to know what the baby will look like, or what it will grow up to be, there are some pretty safe bets about some of its basic features that are no more speculative than saying a human baby is likely to have two arms and two legs and no tail. In turn, those basic features lead to some reasonably straightforward inferences about problems and opportunities that marketers are likely to encounter. And to draw one overriding conclusion:

Technology continues on the side of Differential Marketing.

One of the common denominators in all descriptions of the new technology is that it will be in some fashion *interactive*. At a minimum, interactivity means that consumers will be able to *respond* to cues or questions that appear on the television screen. To say "yes," for example, to a prompt for more information or a pay-per-view event. And the system will necessarily be able to identify the household that is responding in order to follow up on the requested action. Fully developed, interactivity would allow consumers to *initiate* communications, with various programming services, game channels, information databases, advertisers, and perhaps even other consumers on the system via some form of videophone.

Any level of interactivity will facilitate Differential Marketing.

Interactivity is certain to provide a simpler and faster method of identifying high-profit customers and gathering key information about them for the database. *Electronic questionnaires*, for example, could be employed at any stage of interactive development, including a response-only system. They might be part of a follow-up package sent to consumers who pressed a "more information" button on their remote control upon seeing a conventional commercial. With a more sophisticated technology and a resolution of privacy issues, *behavioral prompts* could be used to judge profit potential and trigger further communication. For example, a flurry of database searches for information about new model automobiles could signal an in-the-market prospect. Or a household's purchase history in an electronic grocery store could be used to identify a heavy buyer.

Interactivity means selectivity.

Interactive households are addressable households. If programs can be directed selectively to individual households, so can advertising. Possibilities range from *selective insertion* of conventional commercials in ad-driven programming, the video equivalent of selective binding, to personalized, in-depth messages in a *video mailbox*, the video equivalent of direct mail.

Interactivity equals involvement.

Higher levels of interactivity will significantly increase the ability of the marketer to involve the consumer with the brand. The kind of involvement through brand-loyalty programs that helped drive the increases reported in Chapter 9 will, if anything, be more important in a video world where there is less overall advertising pressure. And allowing consumers to interact with a video selling message in some fashion is certain to foster that involvement.

To try to forecast the level of complexity of the interactivity would be pure speculation. At its simplest, it might entail the consumer answering a question or two so that the in-depth message might be tailored to his or her specific needs. Full blown, it might provide all the choices and flexibility available on CD-ROM today. But almost any level of interactivity should produce as much if not more involvement than can typically be achieved in a direct-mail package.

In addition to interactivity, another common characteristic of the various visions of the super-highway is a virtually limitless capacity for information and entertainment product. In fact, some forecasters question whether the concept of "channels," as in a "500-channel system," will have any relevance in the new technology. They argue instead that there will be only one channel, which is designed by the consumer, and which draws on a vast library of resources. This is precisely how the Internet works today for computer users.

There's room for advertising at the cyberspace inn.

Marketers are assured that there will be enough *cyberspace capacity* to provide the in-depth information that consumers want and that generates loyalty and sales. This has never before been the case. One reason for the demise of The CableShop was that there was little or no room for new networks on the cable systems that were then common, when fifty or more channels was considered state of the art. And advertisers seeking infomercial time in today's broadcast environment find themselves shunted off to the least attractive time periods.

Marketers still face the challenge of getting consumers into the in-depth selling message. Depending on how the technology develops there are likely to be a variety of methods, from flagging its availability in a commercial on ad-driven television to establishing a permanent residency in some kind of advertising/information cyberspace mall that consumers know about and seek out. Or even to delivering it periodically to high-profit consumers' video mailboxes, like direct-mail brand-loyalty programs are currently delivered.

In any case, the fact that advertisers will not be shut out because of system capacity is critical. Combined with the potential for selectivity and involvement created by interactivity, the thrust of the technology all works in favor of DFM.

THE RETAILING SUPERHIGHWAY

Advertisers are not the only ones facing a challenge:

Media revolution means retailing revolution.

The basis for that surprising prediction is the mutual interest of both key parties. Technology providers see retailing as a potentially enormous revenue stream to tap into, and importantly, one that consumers will welcome. Retailers view cyberspace as a release from the constraints and expenses of brick and mortar and unreliable and expensive human sales help.

Ironically, on virtually all the precursors to the super-highway, such as the early videotex tests and the current on-line systems, retailing has been a problem area. One reason is that the display of merchandise has not lived up to expectations. Until now, photo-quality images have not been generally available. On-line sound and motion video is not available, period. Another problem has been that the telephone connect time that consumers use as they "shop" the service on-line has proved to be an unanticipated drain on profitability. This has been particularly true in a "video catalog" environment, where browsing is simply not as easily accomplished electronically as it is by turning the page.

Because of these problems, consumers frequently shop a printed catalog and then use the electronic service to place the order, turning it into nothing more than a high-tech 1–800 number. Or they don't bother to use it at all. As a result, most of the major on-line services have deemphasized shopping as a key consumer benefit. The only electronic retailing success stories of note are the cable TV home-shopping channels, which are more akin to flea markets than the upscale, virtual-mall experience that is the dream of the retailing industry.

As technology continues to develop, the superhighway may yet become an important channel for selling high-ticket, considered purchases. For example, downloading the "store" into in-home memory for off-line access would solve the costly "browsing" problem. And the kind of images that will become available, perhaps even sound and motion, will be a quantum leap forward from the current generation of computer graphics. But in the meantime, electronic shopping is developing in a quite unanticipated but important direction.

The "electronic supermarket" is first on line for the retailing superhighway.

Grocery shopping was initially downplayed as too complicated or too mundane to adapt to an electronic environment. As it turns out, the order-taking capability of on-line services make them ideal for products that are, in effect, presold, and that therefore can be listed rather than displayed. The convenience of shopping from home, rather than trekking through the supermarket aisles, is also highly appealing, especially to two-income families for whom time is the scarcest resource.

The prototype cybermarket is Peapod, a grocery shopping service currently available in Chicago and several other markets on America Online. In the original Chicago market, everything available at Jewel, a local supermarket chain, is available on Peapod. The service employs a staff of shoppers at a local Jewel store who fill the order, including handpicking meat and produce. The groceries are then delivered to the consumer's home at an agreed-to time, all for a fee of $5 plus 5 percent of the grocery bill. Ominously for marketers, Peapod assures would-be subscribers in its brochure that the additional cost will not be a burden: "You will be able to save more than this amount by using Peapod's powerful cost saving features and by using coupons more easily."

In its initial test phase, Peapod quickly won raves from both consumers and industry observers. In a matter of months it reportedly accounted for 10 percent of the daily volume at the local Jewel. Peapod has now expanded throughout the Chicago area, as well as into other key markets, the first of them San Francisco. Ameritech, the Chicago-based Baby Bell with superhighway ambitions, has acquired a substantial stake in the business. And imitators are beginning to appear in other markets such as New York.

At this point, the effect of these kinds of services on shopping habits is pure speculation. But the statement featured in Peapod's promotional literature rings true.

Price becomes a more important motivator in electronic shopping.

It's infinitely easier to comparison shop a list of available brands, along with their size and price, than it is to struggle through a ten-foot stretch of a supermarket aisle, four shelves high, in search of the best deal. In fact, sale items are flagged on the screen in such a way that they are impossible not to notice. And the consumer can program the computer to sort the category by unit price, from least to most expensive. The store brand is likely to pop up at the top of the screen for virtually every category, setting the bar for the added value the marketer's brand must provide in order to win.

Clearly, that kind of environment is likely to put brand loyalty to a severe test. And if marketers can't sustain loyalty, or think they can't, to tempt them to escalate the price wars.

The danger is that brands will become virtual commodities in a real cybermarket.

It's important to reiterate that systems like these are not pie-in-the-sky, as is so much of the speculation about the superhighway. Even if the superhighway is delayed interminably, new shopping services like Peapod, running on existing on-line systems, are certain to multiply. And as they grow, to increasingly be a deciding factor in the fate of the brand. With the eventual advent of the superhighway, they may even become *the* deciding factor.

If advertisers can't compete with programmers, their best strategy may be to cooperate with retailers.

The opportunity to make the superhighway "the greatest selling tool ever conceived" is not likely to come from providing consumers with better entertainment. But it could conceivably come from providing consumers with a more valuable and rewarding *shopping* experience. Tying together the objectives and the motivations of the retailer and the marketer in a helpful and engrossing cybermarket environment may be the best outlet for marketers' efforts and investments.

In this new video environment, marketers may at last have the knowledge and experience and resources to work with retailers on an equal footing to develop cyberspace for their mutual benefit. Retail presence and sales will probably develop more slowly than advertising applications. Advanced technology may be required for all but the simplest order taking. And substantial investment from a perennially cash-strapped industry will be mandatory. Even grocery retailers, who would seem to have an inside track in developing this new outlet, are likely to be preoccupied with brick-and-mortar concerns and move slowly. If marketers experiment and participate fully from the beginning, they will accumulate a valuable knowledge base to share with their retail customers.

Moreover, marketers are the more logical experts about video, even interactive video. Marketers in general have been much more dependent on television to drive their business than retailers. This expertise ought to mean a faster learning curve and greater skill in the new selling techniques that will emerge, qualities that will be valuable to retailers.

Nonetheless, given the history of the two industries, the ultimate reason for cooperation must inevitably be some form of cost-sharing for mutual gain; in other words, the superhighway equivalent of trade promotion for packaged-goods advertisers or co-op advertising and merchandising funds for soft goods and consumer durables. But rather than mindlessly allowing the current tug-of-war to infect the new selling environment, change means an opportunity to restructure and redefine what marketer–retailer cooperation means. The key to this restructuring and redefinition may very well lie in adopting a new currency.

In a digital world, data is money.

The concept of the retail trading area and everything that goes with it—the window displays, the door-to-door circulars, the high-traffic location—go out the window. In comes the database. Retailing on the superhighway is, by definition, direct marketing. Marketers' ability to share consumer data with retailers, and to receive data in return, could form the basis for a whole new kind of productive relationship.

This is the ultimate payoff for DFM: a continuous loop of more accurate and timely data that benefits all the parties who contribute to it, irrespective of on which side of the desk they sit. This rosy scenario presumes that marketers seize the initiative in exploiting the possibilities of new marketing thinking and new technology, starting today. The Epilogue points the way for marketers who are willing to accept this challenge to change.

EPILOGUE

THE CHALLENGE
TO CHANGE

A small segment of high-profit consumers controls a disproportionately large percentage of category volume and profit. Their loyalty is critical to the current and future prospects of the brand. Yet they have been increasingly underdelivered by traditional brand-building advertising and overwhelmed by price-sensitizing sales promotion to the point where, in many categories, shockingly few high-profit consumers can be considered brand loyal by any definition. The fate of the brand is in the hands of consumers who either don't count or don't care.

All that—and more—has presumably been proved. And a solution has been offered up: building the loyalty and profits of those most valuable consumers by communicating with them more relevantly and more directly in all media. This is the promise of Differential Marketing (DFM). A promise that will grow even more important when the future arrives.

Differential Marketing is not a quick fix. No more than the current brand-hostile environment is an overnight phenomenon. Conditions like those under which we, as marketers, are now operating take years to develop. And years to change. Yet the benefits of DFM for the brand *can begin to be demonstrated* relatively quickly. Modifications in media and promotion are potentially as immediate as the next planning cycle. A brand-loyalty program, or at least the test of a brand-loyalty program, can be gotten underway in six months or less. The database can be initialized and up and running in the same time frame.

A fast decision to say "yes" is imperative for marketers who want to maximize the potential of the DFM concept. The window of opportunity to build new bridges to the retail trade is open *now*, as is the chance to get a significant leg up on the competition.

As every marketer well knows, often to his or her despair, virtually any marketing action can immediately be matched by an equal and opposite competitive reaction. But not necessarily so for DFM. The central role of the database is a key reason. The best and most efficient source of names for building the database is the marketer's on-going marketing activities: advertising, promotion, and in-pack and on-pack response devices. Collecting, classifying, and marketing to these names is clearly a more time-consuming process than instructing a media salesman to draw up a contract. And that time insulates the marketer from a fast competitive response.

Another factor allowing a marketer to get a significant head start is that building and using a database is subjected to only minimal competitive scrutiny. Many of the channels of communications, such as toll-free telephone numbers, are proprietary or virtually so, or private, and thus difficult to monitor, like the mail. Even if a competitor subscribes to a service like *DBM/scan*, it is difficult to know with any certainty how extensive the mailing effort actually was, or who precisely was targeted.

In fact, the "stealth factor" of brand-loyalty programs gives early adopters another significant edge. The high-profit consumer may very well be preemptible. A competitive spot TV or free-standing insert blitz in Cleveland is obviously going to have an impact on sales in Cleveland. And can be met with a corresponding blitz. But the impact of a program directed at high-profit customers scattered around the country is much more difficult to isolate. And to combat.

The first problem a competitor faces is identifying the consumers who have been targeted. The sales loss is not geographical but rather at the household level. And even if those households can be correctly identified, how effective are the available countermeasures to a marketer without his or her own database?

The second problem is changing those consumers' behavior, once they are already part of a competitive brand-loyalty program. Other than in the travel and tobacco industries, situations where two programs are actively competing for the same consumer are still relatively rare. But arguably, the program that involves the consumer first is likely to be the most effective, and in some cases the only program needed, particularly for packaged goods. No matter how interesting or appealing, how much information can a consumer absorb for something like coffee or zippered plastic storage bags? Especially if the original program has been fine-tuned for maximum impact. "Me-too" marketers are likely to find it more difficult to even build a database, much less use it effectively.

Finally, competitive response is likely to be slower than faster because the decision to build the database is almost always a corporate one, rather than that of an individual brand. The database is in essence *a private, proprietary medium*. And someone has to bear the start-up costs that would normally be borne by the media company. An analogous situation is advertiser-created programming on commercial television. The up-front production costs are covered by the corporation, and then passed on to the brands on a pro rata basis when their commercials are aired. The most successful marketing databases have been established in precisely the same manner—funded initially at the corporate rather than the brand level. And charging the brands on an "as used" basis, or, early on in the process, not charging them at all.

This litany of benefits makes it sound as though the database might be the holy grail of marketing for early adopters—a sustainable competitive advantage. And in a sense it is, or can be. But there is an even more significant advantage, an advantage that is harder to match than any database ever can be.

The critical issues for the successful implementation of DFM have little to do with the relevancy of the findings of this book for the brand. Rarely will they not be relevant. The critical issues have everything to do with the relevancy of the findings for the *organization* that markets the brand, and which has been marketing it differently, even relatively successfully, for some time.

Virtually every marketer cited in this book started with a single test. And in all instances where Ogilvy & Mather participated, the test was successful. But not every successful test was expanded into a meaningful program. Nor were all programs continued indefinitely, despite their continuing success. A new management broom often sweeps clean, if for no other reason than to prove that "new" is "different." This sad history reaffirms the truism of our business that it is always easier to find reasons to say "no" than to say "yes."

Perceptions and habits do not change overnight. Nor do ways of thinking. Differential Marketing flies in the face of some of the most cherished habits and beliefs left over from the mass-market world. It takes vision to recognize the worth of DFM, courage to implement it, and a deep keel to sustain it. And all these qualities must be found not in one person but throughout the organization.

Starting early, and small, and growing in understanding and appreciation as the successes grow, is the best prescription for getting the concept of DFM to "take" throughout the organization. Do that and you will be rewarded with the real sustainable competitive advantage—leadership in implementing this new and powerful strategy for brand loyalty and profits.

ENDNOTES

CHAPTER ONE

1. Larry Light, *The Trustmarketer's Road to Enduring Profitable Growth*, Coalition for Brand Equity, New York, 1993, p. 13.

2. Steve Yahn, "Advertising's Grave New World," *Advertising Age*, May 16, 1994, p. 1.

CHAPTER TWO

1. Michael McDermott, "Marketers Pay Attention! Ethnics Comprise 25% of the U.S.," *Brandweek*, July 18, 1994, p. 26.

2. U.S. Census Bureau statistics, 1994.

3. Mediamark Research, Inc., Doublebase 1993.

4. Ogilvy & Mather New York, 1994 media department estimate.

5. *Progressive Grocer*, "Fact Sheet 1993," April 1994, p. 34.

6. Gretchen Morgenson, "The Trend Is Not Their Friend," *Forbes*, September 16, 1991, p. 115.

7. Donnelley Marketing, Inc., *16th Annual Survey of Promotional Practices*, 1994, p. 17.

8. "Coupon Redemptions on the Slide," *Promo*, February 1995, p. 1.

9. O. Burtch Drake, executive vice president, Chief Operating Officer, American Association of Advertising Agencies, *"Coalition for Brand Equity Publishes Research Results."* AAAA Bulletin, January 25, 1994, p. 1

10. Stuart Elliott, Advertising Column, *New York Times*, October 20, 1993.

11. Alexandra Ourusoff, "Brands—What's Hot. What's Not," *Financial World*, August 2, 1994, p. 44.

CHAPTER THREE

1. Mediamark Research, Inc., Doublebase 1993.

2. Ibid.

3. Edmund Andrews, "No-Holds-Barred Battle for Long-Distance Calls," *New York Times*, January 21, 1995, p. 48.

4. Mediamark, op. cit.

5. Brian Woolf, *Measured Marketing, A Tool to Shape Food Store Strategy*, The Coca-Cola Retailing Research Council, 1994, p. 6.

6. Mediamark, op. cit.

CHAPTER FOUR

1. Magid Abraham and Leonard Lodish, *Advertising Works, A Study of Advertising Effectiveness and the Resulting Strategic and Tactical Implications*, Information Resources Inc., 1990, p. 1.

2. "IRI Pinpricks Promotion Balloon," *The Media Report* (now published as *The Marketing Pulse*), November 1988, quoting an unnamed IRI spokesperson reporting at an Advertising Research Foundation symposium. Neither IRI nor *The Marketing Pulse* was able to further identify the source.

3. Robert D. Buzzell and Bradley T. Gale, "Market Share, Profitability and the Advertising/Promotion Mix," published in a booklet, *Advertising, Sales Promotion and the Bottom Line*, The Ogilvy Center for Research & Development, March, 1989, pp 18–19.

4. Larry Light and Richard Morgan, *The Fourth Wave*, Coalition for Brand Equity, New York, 1993.

5. Mediamark Research, Inc., Doublebase 1993.

6. William R. Diem, "Bond Stronger with Age," *Advertising Age*, March 28,

1994, p. S-6, citing J.D. Power & Associates survey commissioned by *Automotive News* and *Advertising Age*.

7. Ibid.

CHAPTER FIVE

1. William R. Diem, "Bond Stronger with Age," *Advertising Age*, March 28, 1994, p. S-6, citing J.D. Power & Associates survey commissioned by *Automotive News* and *Advertising Age*.

2. Retained buyers represent 49% of 1992 buyers. Lapsed buyers are the equivalent of 45% of 1992 buyers. Together, these two groups constitute all of 1991 buyers. 45% is almost half of 45% + 49%.

3. Diem, op. cit.

4. Ibid.

5. −20% of Retained High-Profit + −18% of Lapsed High-Profit equals a total loss of 38% from these two groups. If that were reduced by half, the loss would be 19% of 1991, and also a 19% improvement compared with the current loss of 38%. Adding that 19% improvement to the current overall 18% loss produces a 1% net gain.

6. A. S. C. Ehrenberg, "If You're So Strong, Why Aren't You Bigger?" *Admap* (NTC Publications, U.K.) October 1993, pp. 13–14.

CHAPTER SIX

1. Andy Tarshis, President, NPD/Nielsen Inc., "How to Make Advertising Work Better," a speech presented at the Advertising Research Foundation Workshop, November 6–7, 1991.

2. Beth Lubetkin, "Additional Major Findings from the 'How Advertising Works' Study," a speech presented at the Advertising Research Foundation Workshop, November 6–7, 1991, summarizing results from "How Advertising Works" (1990), a study co-sponsored by Information Resources Inc. and a consortium of advertisers, agencies, and trade groups.

3. Ibid.

4. Holly Heline, "Brand Loyalty Isn't Dead—But You're Not Off the Hook," *Brandweek*, June 7, 1993, p. 14; reprinted from *The Public Pulse*, The Roper Organization, 1993.

5. Ibid., p. 15.

Chapter Seven

1. Stanley Resor's definition of advertising as "the news of the marketplace" was common knowledge among J. Walter Thompson executives in the 1970s, when the author worked there.

2. David Ogilvy, "A New Deal for Your Clients," *Journal of Advertising History*, date unknown, about 1980, p. 7.

3. Stephen Fox, *The Mirror Makers*, William Morrow and Co., New York, 1984, p. 55.

4. Public Relations Department, DDB Needham, New York.

5. *Good Housekeeping* survey, "Inside the Mind of the New Traditionalist," The Roper Organization and the Hearst Corporation, 1992, p. 40.

6. Ibid.

Chapter Eight

1. Donnelley Marketing, Inc., *16th Annual Survey of Promotional Practices*, 1994, p. 41.

2. David Ogilvy, *Confessions of an Advertising Man*, Atheneum, N.Y., 1976, pp 97, (1st printing 1963).

3. Alexander Biel, *Creating Long Term Attitude Change*, The Ogilvy Center for Research & Development, 1990.

Chapter Nine

1. Personal conversation with author, March, 1995.

2. Personal letter to author, March, 1995.

3. The "How Advertising Works" study conducted by IRI was first made public at an Advertising Research Foundation conference in New York in November, 1991. The results were also published in a booklet by IRI, coauthored by Dr. Magid Abraham of IRI and Dr. Leonard Lodish, the Samuel R. Harrell Professor of Marketing at the Wharton School, University of Pennsylvania, and copyrighted in 1990.

4. Many of the IRI BehaviorScan tests that formed the basis for the original findings of the "How Advertising Works" study had cells of multiple pairs. In other words, there was more than one copy or weight scenario being tested. Success rates in the original study were based on *any* pair in the test that

had successful results. Dr. Lodish and his colleagues have now reanalyzed the data based on *random pairs* chosen from each test, which were evaluated as either successful or unsuccessful. This methodology has resulted in somewhat lower success rates than those originally reported. Their new results appeared in the *Journal of Marketing Research* in May, 1995.

5. Dr. Leonard Lodish, "Key Findings from the How Advertising Works Study," a speech presented at the Advertising Research Foundation Workshop, November 6–7, 1991, p. 28.

6. Ibid.

CHAPTER TEN

1. *Business Week*, September 5, 1994.

2. Donnelley Marketing, Inc., *16th Annual Survey of Promotional Practices*, 1994, p. 49.

3. Personal conversation with author, February, 1995.

4. Ibid.

5. Personal conversation with author, June, 1995.

6. Personal conversation with author, February, 1995.

7. Personal communication to author, March, 1995.

CHAPTER ELEVEN

1. Dr. Leonard Lodish, "Key Findings from the How Advertising Works Study," A speech presented at Advertising Research Foundation Workshop. November 6–7, 1991.

2. Sonia Yuspeh and Garth Hallberg, "The Radical Potential of Cable Advertising," *Journal of Advertising Research*, August/September 1983, p. 51.

3. Andy Tarshis, President, NPD/Nielsen Inc., "Establishing the Analytical Framework for Delivering on the Single Source Promise," a speech presented at the Advertising Research Foundation Annual Conference, New York, 1990.

4. Ibid.

5. Ibid.

6. Simmons Market Research Bureau, Inc., Survey of Media and Markets, 1993–94, courtesy of Marketing Information Technologies.

7. Yuspeh and Hallberg, "Cable Advertising."

CHAPTER TWELVE

1. Donnelley Marketing, Inc., *16th Annual Survey of Promotional Practices*, 1994, p. 23.

2. Personal conversation with author, March, 1995.

3. Op cit. Donnelly p 41

4. Ibid. p. 23.

5. Harris Gordon, "Retailers Are Ready for Relationship Marketing," *Direct Marketing*, January 1994, p. 38; reprinted from *Retail Insights* (published by Deloitte & Touche).

6. Ibid.

7. Ibid., p. 39.

8. Deloitte & Touche, *Profitable Retailing Using Relationship and Database Marketing*, commissioned and copyright by the Direct Marketing Association, 1994, p. 8.

9. Ibid., p. 127.

10. Ibid., p. 129.

11. Personal conversation with author, March, 1995

12. Op cit. Deloitte & Touche, p. 136.

13. "The Non-Movers," *Food & Beverage Marketing*, December 1994, p. 34.

14. A.S.C. Ehrenberg, K. Hammond, G.J. Goodhardt, "The After-Effect of Price-Related Consumer Promotions," a paper delivered to the Institute of Sales Promotion's annual conference, London, October 12, 1993.

CHAPTER THIRTEEN

1. 21% "New High-Profit" as a percentage of 51 % total "New."

2. 18% "Lapsed High-Profit" as a percentage of 45% "total lapsed."

3. 9% "Declining High-Profit" as a percentage of 25% (16% + 9%) "Retained High-Profit."

4. Simmons Market Research Bureau, Inc., Survey of Media and Markets, 1993–94, courtesy of Marketing Information Technologies.

5. Ibid.

6. Ibid.

CHAPTER FOURTEEN

1. Why does the no-profit segment absorb a disproportionately large percentage of the advertising budget cut? The answer lies in two factors. First, the three other segments must pay to keep spending in the high-profit segment constant. The no-profit segment actually accounts for more than 60 percent of the budget of the remaining segments whose budgets must be reduced. So if they were reduced in proportion to their current budget, it would provide 60 percent rather than 50 percent of the reduction. Second, the budgets of the remaining segments are not reduced proportionately. The no-profit segment is reduced by the greatest percentage. If targeting is improved against the high-profit segment it is logical to assume that targeting will also improve, although not as dramatically, against the medium-profit. So instead of a 12 percent budget cut, that segment's cut is only 6 percent. Assuming the low-profit segment absorbs its full share of the cut, roughly 12 percent, the no-profit's cut must be approximately 19 percent of its budget in order for the numbers to add up.

2. Dr. Leonard Lodish, "Key Findings from the How Advertising Works Study," a speech presented at the Advertising Research Foundation Workshop, November 6–7, 1991.

3. Magid Abraham and Leonard Lodish, *Advertising Works, A Study of Advertising Effectiveness and the Resulting Strategic and Tactical Implications*, Information Resources Inc., 1990, p. 1.

CHAPTER FIFTEEN

1. Steve Yahn, "Advertising's Grave New World," *Advertising Age*, May 16, 1994. p. 1.

2. Ibid.

3. Stephen Fox, *The Mirror Makers*, William Morrow and Co., Inc., New York, 1984, p. 30.

4. Adrienne Ward Fawcett, "Interactive Awareness Growing," *Advertising Age*, October 3, 1994.

5. Yahn, "Advertising's Grave New World."

6. Fawcett, "Interactive Awareness."

7. Yahn, "Advertising's Grave New World."

8. *1994 Cable TV Facts*, Cable Advertising Bureau, Inc., New York, p. 22.

9. *1992 Cable TV Facts*, Cable Advertising Bureau, Inc., New York, p. 15.

INDEX

Absolut vodka, 203
Achenbaum, Jon, 167
Acura, 64
Adams-Russell Inc., 205
Administrative expenses, 29
Ad-supported programming, 286–287
Advanced Promotion Technologies
    (APT), 230
Advertising, generally:
  creativity, 199–202
  industry changes, 196–197
  involvement in, 202–206
  role of, 195, 197–199
  selective binding, 206–210
  selective television, 210–216
  targeting, 195
  television, 210–216
  types of, 195
Advertising expenses, 23–24
Advertising to promotion (A/P) ratio,
    110–111
Advertising tracking studies, 106
Affinity model:
  advertising cutbacks and, 266
  marketing database, 189–192
  YopleX sales promotions, 256
Air fresheners, 79
AkPharma, 161

American Airlines:
  AAdvantage Program, 122–124
  relationship marketing, 158
American Association of Advertising
    Agencies (AAAA), 11, 20
American Express:
  direct mail, 141, 152
  marketing database, 188, 193
American Home Products, 194
American Popcorn, 161
American Tobacco, marketing database,
    193
Ameritech, 294
Anheuser-Busch, 194
Artzt, Edwin, x, 11, 276–278, 285
Asset value, 22–23
Association of National Advertisers
    (ANA), 20–21
AT&T, 34–35, 123, 281
Attention-getting gimmicks, 203
Attitude and usage study (A&U),
    167–172
Auto dealerships, 56
Avon, 206

Baby boomers, 14, 17
Balance sheet, 23
Barbie dolls, 206

Bausch & Lomb, 194
"The Beginning Years," 119–120,
     125–128, 134, 152
BehaviorScan, 106
Ben & Jerry's, 141, 144
Bernbach, Bill, 133, 136
Boston Beer, 161
Bottom line, trade promotions and, 51
Bounty paper towels, 133
Brand advocacy, 155–157
Brand attitudes, 169–170
Brand awareness, 168–169
Brand Development Index (BDI),
     224–225
Brand disloyalty:
   mathematics of, 110–111
   sales and profits and, 63–64
Brand equity research, 166–167
Brand-hostile world:
   retailers and, 16–17
   short-term solutions, 17–21
Brand loyalty, generally:
   consumer involvement, 8
   equation. See Brand Loyalty Equation
   lack of, 52
   price increases, 50
   price promotion, 50–51
Brand Loyalty Equation:
   advertising spending, 99–100
   creation of, 99–100
   function of, 93
   promotional spending, 97–98
   reallocation and, 263–264
   significance of, 98
   YopleX, 98–104, 247, 263–264
Brand-loyalty programs:
   evolution of, 121–124
   frequent-buyer programs vs., 124–128
   function of, 8–9
   impact of, 267–268
   implementation of, 254–256, 297–298
   listing of, 161–163
   role of, 166
   stealth factor, 298
   target audience, 177
   tests, volume gains, 175–177
Brand management, 3

Brand Opportunity Index (BOI),
     224–225, 256, 265
BrandPrint, 201–202
Brand Profit Matrix, defined, 34. See also
     Profit Matrix
Brand reinforcement, 227
Brand-specific information, 142
Brand Stewardship, 201
Brand volume:
   brand loyalty programs, 175–177
   customer loyalty and, 5
   profit segments, 63–65
Bread-and-butter consumer promotions,
     220–221
Break-even point, 268
Budget(s):
   communications, x
   marketing. See Marketing budget
   for marketing database, 187–188
   P&G's, 283
   sales promotion, 116
   trade promotions, 236, 268–270
Bulk sizes, 48
Burger King, 194
Buzzell, Robert D., 51

"The Cableshop," 205–206, 217–218
Cable TV, 283, 287, 293
Cadillac:
   churn, 84
   dominant brand, 64, 65
Camel Cash, 229
Campbell Soup, 161, 194
Caples, John, 129, 135
Carnation, Good Start Infant Formula,
     144
Carol Wright mailings, 140, 225
Carvel, 161
Catalina Marketing, 230
Catalogs, 158, 232–233
Category buyers, one-third/two-thirds
     rule:
   generally, 32–36
   high-profit, 38–39
Category Development Index (CDI), 224,
     256
Category killers, 20
Category penetration, 39

Category Profit Matrix, yogurt, 39, 99
CD-ROM, 288, 291
Celebrity endorsement, 134
Check-cashing cards, 234
Chesebrough-Pond's:
  brand loyalty programs, 161
  marketing database, 194
Chrysler, 208
Churn:
  defined, 82–84
  YopleX, 248–249
Claritas Corporation, Prizm, 190
Clorets gum, 132
Clorox, 194
Coalition for Brand Equity, 20, 51
Coca-Cola, 22, 194, 281
Coca-Cola Retailing Research Council, 35
Coffee Discovery, 161
Colgate, 132, 280
Communications effect, 105
Competition:
  impact of, 4–5
  share of customer, 57–58
  significance of, 299
Computer shopping, 294
ConAgra, 161, 194
Consumer attitudes, 150, 157
Consumer behavior, changing, 298–299
Consumer database, purpose of, 10. See
  also Marketing databases
Consumer diaries, 165, 172
Consumer involvement. See
  Involvement
Consumer promotion:
  in-store, 230–231
  leveraging, 223–226
  roles of, 220
Consumer service businesses, 186
Coors Brewing, 161, 194
Copy testing, 166, 171, 175–176
Core franchise, 57–58, 65
Cost(s):
  of coupons, 231
  manufacturing, 24
  micromarketing and, 265
  trade promotions, 264–265
Cost per thousand (CPM), 188, 208–209

Coupons:
  advanced check-out counter systems,
    180, 219–220
  Brand Loyalty Equation, 105
  brand-loyalty programs, 174
  cost of, 231
  function of, 106
  in-store promotions, 230–231
  questions on, 183
  redemption, 19, 103, 112–113
  time-release, 229
Creative revolution, 133
Credit cards:
  affinity, 123
  brand-loyalty programs, 124
  as data source, 34, 39, 234
Critical mass, marketing database,
  187
Cross-selling models, marketing
  database, 191
Crystal Light, 82–83, 227
Cummings, John, 141, 181, 186
Current buyers:
  gains from, 197
  sales promotions and, 223
Customer loyalty:
  brand volume, 5
  sales promotions and, 5
Cybermarkets, 293–295
Cyberspace, 291–292

Dannon yogurt, 239, 244
Database promotions, 226–227
Databases. See Consumer databases;
  Marketing databases
Data collection, sources for, 233–234
DBM/scan:
  brand-loyalty programs, 141
  data collection techniques, 183
  development of, 181
  infomercials, 205
  promotion offers and, 223
Deloitte & Touche, 233–234
Demographics:
  significance of, 101–102
  television advertising, 144
Demographic targeting, 120, 213–214
Demonstrations, 154–155

Diet Coke, profit segments, 40–41
Differential Marketing, generally:
    brand growth, 7
    challenge of, 26
    core strategy, 7
    defined, 6
    profitability, 7
Direct mail:
    consumer involvement in, 150
    information superhighway, 274
    selective binding and, 209–210
    traditional media vs., 151
Direct marketing, 136
Direct Marketing Association, 233
Direct response:
    principles of, 130
    selling power, 129–130
Disloyalty. See Brand disloyalty
Dominant brand, 60, 64, 67
Donnelley Marketing, Inc.:
    Carol Wright mailings, 140, 225
    16th Annual Survey of Promotional
        Practices, 230, 245
    Survey of Promotional Practices,
        181
DowBrands:
    direct mail, 141
    marketing database, 194
    relationship marketing, 159
Doyle Dane Bernbach agency, 133
DROCI (Differential Return on
        Communications
        Investment):
    defined, 259
    payoff and, 261–262
    worksheet, 271
    YopleX example, 266–272
Dual-income families, 16

Earth's Best, 161
Ehrenberg, Andrew, 88
Electronic scanning, data collection
        resource, 165, 176
Electronic supermarket, 293–294
Evaporation:
    of profits, 84–85
    YopleX, 248–250

Excessive promotion, impact of, 108,
        116–118
Expenses:
    administrative, 29
    advertising, 23–24
    marketing, 46–47, 119–120
    overhead, 29

Family restaurants, 39
Fixodent, 206
Folger's, 57–58, 65, 89
Ford, 123, 194
Form breaks, 225
Free-standing inserts (FSIs):
    capabilities of, 224
    development of, 223–224
    function of, 105, 221
Frequency, in media planning, 149
Frequent-buyer programs, 233
Frequent-flier programs, 48, 122–
        123

Gains, measurement of:
    brand equity, 167–171
    brand volume, 171–174
Gale, Bradley T., 51
Garvey, Richard, 21
Gatorade, 56
General Foods, 23
General Foods International Coffees,
        154, 159
General Mills, 194
General Motors, 123, 194
Gerber, 141, 154
G. Heileman, 161
Gillette, 2, 194
Glenlivet Scotch, The, 144–145, 203–
        205
Global economy, impact of, 22
Golden Age of Television, 288
Green Stamps, 121–122, 124
Grocery shopping, alternatives to, 16
Gross margin, 48
Gross profit, calculation of, 114–115
Gross Profit Matrix:
    sample, 46
    YopleX, 115–116
Gross Rating Points (GRPs), 182, 184

Growing Healthy, 161
Growth strategies:
  conventional advertising and
    promotion, 87
  high-profit customers and, 87–
    90

Hallmark, 161–162, 280
Hardee's, 162
Hathaway shirts, 130–131, 136
Heavy buyers:
  coupon redemption, 103, 112–113
  panel data, 185
  promotion budget and, 95–96
  purchase frequency, 97
Heavy category buyers:
  brand volume and, 63–64
  loyalty parity, 61
  Profit Cycle and, 79
  significance of, 58
Helene Curtis, Inc.:
  brand loyalty programs, 161, 167
  direct mail, 141
Hershey, 162
High-profit buyers:
  brand loyalty in, 8
  brand volume and, 63–64
  competition and, 7
  core group of, 58
  in database, 189–190
  declines in brand loyalty, 59–60
  defined, 4
  future profit growth and, 65–66
  loyalty parity, 61, 63
  marketing databases and, 185–186
  new buyers and, 73
  one-third/two-thirds rule, 40
  in Profit Cycle, 76–77
  sales promotion expenditures, 96–97
  significance of, 57–58
  unique perspective, in advertising,
    200–201
High-profit segment:
  advertising spending, 111
  brand volume, 172–173
  defined, 37
  profitability, 27–28
  profit and volume, 45–48

shrinking, 38–41
targeting, 120–121
Hiram Walker & Sons, 162
H. J. Heinz, 206
Home-shopping, 204, 293
Home Shopping Network, 204
Honda, 64
Hooker, Richard, 3
Hopkins, Claude, 129–130
Hotel chains, brand loyalty programs,
  123
House of Seagram:
  Absolut vodka, 203
  cooperative mailings, 235
  direct mail, 141
  Glenlivet Scotch, The, 144–145,
    203–205
  marketing database, 181, 188, 193,
    235–236
"How Advertising Works" (IRI), 106,
  165–166, 175–176, 197–198, 267
Huggies:
  "The Beginning Years," 119, 125–128,
    134, 152
  competition, 82

Image commercials, 183
Incentives:
  leveraging, 229
  measurement of, 174
  research studies of, 95
Individual consumers:
  impact of, 25–26
  profit, 25–26
Individualism, 15, 25
Infomercials:
  historical perspective, 132–133
  impact of, 195, 217–218
  involvement and, 203, 205
Information, generally:
  advertising techniques and, 128–129
  creative revolution and, 133
  direct mail, 142–148
  direct response, 130–132
  factual communication, 133–134
  feedback, 152–153
  infomercials, 132–133
  product information, 134–135

Information Resources, Inc. (IRI):
  advertising effectiveness research,
    174–175
  "How Advertising Works," 106,
    165–166, 175–176, 197–198, 267
  packaged-goods purchase research,
    51
Information superhighway:
  advertising and, 284–286
  cyberspace, 291–292
  direct mail and, 274
  economics of, 282–284
  function of, 284
  impact of, 275–276
  interactivity, 289–291
  marketing superhighway vs., 289–292
  retail industry, 292–296
  revolution, 280–284
  as toll road, 286–289
Instant database, 186
Interactive TV, 180
Interactive video, 295
Interactivity, information superhighway,
    289–290
Involvement:
  consumer, 202–206
  effectiveness of, 150
  significance of, 148–149
Involvement device, 154
IRI (Information Resources, Inc.). See
  Information Resources, Inc.
  (IRI)

Jack Daniels, 152
J.D. Power & Associates, 64, 84
Jell-O, 23
Joe Camel, 229
Johnson, Samuel, 3
Johnson & Johnson, 194
Junk mail, 139–141
J. Walter Thompson (JWT) advertising
    agency, 128, 205, 218

Kellogg:
  Corn Flakes:
    Profit Cycle, 75–76, 78–79, 91
    share of customer, 91–92
  marketing database, 193

Kelly, Walt, 108
Key attitudes, 169–170
Kimberly-Clark:
  brand loyalty programs. See Huggies,
    "The Beginning Years"
  direct mail, 141
  marketing database, 194
Kohlberg Kravis Roberts, 181
Kraft Foods:
  acquisition of, 23
  Advanced Promotions Technologies
    (APT), 230
  brand loyalty programs, 119, 124, 162,
    167, 171
  consumer involvement and, 139
  cooperative mailings, 235
  Crystal Light, 82–83, 227
  direct mail, 141
  marketing database, 179, 181, 188, 193
  Miracle Whip Salad Dressing,
    152–153, 199–200
  relationship marketing, 159
  We're Right For You, 227–228
Kuendig, John, 35, 167, 227

Lands' End, 158
Lapsed buyers, Profit Cycle and, 74–75,
    79
Laser scanning, 235
Lasker, Albert, 129, 135
Law of Double Jeopardy, 89
Leaky bucket, 81–86
L'eggs pantyhose, 40
Levi's blue jeans, 40
Light buyers:
  brand volume and, 64
  defined, 36
  loyalty blindness, 53–54
  profit cycle and, 79
  purchase frequency, 98
Light, Larry, 20, 51
Lincoln, 64–65
Loblaws, 16
Long-distance carriers, long-distance
    wars, 34, 123, 281
Lord & Thomas, 129
Losses, 28–29
Loyalty blindness, 52–55

Loyalty equilibrium, 108
Loyalty parity, 58–66
Lucky Strike, 280
Luvs, 82
Luxury car market, 36

Manufacturing costs, 24
Margin improvement programs, 17
Marginal utility of spending, 262
Marketers, as accountants, 24–25
Market Facts Telemation research
    service, 281–282
Marketing body language, 106–108
Marketing budget, 3, 25, 95
Marketing database:
    budget for, 187–188
    complexity of, 183–184
    data collection sources, 233–235
    development of, 181–182
    function of, 182–185
    growth of, 179
    high-profit consumers, 189–190
    information in, 183–184
    information sources, 186, 198–199
    models of, 189–191
    optimizing, 187
    size of, 185, 187, 192–193
    syndicated data, 186
    time factor, 185–186
Marketing expenses, 46–47, 116–117
Marketing Information Technologies
    (MIT), 188, 191, 207
Marketing relationships, 232
Market Metrics, 238
Marlboro Adventure Team, 229
Marlboro Friday, 2–3, 14, 21, 278
Marriage, high-profit consumers, 65
Mars, 162
Martell Cognac, 142
Mary Kay Cosmetics, marketing
    database, 193
Mass-market brands, profits of, 41
Mass-media tax, 37–38
Mather & Crowther advertising agency,
    130, 136, 142
Mattel, 206
Maxwell House, 89, 142
MCI, 34–35, 123, 281

Media:
    advertising, 96, 109
    conventional, 176–177
    planning, 149
    revolution, 279–280
Mediamark Research, Inc. (MRI), 34, 39,
    56
Medium buyers:
    brand volume and, 64
    defined, 36
    purchase frequency, 98
Melitta, 162
Merck, 162
Microeconomics, 262
Micromarketing:
    costs and, 265
    effectiveness of, 237
    objective of, 237
    significance of, 236
    types of, 238
Microsoft, 281
Mileage statement, 122
Mileage wars, 123
Miracle Whip Salad Dressing, 152–153,
    199–200
Mnemonic device, 132
Morgan, Richard, 51
MRCA, research studies:
    brand trials, 239–240
    churn, 83
    dominant brands, 67–69
    function of, generally, 32
    growth strategies, 89–90
    loyalty blindness, 58
    loyalty parity, 58–59, 62
    new buyers, 73
    packaged-goods profit matrix, 42–44
    Profit Opportunity Matrix. See
        Taster's Choice, Profit
        Opportunity
        Matrix
    promotional incentives, 95
    share of customer, 56–58
    soft-goods industry, 108
    special analysis for book, 32
MRI. See Mediamark Research, Inc.
    (MRI)

Multiple brand buyers, dominant
        brands, 60
Multiple-brand considerers, 56

Negative profit-flow, 27
Nestlé:
    brand loyalty programs, 124, 161, 162
    direct mail, 141, 152
    marketing database, 194
Net profit, 31
Net Profit Matrix:
    sample, 47
    YopleX, 115, 117–118
New buyers:
    defined, 74, 240
    recruitment of, 198
    retained buyers and, 77, 222
    search for, 72–73
New products, 18
New recruits, 157
Newsletters, 142–147
"The news of the marketplace," 128–135
Noncategory buyers, advertising and,
        116
Nonloyal heavy buyers, brand volume
        and, 64
NPD/Nielsen, Inc.:
    Scantrack service, 215
    television advertising research,
        210–214
    yogurt research, 101

Ogilvy, David:
    advertising spending, 20
    brand loyalty programs, 130, 135
    consumer involvement, 148
    long copy ads, 120, 134, 136–137
    "news of the marketplace," 141
Ogilvy & Mather, 9, 299
Ogilvy & Mather Direct, 119, 125, 168,
        172, 201–202
Ogilvy & Mather Worldwide, 168
Ogilvy Center for Research &
        Development, 150
Opportunity profit, 74
Oreo cookies, 63
Overhead expenses, 29
Ovitz, Michael, 281

Packaged goods, generally:
    brand loyalty for, 67–69
    price increases, 18
Packaged-goods marketing:
    brand loyalty and, 52
    as white mice, 52, 58, 64
Pampers, 59, 82
Panel tests, 165, 172
Pareto Principle:
    defined, 27
    micromarketing and, 237
    retail industry, 35, 233
Pay-TV, 282
Payoff, 260–261
Payout, 260–261
Peapod, 293–295
Pepperidge Farm, 142, 155
Pepsico, 2, 162, 194
Performance model, marketing
        database, 191
Personalization, impact of, 151–152
Pet Inc., 162
Philip Morris:
    brand loyalty programs, 162
    brand value, 22–23
    marketing database, 182, 193
    Marlboro Friday, 2–3
    promotional incentives, 229
    selective binding, 207
Photography, in ads, 130, 132
Pillsbury Bake-Off Contest, 105
PIMS (Profit Impact of Market
        Strategies), 51
Pinkerton Tobacco, 162
Pizza Hut, 194
Pogo, 108
Point-of-sale, take-one, 183
Polaroid, 162, 194
Pond's Age Defying Complex, 155–
        156
Pond's Age Defying Lotion, 154
Population diversity, 15, 39
Population growth, 14
Positive profit-flow, 27, 39
Potato Board, 162
Price, generally:
    electronic shopping and, 294
    increases, 18

inflation, 13
promotion, 19
Price buyers:
    defined, 97
    loyalty blindness, 53–54
Price-switchers, 53
Pringle's potato chips, 62
Private label products, 16–17
Procter & Gamble:
    Advanced Promotion Technologies
        (APT), 231
    advertising budget for, 283
    brand-loyalty programs, 119, 124–125,
        128
    brand management, 3
    consumer involvement and, 139
    cooperative mailings, 235
    direct mail, 141
    infomercials, 206
    information superhighway and, 11
    marketing database, 179, 181, 193
    samples, 154–155
    side-by-side demonstrations, 132–
        133
Profitability:
    brand names and, 22
    calculation of, 45–46
    consumers and, 7
    degree of, 78
    increasing, 21–22
Profit and Loss Statement (P&L), 23, 26
Profit Cycle:
    brand trial, 240
    brand volume, 172
    defined, 71
    function of, 240
    function of, 73
    "leaky bucket," 74–75
    low-profit buyers and, 78–79
    marketer's point of view, 74
    new buyers and, 198
    profit opportunity, 77–78
    retained buyers and, 75–77
    sales promotion, 222
    YopleX, 248–249
Profit Matrix, see specific types of profit
        matrices
    function of, 32–33

packaged-goods, 33, 42–44
Profit Opportunity Matrix:
    function of, 71, 73, 197–198, 241
    Taster's Choice, 80–81, 84–85
    YopleX, 248–249
Profit segmentation:
    defined, 27
    function of, 53
    potential profit and, 30–32
Prom home permanents, 132
Promotional incentives. See
        Incentives
Promotional targeting, 219
Promotion Profitability Index (PPI),
        225–226, 257, 265
Promotions. See specific types of
        promotions
Public Pulse, 107

Quaker Oats:
    brand-loyalty programs, 162
    marketing database, 193
Quality gap, 13, 17
Quarterly earnings statement, 21
Questionnaires, 155
QVC, 204

Ralston Purina:
    brand-loyalty programs, 162
    direct mail, 141
    marketing database, 193
Ramp-up period, 243
Rationalization, 223
Reader's Digest, marketing database,
        193
Rebate certificate, 183
Recency/Frequency/Monetary Value
        analysis, 236
Redstone, Sumner, 277, 281
Reeves, Rosser, 130, 136
Relationship marketing:
    brand-loyalty programs and, 125
    classic, 159–160
    defined, 158
    samples of, 158–159
Rent-a-car companies, brand-loyalty
        programs, 123
Repeat buyers, 240

Resor, Stanley, 128–129
Retailers:
    information superhighway and,
        292–296
    trade promotion and relations,
        232–233
Retained buyers:
    brand volume, 75–76, 172–173
    leveraging, 91–92
    new buyers vs., 222
    sales, 75–76
    types of, 74
Return on investment (ROI), 6, 51
R.J. Reynolds:
    brand-loyalty programs, 162–
        163
    information technology, 10
    marketing database, 181, 187,
        193
    promotional incentives, 229
Roper Organization, 107, 134
R.R. Donnelley & Sons Company,
    207

Sales promotion:
    brand trial, 239–240
    budget for, 116
    customer loyalty and, 5
    impact of, 94–99, 298
    limitations of, 110
    profitability and, 118
    role of, 123–125
    subsidies, 228–229
    YopleX, case illustration, 256–257
Sam's Clubs, 235
Samples, involvement devices, 154–
    155
Sandoz:
    direct mail, 141
    marketing database, 194
    newsletter, 144
Sara Lee, 163, 194
Scent strips, 209
Schering, 163
Schweppes, 136
Scientific Advertising (Hopkins), 130
Scientific advertising, 136

Scott Paper, 163, 194
Seagram, 163. See also House of
    Seagram
Sears, 158, 233
Sears Brand Central, 56
Selective binding:
    affinity model and, 208
    budgets and, 209–210
    defined, 207
    development of, 207–208
    enhanced impact, 209–210
    function of, 180, 195, 207
    portfolio buying, 209
Share of customer (SOC):
    defined, 55
    dominant brand research, 60
    growth strategies, 88
    overview, 55–58
Share of requirements, 54–58. See also
    Share of customer
Shaw, Richard, 207, 235
Shoebox, 186
Short-term purchase incentives, 222
Simmons Market Research Bureau, Inc.
    (SMRB):
    Study of Media and Markets, 213–
        214
    YopleX and, 251–253
Single-source panel, 211
Situation analysis, 243
SKUs. See Stockkeeping units (SKUs)
SmithKline Beecham, 206
Snyder's of Hanover, 163
Soft-drink category, 40
Soft-goods brands, 34
Soft-goods industry, 108
Sominex, 206
Spectra Marketing Systems, 238
Sperry & Hutchinson (S&H Green
    Stamps), 122, 124
Spontaneous awareness, 169
Spray 'n Wash, 142–143
Starbucks, 163
Statistical modeling techniques:
    marketing databases, 179–180,
        186–187, 195
    micromarketing and, 238

sales promotions, 219–220
Stockkeeping units (SKUs), 237–238, 244
Strategic alliances, 231
Strategic Mapping, Inc., ClusterPlus, 190
Sweepstakes, 154

Taco Bell, 163
Taster's Choice:
 Profit Opportunity Matrix, 80–81,
  85–86
 retained buyers, 191
Technological advances, impact of,
  179–194
Ted Bates agency, 130
Telephone surveys, 160
Television advertising:
 current delivery, 211–212
 effectiveness of, 212–213
 impact of, 214–215
 media negotiations, 214
 NPD/Nielsen, Inc. research studies,
  210–213, 215
 program ratings, volumetric and
  demographic, 213, 253–254
 target groups, 213–215
Television weight. See Weight
  tests
Test versus control, 167
Theme promotions, 105
Third-party data, 186
Thompson, J. Walter, 280
Time, Inc., 193, 208
Times-Mirror, 208
Toilet bowl cleaners, 83
Toll-free telephone numbers, 183, 199,
  293
Toyota, 64, 206
Trade promotion:
 decreases in, 268–269
 as fixed variable cost, 264–265
 leveraging, 231–236
 profits and, 269–271
 roles of, 220
 volume and, 269–270
Trade relations:
 leveraging, 231–236
 promotion of, 220

Travel industry, 48
Tree Top, 163
The Trustmarketer's Road to Enduring
  Profitable Growth, 20
20/80 rule, 27, 54

Unaided awareness, 169
Unilever:
 brand-loyalty programs, 124
 consumer involvement in, 139
 direct mail, 141
Universal product codes, 233
Upjohn, 194
USP (unique selling proposition),
  130

Value-added information, 142
Value decade, 2
Variables, statistical modeling, 190
Viacom, 277
Volkswagen, 133
Volume management, 24
Volumetric targeting, 212–214, 220
Vulnerability model, marketing
  database, 191

Walt Disney, marketing database,
  193
Wanamaker, John, x, 3, 6–7, 29, 100
Warner Lambert, marketing database,
  193
Warranty card, 183
Weight tests, 166, 175
Weight Watchers, 206
Willabee & Ward, 163
Windex, 62
Wunderman, Lynn, 187–189

Yoplait yogurt, 76–78, 239, 242–243
YopleX:
 advertising delivery, improving,
  251–254
 analysis factors, 242–243
 Brand Loyalty Equation, 104, 247
 brand-loyalty program,
  implementation of, 254–256
 coupon redemption rate, 113

YopleX: *(cont'd.)*
  DFM plan, application of:
    DROCI for, 266–272
    funding, 262–265
  magazine list, preliminary, 252
  marketing objectives/strategies
      (1993), 241–242, 250–251
  media plan, preliminary, 246
  net profit matrix, 245
  sales promotion incremental volume,
      256–258

  situation analysis, 243–249
  Profit/Promotion Matrix, 102
Yuspeh, Sonia, 218

Ziploc:
  newsletter program, 146–148, 152
  sales promotions, 227
  unique perspective, 200–201